Molly McElwee is a journalist s[...] [...]
tennis, as well as writing about foot[...] [...]
disciplines. She spent more than f[...] [...]
Daily Telegraph and hosted a podcast called Off The Bench. In
2024 she won the Tom Perrotta Prize, awarded by the International
Tennis Writers' Association (ITWA) to a writer aged 35 or under
who shows excellence in tennis journalism. She is from Gibraltar.

Building Champions

Paths to Success in Women's Tennis

Molly McElwee

First published in 2025 by
Arena Sport, an imprint of
Birlinn Limited
West Newington House
10 Newington Road
Edinburgh
EH9 1QS

www.arenasportbooks.co.uk

ISBN 978 1 913759 23 0

British Library Cataloguing-in-Publication Data
A catalogue record for this book is available from the British Library

Typeset by Initial Typesetting Services, Edinburgh

Papers used by Birlinn are from well-managed forests and other responsible sources

Printed and bound by Clays Ltd, Elcograf S.p.A.

Contents

For Aida and Bobo

Foreword

OPPORTUNITY is everything and *Building Champions* platforms the multitude of options women and girls now have to aspire to and achieve in the top level of tennis. The stories of the women featured in this book, and the different paths they followed to reach the same ultimate dream on the Grand Slam stage, chart the progress of women's tennis today. It showcases the global reach tennis has. From how the Czech Republic continues to punch above its weight, to how immigrant families like Emma Raducanu's can guide their daughter to a New York dream, and the way Iga Swiatek has created a tennis legacy in Poland that had never previously been possible. It also covers the game-changing milestones reached by these women: Kim Clijsters and her motherhood journey, the Williams sisters carving out space for themselves in a majority white sport, all the way through to Coco Gauff giving new meaning to the words 'prodigal talent'. It highlights the power of teamwork within this individual sport through Ash Barty's stellar career and the tenacity it took for a figure like Aryna Sabalenka, who fought through challenging moments on the court for years, to become a major champ.

Their individual stories paint a wider picture about how tennis has continued to grow and change, all the while remaining the leading sport for women to pursue professionally. As someone involved in ownership groups in women's hockey, basketball and soccer, I can see how tennis has influenced the rise of women's sports beyond our courts in recent years. Tennis continues to set a blueprint for what is possible. According to *Forbes*, in 2023 nine of the 10 top-paid female athletes in the world were tennis players. Considering it's more than 50 years since I became the first woman to win $100,000 in a season, this is a remarkable measure of the relevance tennis continues to have when it comes to paying women what they're worth.

There is still such a long way to go across women's sport, and tennis is far from the finished product either. Prize money remains unequal, except at the four major tournaments, and unfair scheduling or even court allocation disparities still creep up at the majors. But that work feels achievable because of the progress we have made so far. The momentum is with us to make those changes too. Shouting from the rooftops about women's sport is crucial to that momentum. It is why, as players, the Original Nine championed the role that journalists and the media could, and would, play in elevating our work, understanding that it could unlock further opportunities. Coverage of women's sport is rising, with some athletes gaining global recognition. A new generation – Angel Reese, Caitlin Clark, Coco Gauff, Aitana Bonmati and Ilona Maher among them – are capturing the imagination of audiences right from the outset of their careers and are also being valued for their personalities beyond the field of play.

In this latest era, in the last 15 or so years, women's tennis has shown itself to be diverse, dynamic and ever-evolving, with more champions, from more nations, bursting into our sport than we've previously seen. This book helps us gain a greater understanding of the way champions were moulded by their culture, community and tennis and are now shaping the sport themselves.

Billie Jean King

Introduction

BARBORA Krejcikova stood on Centre Court clutching the Venus Rosewater Dish in her hands, her mouth agape. 'I think nobody really believes it,' she told the 15,000 people in the crowd, and further four million watching on television across the United Kingdom. 'Nobody believes that I got to the final. And nobody's going to believe that I won Wimbledon.' Her charge to the title in 2024, as the 31st seed, was one of the sport's more unlikely storylines. Only, it was also exactly the kind of upset we have come to expect in the women's game. The truth is, there have been plenty of those in recent times. In the last eight editions of Wimbledon, there have been eight different women's champions. Krejcikova was the latest, and also the seventh consecutive first-time Wimbledon champion. The tournament has never seen such an extended period of changeable results in its 140 years of hosting the ladies' singles event.

That unpredictability extends far beyond Wimbledon too. Krejcikova's victory continued a trend that we have seen in women's tennis for at least 15 years, and close to 20. Winning multiple major titles became extremely rare unless you were named Serena Williams. From 2014 to 2024, only Serena, Iga Swiatek, Aryna Sabalenka and Naomi Osaka won the same Grand Slam event more than once. If you stretch back to the last two decades, from 2004 to 2024, only seven women won the same Grand Slam back to back: Serena, Swiatek, Sabalenka, Justine Henin, Venus Williams, Victoria Azarenka and Kim Clijsters. These results mean that, since the turn of the century, there has been a massive boom in the number of women reaching tennis's holy grail. From 2000 to 2024, 36 different women won Grand Slam titles (compared to 22 men). Just as soon as someone made their breakthrough, the tennis gods were already churning out another young star to nab their spot by the next major tournament. A production line, if you like, of fresh faces with fierce forehands and bruising backhands. At least that is how it has sometimes come to feel.

Winning a Grand Slam title is no mean feat; they are after all the most prestigious prizes available in tennis. In January, players battle it out for the Australian Open on the hard courts in sweltering Melbourne; in the spring, they switch to the clay at the chic Roland Garros club in Paris; in July they adapt to the fast grass and inevitable rain at the All England Lawn Tennis & Croquet Club in Wimbledon, before finishing in September back on hard courts, under the bright lights and heavy humidity of Flushing Meadows in Queens, New York. Taking home the trophy at any of these tournaments entails winning seven matches in a row during a 14 or 15-day period. Unlike at other smaller tournaments (which last between one week and 12 days), every fit member of the top 100 shows up to the majors. The calibre of opposition is the highest it can possibly be. The arenas are bigger, the crowds are much larger too, as is the prize money. At the 2024 US Open, singles champions Jannik Sinner and Aryna Sabalenka pocketed a cool $3.6 million each. If all of that doesn't sound challenging enough, at certain slams players may well be completing their matches way past midnight, if they find themselves scheduled to play in the night session (apart from at Wimbledon, where there is thankfully a civilised curfew).

With all of that at stake, you then add the media attention players receive into the mix. At Grand Slams, it becomes amplified to new levels as the world's press descends on the tournaments. During the weekend before play begins and after their matches, top players are ferried between multiple media engagements. First, a 200-seater press conference room, where they are met by the questions of dozens of journalists after each win and loss. Then there are the multiple studios, where players are mic'd up and quickly moved along on a conveyor belt of national broadcasters. For the top talent, it could add up to a couple of hours' worth of interviews and media commitments every other day, as the hype builds with each round they win. Then, when they get back to their hotel room (if they are brave enough to check), their phone will light up with thousands of social media notifications. Some will be messages of support, but others quite the opposite, as vitriol from furious gamblers or cruel trolls is sent their way.

All of that is to say that the mental focus and physical effort it takes to emerge as champion over an intense fortnight like this is a test unlike any other in tennis. It is a measure of endurance, speed, guile, tactical nous, temperament, psychological strength and skill while under the toughest scrutiny. The challenge to win one Grand Slam is immeasurably difficult, let alone multiple. And yet, because there has been an influx of new winners in recent years, the perceived value of a Grand Slam win has changed. The term 'one-slam wonder' is more commonly bandied about across women's tennis now. Can you really fluke a major title, though? The answer is obviously no, but context is key.

Women's tennis has not always been so unpredictable. Actually, at the turn of the century, things were completely reversed. Jon Wertheim's book *Venus Envy*, which gives a detailed, behind-the-scenes look at the WTA Tour during the 2000 season, paints a completely alternate universe to the tennis world we've seen of late. 'Insiders know that at the Grand Slams, the women's draw doesn't really start until the second week,' Wertheim wrote. 'Unlike the men's brackets, which are riddled with upsets, the women's side invariably follows form through the first week.' As such, from 1980 to 1999, there were only 12 new women champions across the Grand Slams. The numbers don't lie, and there has been an undeniable shift since then. But even back in the 1980s and 90s, women's tennis had plenty of critics. When Martina Navratilova, Chris Evert, Steffi Graf and Monica Seles flourished, women's tennis was accused of being boring. Now that there have been shock results aplenty, the women are regarded (by some) as too flaky.

That is partly because women's sport is never valued entirely in a vacuum. Rather, it is too often based on how it compares to the men's game. The long-term view of tennis history paints an even picture. In pure numbers terms, from 1968 (the start of the Open Era) to 2024, tennis saw 58 different men win Grand Slam titles. During that same period, 60 different women did so. That's 56 years of tennis, where on average each tour saw one new champion crowned per year. So far, so (nearly) identical. But it is the trajectory that differs and, when you break down the numbers, it is the last two decades where we've seen the starkest difference in the two. In men's tennis, we saw the rate of new champions drastically slow down, and in women's we saw it accelerate. A good marker to begin from is the moment tennis changed forever: when Roger Federer won his maiden major title at Wimbledon in 2003. I recognise the irony in beginning a women's tennis book from the date a male player won a tournament, but stick with me.

This most recent period of unpredictable results in women's tennis has been measured – for good and for bad – alongside the era of men's tennis it coincided with: the Big Three era of Federer, Rafael Nadal and Novak Djokovic. Where women's tennis has been highly unpredictable, the men's competition has been the opposite. Where the top end of the WTA rankings have fluctuated and changed on a dime, the ATP's have been more stable (17 new female world No. 1s, to nine male). Where we have seen dozens of women champions emerge – some remaining close to the top, others stepping away or fizzling out – in men's tennis the Big Three rewrote the history books with their three-way rivalry and near-complete monopoly over the Grand Slams. Three men had never previously won as large a share of top titles as this trio did for as long as they did (and, in Djokovic's case, continues to do). Before, there was always room for shock winners and dark horses to slip through the draw and make their mark. Federer's 2003 Wimbledon title began the era of the Big Three (or Big Four if you count three-time major champion Andy Murray). Since then (and up until the end of 2024), only 12 different men lifted a Grand Slam trophy for the first time. In women's tennis, the same period saw 30 different new champions – more than double the rate.

That discrepancy is often used as a stick to beat the women's game with. Critics complain about the lack of consistency. Sport is built on rivalries, they opine, and women's tennis has lacked that in the last 15 or so years. Winning a Grand Slam in men's tennis is more difficult, they argue, simply based on the fact fewer men have done it during this period. There are both falsehoods and fair points across these arguments. For example, rivalries are extremely fun, and it is fair to say that women's tennis has not lucked out in this department in recent times. But it is false to say winning a Grand Slam in women's tennis is somehow easier because more women have done it. For some though, greatness can only be truly, unequivocally exciting when men are involved. It goes without saying that this book is not for them.

The point of this book is not to say that women's tennis is better than men's either, or that one era is better than another, or to pit champions against each other at all. There will be no GOAT debates here, I'll leave that to the last remaining survivors of tennis X to fight out. Rather, my aim is to point out that, when you peel back the men's tennis narrative that has dominated the sport over the past 15 to 20 years, you will find rich stories and individuals who have emerged during this era of women's tennis too. Stories about triumphing against the odds, of career turnarounds that defied expectations, of non-linear paths to success that changed our perception of just what can make someone a winner. This book showcases just how much these women's stories can teach us about the sport and how, looked at together as a collective, they prove one fascinating principle of tennis: there is no one way to build a champion. Coexisting with the Big Three was always going to be a tall order, and it has inevitably given the last two decades in women's tennis somewhat of a bad rap in some quarters. But if you flip that narrative, by bringing to the forefront the women's tennis champions that have risen (and sometimes fallen) during this period, there are many angles left unexplored. There is variety, depth and sheer unpredictability that I believe is worth dissecting.

Since the turn of the century, the global sporting ecosystem has increasingly been driven by where the money falls, and results across too many leagues have become near-certainties. The Manchester City of it all in the men's Premier League for example or Chelsea's dominance in the Women's Super League comes to mind. But I would argue that women's tennis bucks that trend, as underdog wins and wild upsets are more prevalent here than in any other major sport in the world. That open field is what makes it interesting and is an overall strength, in my view, not a weakness. The range of champions makes it truly global too. Since 2014, women's tennis has had champions from 17 different countries (more than double that of men's tennis): Poland, the Czech Republic, USA, Australia, Kazakhstan, United Kingdom, Japan, Canada, Romania, Denmark, Germany, Spain, Latvia, Italy, Russia, Belarus and China. This book captures those stories and unravels the paths that were followed to make it on the women's tennis tour in the past two decades.

In other sports, the route to professionalism is often much more prescriptive. In men's football, top club academy systems have produced the vast majority of the best talent in the modern era. It is a similar story in rugby union and league. Across the pond in the US, college sport has almost exclusively helped to draft professional basketball, American football and baseball players. In individual Olympic sports, talent pathways guide British hopefuls from different age groups, depending on their sport. Coaches are assigned by federations or teams. But in tennis, there is no fixed pathway. On the contrary, there are any number of ways to plough your way to the top. Independent academies, many of which became hugely popular in the 1990s and cost tens of thousands of pounds a year, help some aspiring players. Some national tennis centres, run by governing bodies like the Lawn Tennis Association in the United Kingdom, are hubs for developing especially talented players from a young age too. Other players now go down the American college route, waiting to turn professional in their early twenties, to some success, as with Jessica Pegula and Cameron Norrie. The coaching options available to you will depend largely on where you grow up too, while some will have parents who completely wing it, coaching, steering and funnelling their child towards greatness, with little to no tennis background of their own to speak of. The only prevailing factor in everyone's journey? Going all-in from a young age. For the 34 women so far this century who became first-time major champions, that risk paid off.

I will inevitably fall short of covering every single one of the women who has risen in the ranks over the last two decades. There was Marion Bartoli's brilliant Wimbledon win in 2013, for example, where her quirky two-handed forehand and shuffling footwork prevailed, proving at the most traditional of tennis venues that there really is no 'right way' to play this sport. Or take the late bloomer Flavia Pennetta's US Open triumph in 2015 at the ripe old age of

33 years and 199 days. She remains the oldest first-time champion in the Open Era by almost four years and retired promptly that very same day – the ultimate mic drop moment. Or even Maria Sharapova, whose family's decision to move from north-west rural Russia to Florida in order to chase a tennis dream was rewarded in her becoming a five-time major champion and the most marketable female athlete the world had ever seen. Her story sparked countless others who followed her lead, and she remains a prominent figure in the sport, voted into the Hall of Fame in 2024, even after her legacy was somewhat tainted by an unintentional doping charge. Then there were disruptors like Latvian teen Jelena Ostapenko, who experienced the ultimate purple patch of form over a two-week period, snatching victory from fan favourite Simona Halep's hands at the 2017 French Open. At the 2018 Australian Open, Caroline Wozniacki embodied gritty perseverance in winning her first major title at her 43rd attempt, nearly a decade after losing her first final.

There are simply too many stories to get your teeth into. This book will tell many of the wonderful, strange and awe-inspiring avenues tennis players have navigated to reach the top of this sport, as told by the players themselves or the coaches, colleagues and friends who knew them best. From pushy parenting, prodigal talents, mentality monsters, the mother of all comebacks and arguably the greatest underdog win sport has ever seen, each one of the individuals profiled will tell a wider story about just how many different ways you can build a champion. Turns out, they are endless.

CHAPTER 1

Women's tennis as we knew it

TO TELL you the story of where women's tennis is now, you have to look at how far it has come. Unlike in other sports, women have been a part of the fabric of the game for almost as long as lawn tennis has been established. The first Wimbledon ladies' singles title was contested in 1884, seven years after the gentlemen's version, and has continued to grow ever since. While the rules of the game have largely remained the same, style and personalities over different eras have helped to shape the sport. The first true star of tennis – and that's including men and women – was France's Suzanne Lenglen, who made her name during the 1920s. She was brought up on tennis by her father, whom historians regard as the first pushy parent – or worse – of the sport. Many more, including those featured in this book, have emerged in the century since, following in 'Papa' Lenglen's footsteps.

Aside from her father's influence, Lenglen was a beguiling figure because she was so unapologetically herself. Her game was crafted with aggressive shot-making and an overhand serve, which was much closer to how the men played at that time than her fellow women competitors. Her radical decision not to wear a corset and petticoat like the other women players drew shock too. She preferred to don a short-sleeved dress that ran just beyond her knees, plus a silk scarf wrapped around her bob haircut and a swathe of red lipstick across her mouth. To add to the scandal, she also sipped from a brandy-filled hip flask between sets, until umpires put a stop to the practice.

Most of all, she was the supremely dominant sporting figure of the post-war 1920s. She took the world by storm, collecting 12 Grand Slam trophies in singles and receiving recognition across popular culture – nicknamed '*La Divine*' (the Goddess) by the French press and even getting a mention in Ernest Hemingway's novel *The Sun Also Rises*. Her popularity was part of the reason Wimbledon moved from Worple Road to its current, larger venue on Church Road in 1922 – the fans could not get enough of Lenglen. It was no exaggeration to call her the most famous European celebrity figure by the end of the decade. Notably, she was also the first woman to turn professional in 1926 and cited leaving amateurism behind as like 'an escape from slavery'. During her tour of the US that year, she earned $50,000. Lenglen was a pioneer not only on the court but also in demanding to be paid.

Her breakaway from convention would be replicated 40 years later when the Open Era of professional tennis began in 1968, which quite literally opened up all tournaments to professional players – including the Grand Slams. Throughout this book I will mostly be referring to tennis in what is known as the Open Era, i.e. tennis since the French Open in 1968. Before that, tennis was a mixture of amateur and professional events, with players only allowed to compete in one or the other. Many will debate whether the decades before 1968 should be discounted or not. After all, the four majors ran for decades before then – and in Wimbledon's case, since the late 1800s. The Open Era is not a perfect beginning point as for many years the Australian Open had smaller draws and top players (including Chris Evert and Martina Navratilova) skipped the long-haul travel to the less lucrative Grand Slam regularly. But the Open Era was the start of tennis as we know it today, from a professional sense, so it feels like the most appropriate – if imperfect – point to count from.

A couple of years later, an equally seminal shift occurred in world tennis when Billie Jean King and the rest of the Original Nine broke away from the governing bodies of tennis to form the Virginia Slims Circuit, which became the Women's Tennis Association in 1973. It was arguably the moment that changed tennis – and maybe sport as a whole – forever as it marked the start of women's tennis taking control of its own destiny. Women on tour were sick of being treated like second-class citizens. Their male colleagues were outspoken about how they viewed them as inferior and actively supported their exclusion. Prize money for women at some tournaments was as much as 12 times less than what the men received, and the number of events where women were invited to play had started dwindling as promoters began cutting them out.

The women took matters into their own hands in 1970, when eight leading female players signed a makeshift one-dollar-contract with promoter Gladys Heldman to play a tournament in Houston sponsored by cigarette brand Virginia Slims. Their goals were that any girl in the world, if good enough, would have a place to compete, that women and girl athletes would be appreciated for what they could achieve, not for the way they looked, and that they would be able to make a living. The women took a huge risk by extricating themselves from the established order, defying the United States Lawn Tennis Association for one, risking suspension from the Grand Slam events. It meant leaving behind tournaments that had decades of legacy, security, income (however paltry) and sponsors already involved. Forming an entirely new tour required a massive amount of administration, determination and sheer guts to believe they could make a go of it on their own – without the men.

Later, ahead of Wimbledon 1973, a group of 60 leading female players met at the Gloucester Hotel in London and formalised this breakaway tour more widely. King assigned Dutch player Betty Stove to stand by the door and instructed her not to let anybody in or out. This group of women voted to launch the WTA and then signed on the dotted line to make it official. With the players' buy-in achieved, the WTA had more power than ever to create a sport that benefitted women, and did not limit them.

'For us, a tour with women in charge was a dream come true,' King wrote in her memoir, *All In*. 'From our $1 rebellion, women's tennis grew into a profession where the US Open singles winner earned $3.85 million in 2019.'

Breaking away from the natural tennis order helped propel King to negotiate the first example of equal prize money at the slams at the US Open in 1973. It would take another 34 years before Wimbledon would bring up the rear in 2007, becoming the final major event to put women and men on equal terms. The All England Club were finally convinced after Venus Williams penned an op-ed in *The Times* of London on the eve of the Championships, shaming them for undervaluing women like her. Fittingly, she went on to win the title that year too, after continuing to push for equality during private meetings that fortnight.

In between that period, women's tennis produced some of the greatest storylines in world sport – and its most consistent champions. Those with shorter memories refer to Roger Federer, Rafael Nadal and Novak Djokovic as the sport's greatest rivalry, men who dominated the tour in a way that few had previously been able to do. They were consistent rivals for the best part of two decades (along with the injury-ravaged Andy Murray, who matched them for a few glorious seasons). Federer, Nadal and Djokovic remained atop the pecking order at the same time, gobbling up almost every opportunity for major silverware. In the 10 seasons from 2004 to 2013, the Big Three won 35 out of 40 major titles on offer. In the 10 seasons after that – even as they aged and Federer eventually retired – they still shared 30 of the 39 trophies (one Wimbledon was cancelled due to the Covid-19 pandemic). It is a mind-boggling haul, and one which few expect will ever be repeated.

Before they came along though, it was women who had experienced the most dominant periods in Open Era tennis. Three women – Steffi Graf, Chris Evert and Martina Navratilova – led the list of all-time Grand Slam champions in the Open Era (with 22, 18 and 18 titles respectively), ahead of all male players before the Big Three arrived. Evert and Navratilova shared 22 of 27 major titles on offer between 1980 and 1986, not a number to be sniffed at. They also played a whopping 80 matches against each other, 60 of which were finals (which, by the way, eclipses Nadal and Djokovic's 60 total matches). The Graf era was remarkable too as she won 20 of her 22 Grand Slam titles during a rammed eight-year period from 1988 to 1996. During that time, for three stunning seasons, she was also pushed to the brink by Monica Seles. Their short-lived tussle for the top of tennis (which saw Seles win seven of her nine Grand Slams in less than three seasons between 1991 and 1993) could have been the start of a legendary rivalry, if not for Seles being stabbed on court in 1993, a horrific incident which curtailed her career.

Later, alongside the Big Three, there was Serena Williams's 23-major-title career. She had various worthy rivals over time, including Martina Hingis and Justine Henin, but her rise alongside sister Venus remains one of the best stories global sport has ever seen. As for Serena's overall career, she may have had lulls or time spent away from the court, but it was all the more impressive for its longevity – nearly 18 years separated her first and last Grand Slam titles in 1999 and 2017. Those streaks in the women's game were not always perceived positively while they were happening. In fact, the women's game often came up against accusations of being too predictable and boring. When things completely shifted in the last decade and a half, and women's tennis became more unpredictable than ever, it was derided in some corners for having no outright stars or reliable champions. Quite simply, women's tennis cannot win. Broadcaster and co-founder of *The Tennis Podcast* Catherine Whitaker puts it plainly: 'It feels like everything is looked at through a male lens – where men's tennis would be perceived as fun chaos, in women's tennis it's weak flakiness, or failure from any one person to have the chops to be dominant.' The same applies to the periods of dominance: for the women it was regarded as boring, for the men – and the Big Three in particular – any negative takes are glossed over by their success and popularity. 'I've enjoyed the men's Grand Slam race as much as anyone,' Whitaker says. 'But history remembers week two of the slams: the winners, the incredible matches between them in the latter stages. History is not remembering the completely turgid first weeks of slams on the men's side for 15 years, where everything felt like a procession and a foregone conclusion.'

Whichever way you look at it, this latest era in tennis has seen men's and women's tennis exist on opposite ends of the spectrum: the Big Three have monopolised the Grand Slams in men's tennis, while there have been more winners than ever in women's. There are various theories as to why the rate of women's champions might have accelerated. For one, some top champions took earlier retirement than their male counterparts or self-imposed breaks. 'Something interesting happened,' John Dolan, who has worked in player relations and communications roles for the WTA and LTA, as well as being the author of *Women's Tennis 1968–84*, says. 'Justine Henin suddenly retired at No. 1 in the world, Venus and Serena had breaks from the game – due to injury and mental health, because of the murder of their sister – and Kim Clijsters retired. [Lindsay] Davenport and Mary Pierce had also retired. So very quickly, in 2008, there was a bit of a lull in the women's game. Put all of those things together, and you start to get those surprise winners.'

As Dolan says, Henin retired in 2008 when she was just 25, after her sweep of seven major titles. Kim Clijsters also had hiatuses away from the game in her twenties, during her four-major career. Later, Ash Barty retired at 25 in 2022, while Naomi Osaka won four major titles and then took a mental health break and pregnancy leave, which kept her away for the best part of two years. From a physical standpoint, Whitaker points to the impact of the menstrual cycle as compounding sporting performance too. According to studies, at certain stages in the menstrual cycle, women can be far less coordinated and also suffer from chronic pain – and players including Heather Watson and Qinwen Zheng have referred to their period affecting their ability to excel. Others simply think there are more top level players on tour now than there were before. Opportunities to play and make a living out of tennis as a young woman developed over time, and the decades of growth since King and her cohort established the tour in the 1970s has had a huge impact. 'What people don't understand is there is so much more depth than the eighties – I played then!' 18-time major champion Evert tweeted in August 2024, in response to those critiquing player complaints about the unforgiving player schedule. 'The players now have to bring their A game in the first round; we didn't.'

Speaking at Wimbledon this past year, 2023 US Open champion Coco Gauff agreed with that sentiment. 'I feel like when I look at the past champions of this tournament, you'll see people winning like three, four times in a row. If you're Martina [Navratilova], a couple more than that. I do think when you see seven different champions in the past few years, I think that just shows there's so much depth in the game. I think it's great. I think it makes the sport entertaining. Again, there's no easy matches. I think in the past you would almost look at a player and say, "Yeah, she's guaranteed a spot in the quarter-final," in the past, maybe decades ago. You can't really say that now. I think that's great. I think it pushes me as a player to want to be better.'

Perhaps the most obvious reason for women's tennis producing more Grand Slam champions is that they play best of three sets, while the men play best of five. That has long been the case. But as the sport has evolved since the turn of the century to become a more gruelling test of attrition played at the baseline, with longer rallies and much longer matches – stretching beyond four hours in some cases – across five sets it is simply more difficult for an underdog to beat the top players. The longer you have to keep up with the best opponents, the harder it is going to get to maintain that level. Top men can suffer nerves in a dodgy first set and still have plenty of time to recover. Djokovic has arguably made a habit of dropping the odd set during early rounds of the majors before getting into a rhythm later in the match. But the women's best-of-three format is not so forgiving. 'It absolutely, statistically lends itself to more diversity of champions, more upsets,' Whitaker says of the women's best-of-three format. 'If you take away best-of-five sets for the men at the slams, you would not have had the Big Three/Big Four stranglehold that you had. They became masters at that specific form of the sport, particularly Novak Djokovic.'

The reality is that it is a combination of all of these things. More players being in with a chance of winning does not make it inferior to the men's side. It just makes it different. There are undeniable downsides. For fans, it might be more difficult to root for players if results are harder to count on than in other sports. For sponsors and advertisers, a higher volume of lesser-known champions can be perceived as less star power. For broadcasters and media coverage, it means constantly needing to introduce new characters to audiences, and less rivalry narratives to pin coverage around. Whitaker experienced this in her work, both on mainstream television and hosting *The Tennis Podcast*, which has been running since 2012. 'There's no doubt it's a tougher sell. Obviously some personalities are better than others. Jelena Jankovic at world No. 1 is probably, objectively a tough sell, even taking all the male gaze goggles off. But definitely a lot of those stories, it felt like pushing a rock up a hill to sell them when that shouldn't have been the case. People like consistency; they enjoy a familiarity. With a Grand Slam there's a sweet spot for upsets. One or two is fine, that's fun. But there is absolutely a tipping point of overwhelm and lack of familiarity, where you get to, "Oh, I don't know any of these people," for fans, a slight feeling of underwhelm. That balance applies in the macro-sense as well.' But there is an upside too: 'The positives are pretty obvious: so many of those players are fascinating and have interesting stories in their own right. Also, the more players there are that are genuine threats for a title, you're increasing the odds of something special happening within them, or stories interacting.'

These breakthrough storylines add freshness, raise questions and spark debate. They can catch the media itself off guard too. At the Grand Slams, rows upon rows of individual cubicles house hundreds of newspaper and online journalists within windowless or basement rooms in the bowels of a stadium. The journalists breathlessly scuttle from court to court, trying to capture the biggest stories, with hundreds of options to choose from over nearly three weeks of action. Inevitably, some fall through the cracks. The surprise package player of the tournament will emerge as a contender by reaching the quarter-finals, and suddenly sports hacks will be making frantic calls to contacts and cornering compatriots of the player to gain a slither of insight on said dark horse. Do they have any weird hobbies or interests? What's their cat's name? Who coaches them? And, crucially, how did they get their start in tennis?

That final question is often the most intriguing as, especially in this sport, it could literally be any multitude of ways. 'It's a minefield of options,' former British No. 1 Laura Robson says. 'There are different ways to get to the top. You can work with your parents, through a coach, through an academy. It really doesn't matter; the best ones will make it to the top somehow. There's not one way that's preferred or better than the other. It's about figuring out what works for you.'

Robson, for instance, left school at 13 to be taught at home and headed to the National Tennis Centre in Roehampton, opting against the trendy academy set-ups in sunny Florida which some of her peers went to. To her mind, it all comes down to personality: 'I remember talking about it with my mum when I was younger. I knew I didn't want to go to an academy straight away; I felt my personality may have been a bit lost in a group like that. If I didn't have my mum there I probably wouldn't have asked for additional coaching or things I knew I needed for my game. I went for the more individual route and I had the same coach from age 14 to 18. Equally, Heather Watson did the academy route at Bollettieri's (now IMG Academy) and loved it, went to school there, loved the social aspect, that she could still be in a class and go to training later the same day. I think it's really an individual experience. It's also trial and error.'

One consistent theme across tennis success stories is how early each player specialised. The likes of the Williams sisters were committed to their family dream from the age of five, according to their father Richard's recollection of things. Most of the women profiled in this book started to seriously target a career in tennis from at least the age of 11. Compared to other sports, where you hear of athletes like British runner Anya Culling stumbling into marathon competition in her mid-twenties or Katie Taylor who transitioned from playing football for Ireland to becoming an undisputed world champion boxer, tennis requires players to put the blinkers on as soon as possible. 'You're definitely putting all your eggs in one basket,' Robson says. 'For the ones that don't make it, I always wonder what they're up to.' The risk is huge, but women's tennis provides the kind of rewards few other sports do for female athletes. The women in this book are a testament to that.

CHAPTER 2

Serena Williams and Venus Williams: The family project

12 MARCH 1997. Venus Williams was speaking to the press after playing the 25th singles match of her professional career. 'I don't plan to be on the tour very long,' she said. 'I can't see myself playing through pain and injuries, year after year doing the same thing. I can't see it. I don't want to say that I spent all my youth on tennis and didn't do anything else.' On 28 January 2017, nearly 20 years later, Venus was very much still playing. It marked the end of an era: the day the Williams sisters played each other in a major final for the last time, and likely picked up their last Grand Slam trophy too. Of course nobody knew that for sure at the time.

Serena won a record-breaking 23rd Grand Slam title at the Australian Open that day, and everyone fully expected her to win many more, even though she was 35. Conversely, by reaching a championship match for the first time in eight years, this was the resurgence Venus needed in her career aged 36, after constant questions about when she was planning to retire. She went on to make the Wimbledon final and the last four at the US Open later that year. She is still an active player on tour in 2025, at the age of 44.

Watching the footage of that day in 2017 now, of Venus embracing her younger sister Serena at the net, of Serena graciously paying tribute to Venus in her victory speech, of the pair posing with their respective trophies, there is a sense of this being a full circle moment. Twenty years on from their first season on tour together, and 19 years on from their first ever match against each other on tour, at the second round in Melbourne, Venus and Serena were capping off their last big win at the very same tournament in their ninth Grand Slam final. Serena won 6-4 6-4 in what proved to be a straightforward, if intense, match. 'She's the only reason that the Williams sisters exist,' Serena said of Venus while cradling her Australian Open trophy, her elder sister standing behind, her eyes glistening with tears. It turned out to be the last Grand Slam title of her career, and the pair's final meeting at a major event. A few weeks later, Serena would reveal that she was actually seven weeks pregnant while playing the Australian Open. Despite going on to reach four Grand Slam finals after giving birth to her first daughter in September 2017, 23 remains her total tally of major singles titles.

The last four years of Serena's career were marked by her pursuit of number 24, but looking back now it feels mostly appropriate that her very last major title came across the net from her sister Venus. On one level, they are different players with very separate achievements. Just based on the numbers, Serena's tally of majors far eclipses Venus's seven, for example. But their lives have been lived in tandem with each other and are more intertwined than any sporting siblings in history. On the same day Serena won her first singles title in Paris in 1999, her sister Venus was winning a trophy on the other side of the world too. Nine of their collective 30 major titles were won on the opposite side of the net to each other. Venus lost nine of her 16 major finals in her career – and seven losses came at the hands of her sister. What they accomplished individually and together was phenomenal, and all came as a result of sport's most well-loved family project, a sibling rivalry and a tennis dream realised against all odds.

*

Telling the story of the Williams sisters feels somewhat futile as it has been told countless times before. Even people who have never picked up a tennis racket know the names Venus and Serena. They have transcended the sport like no one before them. Dozens of documentaries have tracked the sisters' lives and books have been written. Even a feature-length Hollywood film, *King Richard*, charted the origin story of these two tennis giants and their family. Telling their story in a new way is nigh-on impossible, but writing a version of the last 20 years in women's tennis without featuring these two players would make it incomplete. For all their fame and the recognition they have received, the way they have shaped the sport is what interests me most. First because of their remarkable rivalry, and then because of how Serena was able to march on ahead without the same challenge of her elder sister.

Much of the discourse in women's tennis over the last two decades has centred on the lack of rivalries compared to the men's game. But for about a decade at the sport's epicentre, there existed perhaps the greatest pair of rivals to ever feature in tennis. If we're talking purely in storyline terms, the Williams sisters' time together at the top of tennis is incomparable to any other. This was not a rivalry that ever had to build or grow with time. There was no sense of a young pretender usurping the elder stateswoman. No contrasting styles or yin and yang personalities to clash at the championship matches. This was a ready-made rivalry, delivered and planned out by their parents Richard Williams and Oracene Price, nurtured on the Compton courts of their youth. Venus and Serena were born only 15 months apart in the early 1980s and were pulled along on this tennis dream when they were still only toddlers. The girls never had to wonder what it would be like to be challenged each day on the court, as across the net was their toughest test: their sister.

Family projects in sport are not unique, let alone in tennis. In almost every chapter of this book, a parent is one of the guiding influences in the player's life, and often the person nudging them towards what, eventually, becomes a shared dream. Suzanne Lenglen's 'Papa' is regarded as the first of the pushy parents in tennis and was said to chastise her with brutal criticism during training sessions. In the 1990s, Mary Pierce's father Jim was known for his outwardly outlandish and privately abusive behaviour – he famously yelled, 'Mary, kill the bitch,' when she was playing a junior tournament. Martina Hingis's mother, Melanie Molitor, who was a former player herself, literally named her daughter after Martina Navratilova, and made it her mission to coach her to tennis stardom from when she was just two years old.

As for tennis siblings, the Williams sisters were far from the first. Former world No. 1 Arantxa Sanchez Vicario had two brothers, Javier and Emilio, who also played professionally. In the early 1990s, Cara, Wayne and Byron Black were a trio of Zimbabwean siblings who reached the upper echelons of the doubles tour, with Byron and Cara both achieving the top ranking. The Maleeva sister trio – Manuela, Katerina and Magdalena – from Bulgaria all reached the top 10 in singles. In the US, John and Patrick McEnroe were the most famous examples of tennis siblings, the former being world No. 1 and the latter reaching the top 30. 'That there were two of them wasn't that unusual,' says John Dolan, who was a WTA communications manager during the early years of the Williams era. 'There's a danger that, to the wider non-tennis public, they could be perceived as the only siblings who had done that. But tennis has always been a family production. You'll have a very invested family force behind them. You cannot succeed unless you've got a very dedicated parent there with your coach too. In some ways it's not a surprise that it goes through families: you invest so much into one sibling, and that knowledge is transferable.'

The Williams family's story took sibling rivalries to new heights though, in that they literally competed in major finals against each other for the most prestigious prizes in their sport. Their story captivated people in a different way from the outset. One obvious reason was race. These were two Black sisters conquering a predominantly white sport in the late 1990s. They were also doing so through the unerring belief of their father, Richard, a man who grew up in Louisiana in the 1940s and '50s, where racism and Jim Crow law impacted his earliest experiences.

Neither Richard Williams nor the girls' mother, Oracene Price, had a tennis background when they first took the girls to the public courts in their neighbourhood in Compton, California. Richard was inspired by watching Virginia Ruzici win a hefty prize cheque during television coverage of a Salt Lake City tennis tournament. He read up on every tennis book he could find and put together a 78-page plan to get his young daughters targeting professional careers. Filling an old shopping cart with more than 500 balls, Richard and Oracene took the girls down to the local tennis courts and started to build their champions. This was no country club, nor were there any professional advisers on hand at the start. It was the ill-maintained courts on a street in a deprived neighbourhood. He called his daughters his 'ghetto Cinderellas', and Venus has recalled she and her sister hitting the ground for cover when a drive-by shooting broke out near their courts. Starting from the age of four or five, neither girl had a choice as to whether they wanted to pursue tennis or not. This path was one picked out by their father Richard, but they quickly adapted to the idea. 'They were our parents and there was a very thin line between being our parents and our coach,' Serena said in her recent documentary series *In the Arena: Serena Williams*. 'Sometimes it wasn't great. But I say at the end it was all worth it.'

Richard's dream was the family dream and he would tell anyone who would listen that his daughters were going to be No. 1.

Journalists with news cameras would descend on the courts to pay witness to the Compton girls who wanted to be tennis stars. The likes of the *Today* show and national newspapers were paying witness to these confident pre-teens and their eccentric father. The *New York Times* first ran a story about Venus when she was just 10, after she won the Southern California junior sectional championships in 1990. Richard was front and centre, telling reporters about their East Compton Park facilities: 'It's a radical neighbourhood. A lot of dope is sold. The gangs look out for Venus and they come and talk to her about the mistakes they've made . . . [Venus and Serena] want to be able to be No. 1 in the world and say they came from the worst neighbourhood.' A few months later, Venus's face was on the front page of the newspaper for a story about child prodigies and the agents vying to sign her up. 'I don't want her to peak at 12 and fall to pieces at 15,' Richard is quoted in the article as saying, when asked why he had rejected all contract offers to that stage. 'Who wouldn't want a million dollars? But I need a healthy daughter more than I need a million dollars.'

There is footage from that time of Richard tossing balls to the girls and telling them: 'This is you serving for the US Open – boom!' He was adamant he had the next two sporting giants in his family and talked them up as such. As much as he was often accused of being deluded and would make outlandish, inaccurate statements, his methods meant he was guaranteed to always get the attention that he wanted for the family mission. 'I think my dad was a marketing genius,' Serena said in recent years. 'He had such a genius way of putting our story out there and making sure it was told. He got my sister out there, and then he started to say that I was going to be better. He used to call me a pitbull. I honestly never believed that he thought I was going to be better. I don't know if it was that I never believed in myself, and that's why I never believed it. I always thought my dad was doing that just so I could get some recognition, to make sure I had an opportunity to play professional tennis.' His wholehearted faith in their destiny to be the best rubbed off on his older daughter, Venus, though. 'I guess I always knew I'd be a champ,' Venus said in a 2002 interview with the *Observer*. 'That's what I was told, and at that age that's what you believe.'

Despite Serena's later success, Venus was the real prodigy of this story. She was tall, nearly 5ft 8in when she was still 11 years old, and yet moved with an agility unheard of for a girl of her height. Her calm disposition in the face of her father's wacky behaviour and the huge attention on her also made for an intriguing character. 'She was the phenom,' Serena said. The family's life changed forever in 1991 when renowned coach Rick Macci flew out to Compton to meet them. 'I never went to see anybody in my life,' Macci says, speaking from his academy in Florida. 'They either came to me or I saw them at a junior tournament. But I had a feeling. I said, "I'll check this little girl out" – it was more about Venus. I flew out to Compton that night, and in the hotel they all came – Richard, Oracene, Venus sitting on one leg, Serena on the other, hugging and kissing. Right off the bat one specific thing that has always stood out to me, how close-knit the family was like no other. I've done this a long time; there's a lot of amazing families. This was way over the top, and just how close they were actually got my attention.' They talked for hours in that hotel lobby. 'I thought I was in a deposition,' Macci says, laughing at the memory. 'Richard pulled out a piece of paper. He was grilling me, you know, asked me all these questions. But I respected it, because if he wanted someone in his circle, he wanted a father figure and a role model, and someone who's been there, done that.'

Macci was just that. He had most recently coached Jennifer Capriati, the girl who broke records in 1990 by reaching the semi-finals of the French Open on her debut at 14 years old, rising to become the youngest ever top 10 player in history as a result.

Macci knew a young talent when he saw it, but even he failed to initially understand exactly what made Venus so special when they went down to the Compton courts the next day. 'The first hour I didn't see it,' Macci says. 'I actually said, "What in God's name am I doing in Compton, California?" Remember I had Jennifer, she was poetry in motion, racket back in the parking lot, low centre of gravity; the ball was on a string for her. And then I've got Venus and Serena out there, arms and legs and hair and beads flying off their head. It was a train wreck. No one can evaluate talent better than myself, and I didn't see it.'

It was only when they stopped drilling and instead switched to playing competitive points that Macci saw the potential: 'The whole landscape changed. This is what stood out to me more than anything: I never saw two little girls try so hard in my life. Now, that doesn't mean you're going to be number one, or that doesn't mean you're going to be great, but that quality that I saw, there was like a rage inside these two little girls I'd never seen, and I haven't seen it to this day. Venus tried so hard to get to a ball, her nose was two inches off the ground. Serena had all this explosiveness that I saw, even though she really couldn't play well. This was crazy athleticism. I started projecting in my mind. Richard was 6ft 3in, so I started thinking about where Venus could be at 17. Once we played the competitive points, I just felt they were bulletproof, because the minute I said "Game on," it went to a whole other level. Now technically they were all over the map, but they did start popping the popcorn, extra butter. Their feet were a little better, but it's what I saw on the inside. It blew me away. I thought not only can these two little girls be No. 1 in the world, they could transcend the sport.' Easy to say with hindsight, perhaps, but Macci did back the girls from the word go.

Macci remembers Venus asking to go to the bathroom mid-session, and walking on her hands and doing cartwheels all the way to the outbuilding. Then he said the line that has been immortalised in *King Richard*: 'I told Richard, "Let me tell you something; you've got the next female Michael Jordan on your hands." He puts his arm around me, and he goes, "No brother, man, I got the next two."'

CHAPTER 3

Serena Williams and Venus Williams: A dream realised

FOUR months after that first meeting with Rick Macci, the Williams family packed up and moved across the country to Florida, after signing a contract with the coach at his academy. It was a huge step to uproot not only their two daughters, but Price's three daughters from a previous marriage, in pursuit of this crazy tennis dream. It also moved them into a more insulated world at a state-of-the-art, expensive tennis facility. It marked a complete shift from the Compton environment where Richard was giving them tough love on the tennis court. 'He wanted the real world,' Macci says. 'There'd be times there'd be broken beer bottles at the back fence, or he'd have his car radio on loud, or he'd yell at Venus, "Don't double fault!" He would do all these things, and he prepared them.'

But the best coaching was the only way to take the girls to the next level. For the first time in Macci's career, he agreed to give the girls completely free stewardship and coaching, as he was convinced Venus at least was the real deal. He had no doubt that his gamble would pay off. That meant working closely with Richard Williams every day. Macci has become seasoned with father–daughter dynamics on a tennis court throughout his career – from the intense to the downright abusive. Richard was intense, for sure, but he stood out for different reasons: 'You've got to remember, I had Capriati, who was daddy's little girl. I've had Maria Sharapova and her father Yuri, Mary and Jim Pierce, Sofia Kenin, who were also daddy's little girls. I've had some fathers from outer space, they're all in. Listen, the parent has to push. You're not going to find a kid that's just going to bang, do it all on their own. So I get all that. But the difference with this family was Richard Williams every day was teaching life lessons. He not only knew about sports and competition, he wanted them to be kids, and every single day he would be joking and laughing. We'd go six hours a day, it was hard-core because I had a lot of work to do, but he was all about life lessons. Every single day they brought their books to the court and, if it rained, he made them go up to my office and study. Every night – good, bad, happy, sad – the girls would say, "Rick, thank you very much." And if they didn't, he'd remind them. Believe me, Serena a lot of times was kind of chippy at the end of practice. You know, she's like a little prankster. Venus was more calm and chilled out. I just had so much respect for Richard as a father. I get along with everybody, but it was different, the way he just treated them. He kept saying, "Rick, they'll only be kids once."'

That sentiment was constantly juxtaposed by the exposure the girls were given in the media from a young age – all of which was led and endorsed by Richard himself. 'We're talking hundreds of interviews,' Macci says. 'I mean, they were legendary before they even did anything.' At night, Richard would set up a tripod in their living room and interview his daughters on camera. He got them to practise fronting up to the media, imagining the press confer-ences they may partake in in the not-too-distant future, or even just answering philosophical questions of his own. 'It prepared you for the world,' Venus said of the pressure these sessions would put them under. 'He would train them to answer the question without answering the question, it was unbelievable,' Macci says. 'Listen, if you're going to do that, all the media and all the hype, you'd better have the thoroughbred to win the Derby. And he knew he had two. We all could have been wrong. They could have got hurt, but I wasn't and he wasn't. And I think what people have to understand is two sisters, same house, same bedroom . . . you can't make it up. It's the biggest story, in my opinion, ever in sports to have that level of greatness.'

Richard was the ultimate hustler, architect of the 'dream big and achieve' story. He was also a total maverick, who famously made statements about being opposed to interracial marriage, told tall tales about investments he had made in the technology industry and often detracted from his daughters' own achievements during their careers with his behaviour. Still, compared with the likes of Jelena Dokic's father, who – as outlined in Jelena's autobiography, *Unbreakable* – was allegedly physically abusing his daughter and being ejected from tournaments for being violent towards staff, Richard telling some silly stories seemed like small fry. In February 1999, though, Oracene Price went to Columbia Hospital in West Palm Beach with three broken ribs. Medical staff suspected domestic abuse, but Richard denied any involvement and no charges were ever brought.

His daughters have remained fiercely loyal to him throughout their careers. Macci to this day calls Richard his 'best friend', while in the same breath acknowledging what a difficult character he could sometimes be to work with. 'I should be in the Hall of Fame just putting up with that guy. It was kind of brutal. But the art of coaching is knowing when to keep your mouth shut also. Richard just liked to bust everybody's chops all the time. He was just that type of guy. But regarding the tennis, he let me do my thing, and he never really interfered, because we were a team, and we were doing this together, but he gave me full reins for everything. At the end of the day, he was the easiest guy to work with, even though he was the most stubborn, because he respected me, and he was my best friend, and Venus and Serena were like my daughters and they still are.'

The girls had every tool at their disposal to succeed at Macci's academy. The perfect facilities, training in the Florida sunshine and humidity (which players from all over the world flock to, or at least try to replicate), private schooling, four hours of tennis lessons one-to-one with Macci per day, top quality adult male hitting part-ners and a host of other hugely talented teenagers to pit themselves against. The likes of future Grand Slam champions Mary Pierce and Andy Roddick were at Macci's academy at the same time, not that the girls became especially close to anyone outside their own family. 'They had, I would want to call it more acquaintances; no one ever went to the mall together, they never invited them over to their house, but they were around other children,' Macci says. 'It was always this, Muhammad Ali, us against the world mentality. They're competitors. They're not there to make friends. I think also, what people have to understand, is I've never seen two siblings so close. Venus and Serena at nine and 10 years old, they're like skipping and holding hands.'

This separation between the Williamses' inner circle and the rest of the tennis world continued in the decisions they took. Richard withdrew them from the competitive junior circuit when they were 11 and 10 years old too, against all advice – including Macci's. Venus had won 63 of 63 matches she had played, but he wanted them to focus on going professional, not playing junior tournaments around the country with other youngsters who were not at their level. He was teaching them how to succeed on the WTA circuit by taking risks and being front-foot players, not by simply keeping the ball in play, as often happened in the juniors. Venus was simultaneously the most talked about young talent in America while also not play-ing any competitive tennis for three years. It meant the Williamses developed somewhat of an unknown aura around them.

When Venus was 13, they briefly switched from Macci's academy to the more star-studded Nick Bollettieri's. It lasted only six weeks as Richard felt wary of the academy's wish to enter into an agreement that would see them benefit if and when the girls made it to the big time. It was at this time that the Williams sisters attended their first USTA player development camp, aged 12 and 13. 'It's good for them to mix with the other kids,' USTA coaching director Stan Smith said at the time. 'They've been something of a mystery and it's good for the kids to see they aren't Public Enemy No. 1.' Former USTA press officer Randy Walker recently published questionnaires they filled out that weekend. Answering who their role model was, both of the girls wrote down 'Myself'. That sense of self-assuredness was startling to people. In a now-famous 1995 interview, Venus fully encapsulated this. She said, 'I know I can beat her,' of an upcoming opponent, and John McKenzie of ABC News replied, 'You're very confident.' In the grainy footage she nodded, smiled serenely and said, 'I'm very confident.' When McKenzie asked her why, her father Richard interrupts the interview, admonishing the journalist for what he perceived as unnecessary prodding at his daughter's self-esteem. 'You're dealing with a little Black kid, she's answered with a lot of confidence, leave that alone,' he said, standing over McKenzie.

Pam Shriver first met Venus and Serena Williams in October 1993, a couple of years prior. The sisters flew out to Baltimore from Florida as they were invited to take part in Shriver's annual charity event. Venus was to play mixed doubles with 41-year-old Jimmy Connors, against Shriver and Jim Courier. At the time, Shriver was an Olympic gold medallist and 22-time major champion in doubles and former world No. 3 singles player, now ranked just outside the top 30. Venus was only 13, but she had already played tennis with the likes of Arthur Ashe, Billie Jean King and John McEnroe, and been profiled by just about every American sporting media outlet going. And yet, a mystery still surrounded this pre-teen prodigy and her sister. There was rampant chatter within the tennis world about just how good these girls, who had been thrust prematurely into the limelight by their father, actually were.

'Prior to Venus playing her pro debut in Oakland in '94, there was a lot of swirling conversations about the skill set of the Williams sisters at age, say, 10, 11, 12,' Shriver says. 'They were coming into our consciousness; stories about two really talented sisters that were 15 months apart, who had a very atypical developmental pathway involving learning tennis in some tough neighbourhoods in LA and then moving to the academy in Florida. We don't know how good they are and there was this rumour that they never practised sets. After I hit with Venus for a day or two, in maybe our third session together, I said, "Hey, let's play a practice set." Venus shrugged and said, "Okay." There was no hesitation, no nothing. So there were urban myths that surrounded them.' Shriver says there was no hint of overawe from Venus whatsoever, but the lasting memory was of how appreciative they were for the opportunity to practise with her. 'I can remember kind of thinking, oh my goodness, I've never heard "thank you" so much. At that point, because they weren't playing junior tournaments, there were a lot of mysteries around them. But year by year, those would be peeled away, and it was just left with two talents that would go on to become No. 1 in the world.'

Aged 14, Venus made her professional debut at the Bank of the West Classic in Oakland, California on 31 October 1994. After years of speculation, and warnings about the likes of Capriati experiencing too much too soon, this was Venus's decision in the end. Interestingly, it went against Richard's own view that she should wait until she was 16. It had been nearly four years since she had played a competitive match at junior level, and she lacked so much experience that she seemed perplexed by the common practice of sitting down between games. She didn't do it during her practice, so why would she do it during a match? 'I don't believe in sitting down,' Venus reasoned with the press after she defeated world No. 58 Shaun Stafford 6-3 6-4. About 900 people were in the stands for this introduction to the girl tipped as tennis's next star. 'Williams Tastes Victory at Prime-Time Debut' ran the *New York Times* headline, and reporter Robin Finn claimed Venus's match had eclipsed 38-year-old Martina Navratilova's final bow in Oakland.

Under the glare of the spotlight, Venus spent the aftermath of the match signing autographs, a wide smile painted across her face. She only played nine tournaments in her first two years on tour, all of them in North America. Her first foray outside of her home country was in May 1997, when she played at Roland Garros after finally breaking into the top 100 – at the ripe old age of 16. It came after her run to the Indian Wells quarter-final, scoring her first top 10 win over Iva Majoli. In September, her true breakthrough happened at the US Open in New York where she made it all the way to her first Grand Slam final ranked just 66th in the world, ending in a 6-0 6-4 loss to Martina Hingis.

Serena's own debut was in October 1995 in Quebec, after a chaotic journey which saw her miss her original flight. Compared to Venus's Oakland match, this was a far less flashy, third-tier event, and she lost 6-1 6-1 to world No. 149 Anne Miller in the Canadian Open qualifying in front of barely 50 people. Miller uncharitably said post-match of Serena's early fame, 'I guess I played a celebrity,' and suggested she get back to the junior circuit. For Serena, this was a brief dipping her toe into professional tennis. She waited nearly 18 months before playing again, and it wasn't until October 1997 that she finally managed to battle through to the main draw of a tournament at the Kremlin Cup. A week later, her breakthrough came in Chicago where she used her wildcard to inspire her wins over top 10 players Mary Pierce and Monica Seles in a run to the semi-final. If 1997 was the Williams sisters' true starting point in the big leagues, 1998 and 1999 was when the story got really good.

CHAPTER 4

Serena Williams and Venus Williams: From sisters to rivals

IN 1998 the Williams sisters played their first ever match against each other on tour. It came at the Australian Open second round, and Venus won 7-6 6-1. At the end, she lifted her younger sister's arm in the air at the net and got the crowd to applaud her. The following month Venus won her first title in Oklahoma, including finally beating world No. 2 Lindsay Davenport after three consecutive losses to her. She followed that up with another title in Key Biscayne. She did it by ousting teen Queen Bee, world No. 1 and four-time major champion Martina Hingis, as well as superstar Anna Kournikova. She made her top 10 debut as a result and all signs pointed to Venus finally fulfilling her promise on the biggest stage – at a Grand Slam. But quarter-final losses at Roland Garros and Wimbledon followed, before a semi-final defeat at the hands of Davenport in New York.

There was more of the same in 1999, but again Venus fell slightly short at the Grand Slams, including another semi-final loss to Hingis in New York. Serena had barely made a ripple at the Grand Slams up to that point but had beaten the likes of Hingis and Steffi Graf that year and steadily climbed into the top 10 too. Somehow, 1999 became her year at the US Open: she beat three major champions in

Conchita Martinez, Seles and Davenport, before coming up against top dog Hingis in her first major final. 'I never felt like this again, but I knew before the tournament started that I was going to win,' Serena said on *In the Arena.* 'It had already happened for me. It was like a premonition.'

Serena had watched from the stands as Hingis beat her sister Venus, standing in the way of a history-making final between the pair. She immediately went to the practice courts afterwards, in what she has since described as mind games she hoped might affect Hingis. Standing in the arena on the day of the final, across the net from Hingis, the mind games were less subtle from Serena: 'I lose the coin toss and the referee says to Martina, "Serve or receive?" She said, "I'll serve." And I looked at her and said, "Are you sure about that?" She was startled. Years later I remember thinking, I can't believe I said that.' Serena won the first three games of the match and never looked back, 6-3 7-6. As the final point went her way, Serena held her hand to her chest and cried out in a mixture of relief and sheer unadulterated joy. She was the first African-American woman to lift a Grand Slam trophy since Althea Gibson in 1958.

'She finally grew and became a monster on the court, in the best and most beautiful way,' Venus said of that moment. In the stands, with a hoodie fixed over her head and shading her eyes, Venus seemed a world away as she watched her sister defy the natural order of things. The younger Williams girl, the one who had not been tipped as the prodigy, the one who did not have the same height and graceful shot-making, had nudged herself ahead of her sister to the biggest trophy in their sport. Some questioned how it might impact their relationship or affect their closeness. But the Williams sisters proved that their rivalry was only ever playing out on the court, as no jealousy ever seemed to impinge on their sisterhood. If anything, it brought them closer together. 'The best thing that happened in my career was coming up behind my sister,' Serena has said since.

'Everyone was expecting her to do good. I cannot imagine the pressure she felt as a 15- and 16-year-old. I don't know if I would have handled that pressure the same. I was able to go so much faster because of everything that she went through.'

Venus's time came the following year at Wimbledon, where she won her first of five titles at the All England Club. To get to the championship match, she prevailed over Hingis and then her sister Serena in an awkward semi-final. Ahead of their match, they spent 30 minutes warming up together on court. During the match, there was a notable absence: their parents. Their mother Oracene was in the States while Richard had taken a long walk around Wimbledon village during his daughters' semi-final as he found it too difficult to watch. Venus was subdued even after winning. Conspiracy theories were rife at the time that the Williams family would decide pre-match who would win, but Serena's despair at losing that year should have put those rumours to bed. 'It's really bitter,' Venus said after. 'But someone had to move on. In this instance it was me.'

Richard was in the player box alongside Serena to watch Venus triumph the following day over defending champion Lindsay Davenport 6-3 7-6 in a commanding performance. At the winning moment she pranced around the grass, leaping in glee, at finally having won the slam she had been hunting for, despite still only being 20 years old. She then ran up to the stands to celebrate with her family, her younger sister the first to wrap her arms around her. It made the Williams sisters the first sisters to each own a Grand Slam singles title. 'I think I was probably happier than her when she won Wimbledon, because it felt like okay, I'm not stealing anything,' Serena said recently, reflecting on that moment.

Off the court, nothing about their relationship seemed to change. In the midst of all that initial success, the pair moved into a shared home in Florida – with two sides, one for each sister. They attended an arts school together too. At tournaments, they continued to stay at the same home or hotel, eat with each other and practise with each other. At the US Open in 2000, one big change came when their mother Oracene revealed to the sisters that she intended to file for divorce from Richard. Venus still went on to win the title. When President Bill Clinton called to congratulate her, she said, 'What happened? Where'd you go?' referring to him exiting the stadium before their match started.

Afterwards, she signed a $40 million five-year contract with Reebok, the single largest endorsement deal ever signed by a female athlete. She was officially the most marketable prospect in tennis, and her star power was extending beyond her sport. Though Serena did not seem affected by envy, the Williamses' success did not endear them to the rest of the WTA Tour. Their circle remained close-knit in those early years, what Jon Wertheim referred to in his book *Venus Envy* as 'House of Williams'. The Williams family did not seem to care much about the feathers they ruffled or the way they were viewed. 'I don't come to make friends, I come to win matches,' Venus told Wertheim. That aloofness brought criticism. 'They lack humility,' John McEnroe said in the early noughties. Other leading players including Lindsay Davenport and Martina Hingis made no secret of their pact to try to tag team during tournaments to beat the Williams sisters at every opportunity. One player would struggle to beat them both in a tournament, but together they had more luck. Hingis even famously said that 'being Black only helps them', after Richard said his daughters experienced racism at Indian Wells. Their elder sister, Isha Price, a constant presence with Serena and Venus, recalled the early years in *In the Arena*: 'The tennis scene, when we first entered it, it wasn't kind. When people are purposely isolating you, or putting you in a category or over there, then you bring your team in. It would be all of us [as a family] walking through the players' lounge. In that way we were our own team. A lot of the time it extended to the crowd. We approached it from the standpoint of definitely us against the world, because that's what it felt like at the time.'

John Dolan remembers Serena's first French Open in 1998 when she was only 16. She reached the fourth round and played fourth seed and former champion Arantxa Sanchez Vicario. During a close net exchange, Serena drilled a ball right at her Spanish opponent. 'You'd never seen that before in women's tennis,' Dolan says. 'That's confidence; it's brash. But the rest of the players in the locker room see that and think, woah, that's stepping over the line here. At the press conference afterwards, there was a real kerfuffle as Arantxa really went for her; she said it's a lack of respect. That was a reputation Serena had for a while. This spice only added to the profile of women's tennis. It was a PR person's dream as it meant women's tennis was getting all these headlines but, maybe unfairly, these two teenage players were getting a bit of a bad rap. To be fair to Venus and Serena, I don't think anyone ever took them to one side – certainly not any of the players – to say this is not the way things are done. Maybe the players saw them as such a threat because they were so strong, physically developed and had so much confidence and potential which we'd never seen before. That was something new in the women's game. Before, it had been, "Let's be nice and demure."'

Those same expectations did not exist on the men's side of the tour. 'Were they male, we would applaud their "intensity", their "competitive streak", their "ferocity". Because they are women – Black women, no less – they are "catty" and they are "trash talkers",' Wertheim wrote in *Venus Envy* at the time. Serena sometimes got drawn into back-and-forths with other players via the press, while Venus mostly kept herself to herself. She often appeared unbothered by all the fuss, all the talk that surrounded their travelling circus. Dolan was often the man ferrying them to and from press conferences, and could get a sense of the dynamics between rival players on tour. 'A lot of the times when the players talked about Serena or Venus they used the word "they",' Dolan says. 'I often wonder if there was just one of them whether they would have forced themselves to integrate a bit more into the tour. But there was a real mystique and mystery about them. Because they had each other, they were often quite separate from everyone else. And not only that, also they had their mother or their father, who were always with them on tour. It was very clan-ish, more so than some other families. That was maybe to protect them as well. As Richard used to say, there were a lot of "sharks" around. But that prevented the rest of the tour from, I think, really getting to know them. Venus was always an introvert, whereas Serena is a borderline introvert. The first couple of years of their careers were very insular. But maybe that was protective, because they had no clue what they were letting themselves in for – nobody did.'

Macci says the rest of the tour did not warm to the Williams sisters because of a rooted jealousy about how much attention and marketing dollars they attracted from the outset – before they had ever really achieved anything. 'Eight months after Venus's debut, she got a $12 million [Reebok] contract,' Macci says. 'You've got to understand, no one had something like that in [women's] pro tennis. You know how it is, people, they'll tell you good luck, but they want you to lose. It's brutal, but there's a lot of that.'

The Williams sisters were further ostracised in 2001 at Indian Wells, when Venus pulled out of the semi-final she was due to play against Serena, citing a knee injury. The problem was she only did so four minutes before the start time. The fans were already seated and ready for a popcorn showing. When it was announced they would not be getting what they paid for, they were angry. Accusations of Richard orchestrating it all behind the scenes and fixing the result were swirling again. It led to the largely white, older crowd turning on Serena in the final, which she played against Kim Clijsters.

She was booed throughout the match and Richard and Venus were both jeered when they arrived in the stands. He later said punters shouted racial slurs at him. It was a horrific episode for 19-year-old Serena, but somehow she still won the tournament. She did not return to Indian Wells for 14 years as a result.

That was Indian Wells's great loss as the Williams sisters had established themselves as tennis's hottest ticket. At the US Open later that year, their first ever joint Grand Slam final came to pass. It was the first time sisters had played for a major title since the Watson sisters, Maud and Lilian, competed for the inaugural Wimbledon ladies' singles title in 1884. That year, 19-year-old Maud went home with a silver flower basket as her prize but, after 117 years, this latest meeting of sisters in New York was a significantly higher profile affair. More than 7 million Americans tuned in and a host of A-listers watched from the stands, including Mary J. Blige, Spike Lee and Jay-Z. None other than Diana Ross kicked off the show by singing 'God Bless America' and a fireworks display preceded these two Black sisters from Compton walking out on to a court named after another African-American tennis icon, Arthur Ashe.

The match was nothing to write home about in the end, a 6-2 6-4 win for Venus against her error-prone younger sister. But their 'I love you' at the net and Venus breaking from tradition to sit alongside Serena while they waited for the trophy ceremony was what touched fans. Venus was undoubtedly the best player in the world, this being her fourth major title in the last six tournaments. The following February, she finally fulfilled her childhood promise and family's dream by ascending to the world No. 1 ranking. But her sister Serena did not allow her to get comfortable. At a Florida tournament that March, she finally beat Venus, in the seventh attempt of her professional career. It was a 6-2 6-2, 50-minute schooling. It set into motion a shift in the Williams hierarchy.

Roland Garros 2002 marked the beginning of one of the most remarkable streaks tennis had ever seen as two sisters monopolised Grand Slam finals for four tournaments in a row. But unlike the US Open the previous year, little sister Serena won each and every one of them. It was the first time she had won a Grand Slam event since her victory in New York in 1999, and the near-three-year wait proved worth it as she swept the majors. It was the first 'Serena Slam' of her career, in which she held all four major trophies at the same time – the first woman to do so since Steffi Graf in 1994. The only problem was that it meant snatching victory from her sister each and every time, including the world No. 1 ranking, which Venus would never reclaim.

As incredible as their run of finals was, the actual tennis often did not live up to the hype. Serena said she found a way to win at the French Open by deploying a new tactic when playing Venus: not looking at her. 'She's so classy and I'm so crazy,' Serena has said of their contrasting on-court demeanour. 'Playing her is so annoying because here I am, eyes out, and she's like, you hit a winner and she just moves on to the next shot. I'm like, aren't you mad? It's the most frustrating thing in the world.' To help her separate herself from her sister on the court, she opted to act as if she was not there at all. This was a complete departure from the ferocious, impassioned celebrations and frustration that Serena usually brought to her matches. She would psych out many opponents with her imposing behaviour. It was part of what made her so awesome to watch throughout her career as she let every emotion run free – for better or worse. Against her implacable sister though, she recognised it did not have the same impact so she reined it in. It was the best thing she ever did when it came to the results, but it could make the match-up between them feel flat. They rarely brought the best out of each other, and their finals were often described as messy or lacklustre. The crowd struggled to feed off their energy, and the occasion never quite lived up to the epic storyline. There was no venom between the two sisters.

After Serena wrapped up her first French Open, thanks in part to a sub-par showing from her older sister, Venus stood with the line of photographers, holding her own camera to snap photos of the champion. It brewed some disgruntlement, not to mention from other players who were being blocked out of the major finals. Their next final at Wimbledon appeased some, due to the higher quality match that played out, but still the apathy that surrounded them did not go unnoticed by the Williams sisters. 'It was us against the WTA,' Serena said. 'We didn't have people talking to us, people were avoiding us. We were literally winning every week and people were saying, "This is boring, we don't want to see another Williams final." What Venus and I did was unprecedented.'

Stephen Capriati, Jennifer's brother, was one such person who spoke out about how 'boring' their dominance was growing, as had players including Justine Henin and Amelie Mauresmo. Perhaps the public swipes were to be expected in a sport dominated by literal teenagers, who were being asked their opinions by the world's media. Other tennis insiders who had less skin in the game could appreciate their brilliance for what it was. 'I can compare it to if Tiger Woods had a brother who was No. 2 in golf,' former player-turned-analyst Mary Carillo told the *New York Times* in 2002. 'It's so improbable that it almost seems impossible.'

As Serena wrapped up her haul at the 2002 US Open and 2003 Australian Open, there was no doubt that the Williamses' success had undeniably transcended the sport. Serena was turning heads by donning unitard tennis outfits, and both sisters counted Wrigley's chewing gum, Avon cosmetics and McDonald's as companies they were endorsing, alongside Reebok (Venus's apparel sponsor) and Puma (Serena's). In 2003, Serena jumped ship from Puma, her sponsor of six years, and signed a $55 million deal with Nike, which proved the start of a long and hugely successful partnership between the brand and herself. They were still earning less than top male players like Andre Agassi (which Venus pointed out at the time was due to the gender inequality that was ingrained in sport), but they were certainly attracting lucrative deals beyond what women athletes could generally hope for.

Those three years marked the most sustained period of direct rivalry between the two sisters that we would ever witness in their careers, as Serena backed up her Wimbledon title in 2003 by beating Venus 4-6 6-4 6-2. In six major finals against each other, Serena led the head-to-head 5-1. Macci says it is a testament to their parents that it never ruptured their relationship. 'Think of all the things that could have blown up,' he says. 'You've seen families blown up for their siblings, the money, boyfriends, fame, the winning as well. They played 31 times. But that goes back to Richard and Oracene; the parents deserve credit when they should have credit. This thing could have gone in the other direction so fast. It's unbelievable with all this stuff involved that it didn't.'

But there were major low points throughout their lives and careers to come. The first was the most tragic: the murder of their older sister, Yetunde, in a September 2003 drive-by shooting. It sent them spiralling into a pit of grief that, despite trying to power through the tennis as they always had done, took time to adjust to. Neither sister would win a major again until 2005. From 2000 to 2003, they won nine major titles between them, but between 2004 and 2007 they won four. Their era of dominance had waned, and the likes of Justine Henin, Maria Sharapova, Kim Clijsters and Amelie Mauresmo took it as their opportunity. There were still moments of magic though, like Venus's 2005 Wimbledon comeback win over Lindsay Davenport, in a final regarded as one of the greatest ever played, ending 9-7 in the deciding set.

Their influence went beyond just winning though. Venus scored perhaps the biggest victory of her life in 2007, when she success-fully lobbied for Wimbledon to bring the women's prize money in line with the men's. Wimbledon remained the only major to not have equal prize money, and Venus made it her mission to change that. She gave a speech to the All England Club committee on the eve of winning the 2005 title, asking them to close their eyes and imagine telling their daughter they were to earn less than their son. Then she wrote a column in *The Times* of London in 2006 imploring the All England Club to reconsider their prize money policy, which in 2006 saw Amelie Mauresmo win 95 per cent of the $1.7 million that Roger Federer earned as champion. Even British Prime Minister Tony Blair weighed in, supporting Venus's cause. In 2007, they finally adopted an equal stance, and Venus was credited as the leading force for change, who completed what Billie Jean King had started at the slams in 1973. Fittingly, she also won the title that year. It was a measure of how Venus saw her role evolving on the women's tour, and showed the savvy negotiation and skilful advocacy she wanted to incorporate into her career. She and Serena had never just been about the tennis. In fact, their time working in fashion, going to art college and engaging in business opportunities often earned them criticism when their tennis results slipped. But they shrugged it off. They needed the balance away from the court.

The next Venus v Serena major final came in 2008 at Wimbledon, following a five-year gap. After five losses in a row, Venus finally came up trumps in a tight 7-5 6-4 win in gusty conditions, clinch-ing her fifth Wimbledon title and seventh major overall. It would prove to be her last. The following year, they met in the Wimbledon final again, with Venus on a 20-match, 34-set streak at the All England Club. But Serena was the woman in the ascendancy, and never lost her serve in the 7-6 6-2 victory. It meant she had won four of the last five majors, re-establishing herself as the woman to beat in world tennis. After all their dominance, 2010 proved the start of a downward trajectory for them both. Venus's career was curtailed by Sjögren's syndrome, an autoimmune disease that affected her strength and endurance. She was diagnosed in 2011, but had been feeling the effects of it for years. She dropped from top five to outside the top 100. Meanwhile, Serena in 2009 landed in hot water after an outburst at the US Open semi-final. She lost 6-4 7-5 to Kim Clijsters after she was docked a point on match point for hurling abuse at a line judge who called her for a foot fault. 'I'll fucking take the ball and shove it down your fucking throat,' she is reported to have said. Afterwards, she was fined by the tournament. She was even reprimanded by the Elders in her church, as a staunch Jehovah's Witness throughout her life.

The following year she suffered a freak accident when she cut her feet on broken glass while at a restaurant in Munich during the summer of 2010. She had just won her fourth Wimbledon title, but this would curtail the next year of her life and two years of her tennis. She had two operations on her feet, then suffered from blood clots in her lungs a few months later and a subsequent hematoma, both of which left her completely wiped out. At the time she was a 13-time major champion, but some questioned whether her career was over as she took almost a complete year off to recover. At the time, she said it was 'more mentally tough than a lot of things I've been through, including my sister dying'.

In 2011 she got back to a Grand Slam final at the US Open, but lost to Australian Sam Stosur – only the second time she lost a major final to anyone other than her sister. The following season's last-16 exit in Melbourne plus an opening round loss at Roland Garros – the first time that had ever happened in her career – caused her to do some soul-searching. Though her mother and father remained constant sounding boards during her career, she was lacking in a full-time coach. While trying to pick herself back up after her humbling loss in Paris, she met French coach Patrick

Mouratoglou, who owned an academy there. She asked him to travel to Wimbledon with her and somehow she won. It was one of the most impressive serving fortnights ever seen, and she broke the record for aces at Wimbledon with a tally of 102. In the final against third-ranked Agnieszka Radwanska she hit 17. So began the second half of Serena's career, but she was out on her own. Injury was stopping Venus from playing much between 2011 and 2013. Entering her mid thirties, her star was waning while Serena was just getting started again. With Venus out of the mix, there were few rivals to speak of for the next decade. People tried to talk up Serena's rivalry with Maria Sharapova, but her 18-2 record against the Russian speaks for itself.

'It was a situation of this is either the most predictable thing ever, i.e. Serena's going to win, or it's almost a free-for-all,' tennis broadcaster Catherine Whitaker says. 'If it's not Serena it's Marion Bartoli or Sabine Lisicki. Both completely predictable or completely unpredictable.' Even Serena recognised how things had shifted. 'Girls would talk in the locker room about how they had to beat us [her and Venus]. Eventually it became me against everyone else. It was, "We don't care who wins, we just don't want her to win – that's the girl to beat, we're going to do everything we can to take her down." That target got to be a blessing. If I didn't have that target I would never have been Serena Williams.' Across her 33 major finals, she faced 18 different opponents. It is the most of any player who contested 30 or more finals in the Open Era (Chris Evert had 13 opponents, Martina Navratilova 11, Steffi Graf 11, Roger Federer 13, Rafael Nadal 11, Novak Djokovic 14). She found ways to deal with most of them. Hard-court specialist Victoria Azarenka could rarely match her for power, pushers like Caroline Wozniacki and Angelique Kerber could hardly ever outlast her, while statuesque players like Garbiñe Muguruza and Maria Sharapova still lacked the agility that Serena continued to possess even well into her thirties. She reached 16 major finals after turning 30, winning 10 of them.

Venus reached two by comparison, both 2017 losses when she was 36 and 37. While their rivalry had fizzled in later years, the truth was that Serena was simply an out of this world talent that no one could keep up with consistently for two decades. She never claimed to be perfect. That came into sharp focus in 2018, at the US Open final which now exists in notoriety. What should have been the story of Naomi Osaka's astonishing arrival aged just 20, as Japan's first major champion, is instead remembered for Serena's clash with umpire Carlos Ramos. It began when she received a code violation for on-court coaching due to Mouratoglou signalling at her from the stands. 'I don't cheat to win,' she shouted at the umpire. 'I would rather lose.' At this point she was already a set down and she continued her outburst by telling him he was questioning her integrity. Her second code violation came for a racket smash not long after, causing a point deduction. When she implored him to apologise and then called him a 'thief' she was handed her third violation and was deducted a game, putting her 5-3 down. When Osaka served it out for 6-2 6-4, all hell broke loose. Osaka sat crying in her chair while the crowd booed. Though Serena asked them to stop booing during the tearful trophy ceremony, it was a complete shambles. Though Serena maintained she did not receive coaching, Mouratoglou later admitted to committing the offence – whether Serena clocked on or not. Regardless, her reaction proved one of the most divisive moments of her career. She reached two more major finals, but never won another.

*

In terms of the Williams sisters' legacy, it is difficult to summarise what an impact they had on the sport. You could measure it by the number of Black women to follow in their footsteps and win major titles: Madison Keys, Sloane Stephens, Naomi Osaka and Coco Gauff. Of the latter two, their stories were literally built around the legend of the Williams sisters. Osaka's father took inspiration from Richard Williams and set out to make champions of both of his daughters, coaching them as children and achieving the goal with his youngest. Gauff's father Corey also moved their family across the country to Delray Beach, Florida, to coach his daughter on the very courts that Venus and Serena frequented. In an echo of the Williamses' story, Gauff was telling anyone who would listen that she wanted to be 'the greatest' before she was even a teenager.

You could also look at the conversations they sparked about race and body image as a lasting reminder of the barriers that the sisters were constantly coming up against during their careers. They dealt with ludicrous conspiracy theories that they were actually men, based on their muscular appearance. Even within the tennis establishment, the president of the Russian Tennis Federation Shamil Tarpischev referred to the sisters as the 'Williams brothers'.

For Serena, her achievements after becoming a mother have added an entire other layer to her story. She reached four major finals after nearly dying in childbirth in 2017, and continues to be held up as the athlete that shifted the conversation around mothers in sport. Even now, in her forties, Venus continues to play on tour on occasion. She never officially retired. In an interview in 2024, Serena said her older sister would have won 'at least 15 Grand Slams' if they had not played each other. But what a rivalry the rest of us would have missed out on. In a *New York Times Magazine* profile on Venus as recently as 2019, Richard was still courtside during her practice session, coaching from the sidelines and complimenting her game. The sisters own homes in the same areas, even buying neighbouring plots of land. 'We've got the most codependent relationship you've ever heard,' Venus said in 2019. Some things never change.

CHAPTER 5

Kim Clijsters:
The mother of all comebacks

KIM Clijsters is running around an athletics track in Bree, just a stone's throw from her home in the east of Belgium. Her icy breath is visible with every gasp, and she breathes heavily. Her trainer Sam Verslegers is bounding along beside her, trying to get her to talk through their training plans for the next few months. It is February 2009, almost a year to the day since Clijsters gave birth to her first child, Jada, and, sadly, barely a month since the death of her beloved father and mentor Lei. It is also nearly two years since she retired from tennis, aged just 23. Local physiotherapist and osteopath Verslegers has known Clijsters since she was a teenager breaking into the WTA Tour, when he was introduced to her via her younger sister Elke. He helped treat Clijsters' injuries prior to her retirement and has agreed to help her get back to fitness for an exhibition event at Wimbledon in the summer. He thought an hour's run would be the best bet to talk through plans. But Clijsters is in no fit state to chat. 'My plan was to talk a bit during the jogging about what she wants and how I see it,' Verslegers recalls. 'But we started jogging and Kim couldn't talk; there was no conditioning at all. I said this isn't going to work, we'll talk after.'

After calling time on her career with one major title to her name, Clijsters had spent the past year caring for her new daughter as well as for her father during the last months of his illness. Agreeing to play the exhibition event at Wimbledon that summer, to mark the opening of the newly built Centre Court roof, was her way of bringing some normality to her routine. But within weeks, her appetite for real competition had returned. And, barely six months after this laboured jog with Verslegers, Clijsters would be juggling the US Open trophy and daughter Jada on each hip, as confetti rained down on her on the Arthur Ashe Stadium court. The victory was not only Clijsters' triumphant return to the tour, but it also marked the first time in 39 years that a mother had won a major tennis tournament post-partum. In the 15 years since Clijsters' victory in 2009, no other woman has been able to repeat the feat. 'Maybe it looked easy,' Verslegers says, 'but it isn't easy at all.'

Clijsters never intended to become tennis's poster girl for motherhood. When she retired in 2007, she genuinely believed she was done with the sport. She had reached her goals: she won her long-awaited major title in 2005 at the US Open, after losing her first four Grand Slam finals. She had reached world No. 1 in both singles and doubles, and she had enjoyed brief rivalries with compatriot Justine Henin and the Williams sisters. Now, she wanted to get married, have a family and move away from the nomadic lifestyle required in her profession. Even in those final months of what she now dubs her 'first career', she struggled to find motivation. Wim Fissette was her hitting partner that season, and remembers 'everything had become difficult' for Clijsters. She lacked motivation and getting her on the practice court six days in a row was a challenge as she was dogged by persistent injuries. Her father tried to get different friends and family to travel with her to add a bit of variation to the grind of daily tour life. But within herself, she knew she lacked that internal drive. After a hip injury blighted most of the spring of 2007, she called time on her career when she lost in the first round in Warsaw. 'The recurring injuries, having difficulty in getting out of bed in the morning, needing about an hour to get all the muscles warmed up, the demanding preparations of the marriage with Brian. It all makes things a bit difficult to keep on going,' she said in her statement. 'It has been more than fun, but the rackets are being hung up.'

Fissette was not surprised in the slightest: 'She definitely needed a break.' He had known Clijsters since he was a talented 15-year-old junior player, and she was the prodigious 12-year-old who practised with the boys. In early 2007, he quit his office job to travel on tour with her full-time, so her sudden retirement was not exactly ideal for him on a professional level. But Fissette was not completely convinced Clijsters was actually done. 'From the beginning, I always had the feeling, this is not the end,' he says. When he got a call from her agent in early 2009 about helping her get fit for an exhibition, he was game and joined up with Verslegers and Clijsters in Bree.

A couple of weeks into their sessions, Clijsters started to get the itch to compete. Though no one in her camp was shocked, she was the most surprised when the idea of a comeback became hard to shake. 'It's the challenge I felt within me that got triggered,' Clijsters says. 'My gut instinct really. I lost my dad, then I got invited to come to Wimbledon when they had the new roof on Centre Court, so me preparing for that made me think, hmm, this is fun – where could this take me? I'm too young to just do exhibitions. It triggered the will to compete. I still love hitting the ball, the hunger to take on that challenge and see how far I could go became very strong – to the point where I had to start telling people around me from my team. I was a bit nervous about it in the beginning.' Other than her husband, Brian Lynch, the first person she confided in was Verslegers: 'Whenever I lay on the table when he was treating me, that's when all my thoughts would come out. He was kind of like my psychologist; I would call him my communicative wall. After a few weeks I said: "Sam, I need to tell you, I'm feeling this, I want to take this challenge on." And he said: "You still have a long way to go if that's where you want to go, so let's see how it feels."'

Verslegers cannot remember the exact conversation. But he does remember a feeling of inevitability. 'I was surprised and not surprised,' he says now, chuckling. 'I thought, let's start with the exhibition. But for her the exhibition was nothing; she wanted real competition.' Verslegers is not prone to hyperbole. He is rather understated and has an endearing humility about him, despite forming a key part of one of tennis's greatest stories in recent memory. So when Clijsters turned to him for advice, he was cautious about his own expertise and even had a sense of imposter syndrome. Verslegers recalls: 'She said: "I want to see and feel if I can beat these girls again. I want to work for that. Do you think it's possible?" For me, that was hard to tell,' Verslegers says. 'I'd never travelled with an individual athlete; I'd never even been at a Grand Slam tennis tournament from beginning to end. Who am I to say this is possible, Kim? But I saw already on the court that, for me, she played the same. Then I said: "Probably when you work on your physical, get you to a point where your cardio, physical strength and flexibility is where it has to be, you have a real good chance to beat these girls." From that moment she started working out harder.'

News of her comeback broke in late March, and made headlines nationally, as well as around the world. Clijsters said she was eyeing a return during the late summer US Open swing, and accompanied the announcement with a confident statement: 'I don't plan to go there as a tourist and come back home after one or two rounds.' As strong as that sentiment was, she mostly stayed away from the limelight and did not rush things. Instead she spent six quiet months in sleepy Bree, a small city on the east Belgian border with the Netherlands, which is home to barely 16,000 residents. As a former US Open champion, Clijsters was one of the most recognisable figures in Belgian sport, even then. At Verslegers' clinic though, she was like any other of his clients. She would diligently work out at the tiny 80 square-metre gym – not even half the size of a tennis court – completing her weight sessions squeezed in alongside a middle-aged non-athlete, recovering from a heart attack, and a young teen cyclist, hoping to make a splash at regional level. 'Everybody was coming as normal, and then you had Kim Clijsters in the middle,' Verslegers says. 'Everybody still knows who Kim Clijsters is but, to be honest, in Bree in my office where she worked out, she never got asked for a picture or autographs. They just left her to do her stuff, left her alone. They said: "She's Kim, she's one of us – we know her, she's great."'

Verslegers and Fissette had a grand total of four hours each morning to work with Clijsters – including tennis training, fitness work and body treatments for any niggles that cropped up. By lunchtime, she wanted to be home with Jada, prioritising family time. The limited window they had to work with makes her comeback all the more impressive. 'It was not an easy job to fit everything in,' Verslegers says. 'For an athlete who's completely out of shape, you want six hours a day to work on them and build. We had only the morning. But it was all quality, and it worked. She was better every session, every week she was growing and getting better in shape, getting stronger. Everybody could see she was making progress. I could see it and she could feel it. Feeling those steps she was making gave her more hunger to be even better.'

On the tennis court, Clijsters was firing on all cylinders pretty quickly. She was more focused than Fissette had seen her in years. 'It was the opposite of 2007; it was like an extreme internal motivation. The happiness of being back on the court, finding back the love for the game. Everything she did was with full intensity, you never had to push her. It was more like you had to stop her. Another big difference was she was very coachable; she wanted to learn, develop more. She wanted to become a better player. The work ethic was very different.' Her childhood coach, Bart Van Kerckhoven watched her train during one of those early sessions. 'Playing like that, you'll reach the US Open finals this year,' he told her. She laughed, replying: 'If I make the finals, I will fly you to New York.' Clijsters was not necessarily banking on having to keep that promise, as she did not anticipate such swift success. But just a couple of weeks into training she was goal-setting with Fissette and painted an ambitious picture. This was a woman looking to push herself much further than anyone had previously done post-pregnancy in tennis in decades. Fissette recalls their conversation while standing on the tennis court in Bree, where she outlined her three top goals for this 'second career': winning a Grand Slam as a mum, beating the best players in the world and becoming world No. 1. It was music to Fissette's ears. 'When she left the tour, she was still a top player, right? So she was confident that she was definitely going to be a top 10 player. The question was if she was able to beat the best players in the world, like Serena and Venus at that time.'

While Fissette saw the potential, he says the tennis needed to take a back seat at the beginning of their seven-month training block. It began with 90 per cent physical work and 10 per cent tennis, that balance shifting every week, until they got to 50/50 – but never more than that. That was partly because of how tight the daily schedule with Clijsters was. Verslegers had his work cut out. From a cardio perspective, Clijsters was starting 'from zero'. She was also easily bored by fitness sessions, so he had to be inventive: running, biking, mountain biking, kayaking, swimming and aqua jogging all figured into their programme. At the gym they would combine speed and strength-based training. When time was especially tight, they would do it all on a tennis court, using combination exercises that saw her work with a racket in hand, plus a medicine ball and resistance bands. Her favourite sessions, though, were spent in a nearby woods, 15 minutes outside of Bree. In the middle of the trees there was a large sand hill with a plateau at the top. Verslegers would have her doing speed, jumping and acceleration training in the sand, and running sprints up the dune itself. 'I would tell her: "I'll pick you up at 9 a.m. tomorrow – bring your tennis shoes, running shoes and an extra T-shirt, because you'll sweat through the first one,"' Verslegers recalls. 'We'd practise there for hours – really tough, but also really fun.'

For Verslegers, one of the main challenges was not just that Clijsters had zero conditioning. It was also that her body had experienced major events like pregnancy and childbirth – and he had never worked with an elite athlete aiming to return to the top of their sport as a mother. There was very little scientific research to support him either. Other athletes have experienced this too, including the poster girl for British Olympic sport Dame Jessica Ennis-Hill. She became the heptathlon world champion in 2015, just over a year after giving birth to her first child, but has since described the lack of information available to help guide new mothers that happen to be elite sportswomen. Mastering her seven disciplines involved strength, twisting, explosive power and endurance, and trying to reclaim those skills in a way that was safe for her body was a minefield.

Personal trainer Baz Moffat is co-author of *The Female Body Bible* and chief executive of The Well HQ, which is dedicated to female athlete health expertise. She says the dearth of information and training available on pregnancy, as it relates to elite sport, remains an issue to this day. 'What has absolutely happened over the last 10 years, because of pioneering women like Serena Williams, Paula Radcliffe, Jess Ennis-Hill, is women think, oh we can do that, and that is now filtering down to grassroots sport. But what is missing is the system. There's still a huge amount of confusion about what pregnant women can or can't do. In the UK only 8 per cent of personal trainers have a pre- or postnatal qualification. One of the critical gaps is between the evidence and the practitioners. The evidence is starting to come out about how it's safe to train during a straightforward pregnancy. And actually, women do have the capability to lift weights and do high intensity training. When you come to elite sport they don't know what to do, because there isn't a clear return-to-play guidance. There's a massive gap between telling the practitioners on the ground what to do in most sports.'

When Moffat was seeking out her own qualifications in pre- and postnatal exercise back in 2011, her teacher was considered 'a bit extreme' by some in the industry for promoting the idea that pregnant and postnatal women could do functional movements like squatting, deadlifting and lifting weights. 'At that stage, the messaging for pregnant and post-partum women was very much "rest is best, do some aqua aerobics",' she says. That was the landscape when Verslegers was starting his own work with Clijsters, and he admits it was completely new territory for him. 'At that time I was working with a number of athletes from different sports, but never before with a female athlete who wanted to get back to the top after pregnancy,' Verslegers says. 'There are enough books about postnatal exercises and recovery, both mentally and physically, but little was or is known about the road to top sport after pregnancy. It wasn't just post-pregnancy, but Kim's father had also died in 2009. It was mentally and physically really tough at the beginning.' He had to apply what he knew about the impact of pregnancy on the average person's body, and adapt that to work for an athlete of Clijsters' calibre. 'In the injury prevention I did a lot of tests on her stability in her pelvis and her lower back. She had problems with the stability of her pelvis due to pregnancy and the delivery, so we had to work on glutes, abdominal, core and pelvic stability exercises. You would do it after pregnancy with regular people, but with athletes you go to higher levels, higher loads, to get everything stable when they're trying to get faster and more powerful.'

One thing he tried – but failed – to block Clijsters from doing was her trademark shot: the splits forehand. 'Kim has very lax joints naturally. By the pregnancy, it was getting even more lax and that was a disadvantage. She was great at defensive balls, the famous stance where she's in the splits when hitting the ball. It's good she can do it, that's an advantage, but it's a disadvantage that every time she does it she has the rotation of her pelvis. After pregnancy it was even looser. I told her many times: "No splits, please; use your legs, don't split." She didn't listen all the time. When she used that a lot in a match it was always that I'd have to adjust something in the pelvis or back, or both, after the match. It did have an effect. But that's her move! And she won important points with that too, eh?'

With those intensive months of work behind her, it was now about what could transpire on the court. Clijsters and the team – which now included Verslegers, Fissette, her agent John Dolan, her husband Brian, daughter Jada and the family nanny – packed up their bags and headed Stateside.

CHAPTER 6

Kim Clijsters:
Mastering the juggle

BEING a mother and an athlete has always been tangled with challenges. It is why, in tennis's Open Era, only two women other than Kim Clijsters had ever become a major champion after becoming a mother: Evonne Goolagong Cawley won Wimbledon in 1980, three years after childbirth, and before that it was Margaret Court in 1973, who won three major titles in a single year after giving birth to her first child. Across the sporting world there have been other examples of women succeeding despite the barriers in place for mothers. Paula Radcliffe won the New York Marathon in 2007, 10 months after giving birth. Golfer Catriona Matthew won the 2009 British Open just 10 weeks after her second daughter was born.

Success though is often punctuated by barriers. Nearly two decades earlier, Scottish distance runner Liz McColgan famously became 10,000 metres world champion a mere nine months after giving birth to her daughter Eilish in 1990. She did it after allegedly being dropped by her sponsor Nike, via letter, as soon as she broke the news that she was pregnant. That attitude continued for decades. As recently as 2017, American sprinter Allyson Felix was refused pregnancy protections in her contract by Nike, despite being a six-time Olympic gold medallist at the time of negotiations. In

2019 she joined a chorus of athletes that blew the whistle on poor maternity conditions provided by the sportswear giant, and Nike was forced to apologise and improve their provisions for female athletes who may want to start families during their careers.

Behind the scenes, Clijsters experienced some of that reluctance from brands. Though she had retired from tennis before getting pregnant, so never wrangled over contractual maternity issues, upon her return to the tour it was not easy to get sponsors onside. Even though she was a former Grand Slam champion in her own right, one of the most recognisable names in women's tennis and, not to mention, still only 25 years old, her agent John Dolan remembers being shocked by how difficult it was to get a clothing sponsor on board. 'I asked her what she wanted and she said I'd love to go to Nike, Adidas and I've previously been with Fila,' Dolan, who worked with Clijsters from 2009 to 2011, says. 'But it was a real challenge to get clothing companies to buy into her story. They really didn't believe, even with the narrative of being a mother; it was a real struggle. Eventually Fila remained loyal to her, but she probably didn't get the base compensation that she was looking for. Luckily there were bonuses tied in, so when she won the US Open that was all fine. I don't think they were expecting to pay a bonus so quickly into their tenure!'

Dolan had moved from a WTA communications team job to working with Clijsters as his first client, and momentarily wondered whether his own instincts were misguided. 'I didn't think it was a leap of faith to work with her, but I remember being surprised by the reaction of some brands, and questioning myself thinking: "Oh golly, have I read this wrong here? Other people aren't quite believing." But quickly after Kim beat Serena Williams at the US Open, everyone came knocking at her door.' It is hard to imagine such wariness among sponsors about a mother returning to tennis, considering the current landscape. It may sound crass, but since 2018,

Serena Williams has slowly transformed the 'athlete mother' tag into a marketer's dream. Her influence on world sport is such that when she made her comeback and spoke in earnest about recapturing major titles, her every word, move and decision was tracked with interest around the world. Nike outfits were created to aid her body's post-partum recovery, her press conferences centred on the 'mum guilt' she was experiencing, and on court she crafted a new chapter of her career with her daughter in the stands. It took time, but Williams's impact made brands want in on the motherhood experience, which is finally, rightly, being celebrated – at least at the top of women's sport.

Before Serena, there was Kim. 'It was 100 per cent a different landscape to now,' Dolan says. 'I was surprised, coming from a marketing and comms background. I felt like are they missing a trick here? Yes, they were. But with branding companies, sometimes they're a little behind the eight ball. There's no doubt in my mind that Kim paved the way for Vika [Azarenka], Serena and [Naomi] Osaka coming back. She showed what was possible. Also the earning potential a mother could have because of the storyline, all of those things. But, like for so many mothers in sport, it was tough for Kim at the start. I don't think it bothered her much to be honest because she was so focused on the tennis. It kind of bothered me, we all were biased as we believed 100 per cent in her. But the landscape was nowhere near where it is now for mothers. Credit to Fila that they stepped up but other companies didn't see the potential – which then very quickly became apparent.'

Watch back Clijsters' press conferences from that North American run in 2009, and not all that much attention was being paid to her new mum status until the US Open. Maybe that was because, based on the way Clijsters was storming through her first few tournaments, she was making it look seamlessly easy. She played her first competitive match in Cincinnati – less than three weeks before the US Open began – against world No. 13 Marion Bartoli. Fissette remembers delivering a rousing pep talk. 'Honestly, the way I see it, you are ready to completely dominate women's tennis for the next year,' he told her. 'The way you are playing, the way you hit your groundstrokes, nobody's coming close to where you are.' She proved him right. Wild card Clijsters beat Bartoli 6-4 6-3, skipped past world No. 20 Patty Schnyder in straight sets too, and outlasted Russia's Svetlana Kuznetsova, then ranked sixth, in a three-set tussle. She only ran out of steam in the quarter-finals against world No. 1 Dinara Safina. In Toronto next, she won two more matches – including her second top 10 win of the comeback, against world No. 9 Victoria Azarenka – before falling to fourth-ranked Jelena Jankovic in the last 16. To her team, it told them everything they needed to know. 'From the first match in Cincinnati, winning was like normal,' Fissette says. 'For me, she was that good.' In his mind, she was already showing that she was a 'better player and athlete' than she had been before her retirement. 'I think the serve was better, the groundstrokes were better. I mean, you have to. Tennis always evolves. It gets better every year. When she came back, she was the best player in the world. That was clear.'

Her rivals began to take notice too. Arriving in New York for the US Open, Clijsters' path to the final was anything but easy. She made light work of world No. 79, Ukraine's Viktoriya Kutuzova, beating her 6-1 6-1 within 54 minutes. The second round against Bartoli was trickier. The Frenchwoman's quirky technique, in particular her two-handed forehand, was a nightmare to come up against. After losing an error-strewn first set, Clijsters recovered, taking early breaks in the next two and storming to a comeback, 5-7 6-1 6-2. Next she obliterated her compatriot Kirsten Flipkens for the loss of only two games, and set up a blockbuster fourth round against Venus Williams. They had played each other 10 times before, with Venus holding a 6-4 winning record. But their last meeting was at the US Open in 2005, which Clijsters went on to win – and was the last time she had played in New York. It gave her a good feeling. Venus had been struggling with a left knee injury, and had heavy strapping on that leg for her match against Clijsters. When Clijsters blasted through the first set 6-0, it looked like it could be an ugly end for the American. But third seed Venus took control then, answering with her own 6-0 set to push the match to a decider. In a high level third set where the pair went toe to toe, Clijsters' supreme athleticism and cool head won out, the final score 6-0 0-6 6-4. Immediately after, in the on-court interview, the magnitude of her win hit. 'You've played Venus twice at the US Open before, and the winner has gone on to win the title,' Mary Joe Fernandez told her. 'Do you now feel you are in this with a big chance?' The crowd cooed at that. While Clijsters batted away the suggestion, saying she was taking things one match at a time, this win marked her first over a Williams sister since her comeback, ticking off one of her big goals.

Without the likes of the Williams sisters dominating the tour, Fissette does not believe Clijsters would have been as hungry to return. 'The best players in the world, they want to beat the best players in the world,' he says. 'That's why they do all the hard work to be on Arthur Ashe in a semi-final in the full stadium and be able to beat someone like Serena or Venus. That was definitely a very high motivation. That was goal number two, even ahead of being No.1 in the world.' While these huge goals were becoming achievements, behind the scenes, Clijsters' new life on tour was more complex than ever. Any parent of a toddler who has travelled abroad can empathise with Clijsters here. She was new to navigating everything: a toddler screaming on plane journeys or how to manage family time versus player time at a slam. She ended up turning to fellow WTA player and former world No. 1 Lindsay Davenport, who famously returned to the tour just six weeks after undergoing her Caesarean section for the birth of her first child in 2008. 'I spoke to Lindsay prior to travelling as she had been doing it with her son,' Clijsters says. 'Even just booking hotel rooms I was like huh, what would I need? As a first-time mum, I just didn't know. I would ask Lindsay so many questions, woman to woman. Travelling with a child, that was an added thing to try to solve at the time. Dealing with a baby that has jet lag is not fun when you have to play or when they get sick on the road. There's so many things where you have to adjust. But I had women on tour. I could go to the physios when Jada was sick at night and ask for them to get me a doctor. Those things make it so much easier on the travelling circus. It was trial and error, and not getting too upset about doing things wrong. We were just winging it.'

Dolan recalls the manoeuvring that happened on a daily basis to ensure Clijsters could perform at her best. 'The logistics were paramount. One of the reasons I think she hired me is because I'm quite meticulous. My mantra was 'never leave a stone unturned'. I asked Kim, what do you need? She was one of the only ones at that level travelling with a child at the time. Making sure she was in the right headspace to compete was a mantra of ours. Kim talked about feelings a lot; she was a very intuitive person. She said I want to have the same feeling as I did in 2005. The first thing I did was call up the same boutique hotel in New York that she stayed in the last time she'd visited four years prior, when she won the tournament. She wanted all of us on the same floor and that was a logistical challenge to have that layout: the suite, with the nanny who always had to be next door, the physio one door away; I was next to them. There were eight or nine of us and she created this family atmosphere on tour. Jada was obviously always the priority; she wanted to make sure Jada was always comfortable.'

That applied beyond the hotel too. Most players would usually spend every day on-site at Flushing Meadows, practising on court even on their days off, but Clijsters opted out of what she deemed unnecessary trips to Queens, which took at least an hour each way in New York traffic. Instead she jogged to Central Park with Verslegers and did resistance band training and plyometrics on the grass for a couple of hours, before spending the rest of the day with Jada and Brian. 'That's something that was in her head from her dad,' Fissette says. 'Where all the players think, "I played really well today, so tomorrow I have to play to keep that feeling," her father used to say the opposite: if you play fantastic today and tomorrow you don't play, it means you can't lose your rhythm.' Whether that theory is right or not, in opting out of travelling to Queens, Clijsters retained the 'four or five hours of physical and mental energy' by Fissette's estimation. He believed it kept her 'more fresh' by the end of the tournament. 'It was a smart way to think,' he says.

As much as Clijsters was ploughing through her stacked side of the draw, there were milestones happening back in Manhattan with Jada too, and she did not want to miss them. Dolan recalls one night in particular, when Clijsters came screeching down the hotel hallway and everyone rushed to their doors in a panic. 'It's one of my overriding memories of that US Open: Kim coming screaming down the corridor, saying in Flemish and English: "Jada's just done a poo in the potty!"' he says laughing at the memory, 'It was just bonkers.' That familial dynamic extended to the team, and Clijsters always tried to make their time on the road fun. Between Cincinnati and New York, she invited the entire team to Kings Island, a Six Flags theme park nearby. Dolan remembers stifling his screams on the roller coasters as Clijsters cackled with laughter. She also regularly made bets with her team. On one rainy day at an exhibition in the Netherlands earlier that summer, Fissette agreed to shave his head and Verslegers said he would grow out his hair to his shoulders if she won the US Open. They all shook on it, as if Clijsters needed further motivation. Whereas her final months on tour in 2006 and 2007 had felt strained and stifling, her approach to her second career was about making the most of their time.

But she was also managing the very raw grief from her father's death earlier that year. Speaking on Andy Roddick's *Served* podcast in early 2024, she shared that she even found herself dialling her father's number during the US Open that year, as that had been how she previously coped with nerves before a big match. Despite all of the emotions she was juggling off the court, Clijsters continued to excel on the court. After her win over Venus, she scored a straightforward quarter-final victory over Li Na, a top 20 player at the time and future Grand Slam champion. With that win, Clijsters made it to the last four, where she would face what she classed as the ultimate test: Serena Williams. She had always proved one of the trickiest opponents in Clijsters' career. It was going to be their ninth meeting on tour, and Clijsters had only ever beaten Serena one previous time, back in 2002 at the championship match of the WTA Tour Finals. Their matches were often close and physical, and Clijsters had twice lost to Williams 7-5 in the deciding set at previous slams. The hype around this latest encounter – which proved to be their final ever match – was big. And Serena admitted that she had been impressed by Clijsters. 'I saw how well she moved [against Venus],' Serena said in her press conference before their semi-final. 'It seems like she's even faster than she was before. I was thinking maybe I should have a baby and then I'll come back faster. That was my observation; I'm thinking about it.'

The members of the media in that room laughed and Serena smirked too. Clijsters was clearly making this motherhood thing look easy but Serena remained the heavy favourite. She was the reigning champion and had that hefty 7-1 winning record against Clijsters. The difference was, this time, it was Clijsters 2.0 she was dealing with. When Clijsters was asked what level she was playing at 12 months prior, she described a disastrous leisurely hit she had had back in Belgium. 'Moving even two steps were terrible,' she said. 'I felt like an elephant sometimes.'

Clijsters had come a long way. Her confidence was boosted by her win over Venus, but she remained wary of this big test against Serena. Her agent Dolan remembers her voicing her fears the night before the semi-final. 'I don't know if I can trust myself. Am I going to choke again if I get into a winning position?' Clijsters said to him. Dolan was not entirely sure himself, but he was bullish in his reply to her: 'Remember this, you've buried your father, gone through childbirth, dealt with a hell of a lot of worse things than playing a Grand Slam semi-final; there's no need to be nervous. Serena's never gone through any of that.' Fissette was even more confident. 'I said to her again: "You're ready to dominate women's tennis – you're that good." But she said: "Serena is just next level." Serena is Serena, right? There's no player in the world that would go on the court with Serena and not be intimidated. I didn't want to disrespect Serena, but I said: "You hit a way bigger ball than she does; I want you to show that in the match." That's the mindset she took into it and she was the better player that day.' They did not step on to the court until after 9 p.m., following a rain-soaked day in New York. That may be a standard start time for tennis these days, where post-11 p.m. has become normal, but in 2009 the crowds were less keen. Though this was a highly anticipated match, the weather delays meant the stands were sparser than the players deserved. Those who stuck around were in for a treat and a match they would never forget.

Most remember this match for Serena's outburst at the end, which I will get to, but that selective memory does not give enough justice to Clijsters' supreme performance. Her agent Dolan remembers it as 'the best' he had ever seen Clijsters play. 'She was like a woman on a mission the whole match,' he says. She was rapid, precise and persistent as she drew errors off Serena's racket. She was causing the American all sorts of problems, and when Serena hit two of Clijsters' returns into the net to hand the Belgian the first set, she smashed her racket to the ground in abject frustration. It earned Serena a warning which would prove pivotal later on.

For now, though, this was simply an absorbing contest. Even though Williams went a break ahead twice in the second set, Clijsters kept clawing back. She forced Serena to cover every corner of the court, and memorably made the world No. 2 look slightly foolish when she lobbed a ball just out of reach and sent Serena stumbling on the back-pedal. With Clijsters 30-15 up at 6-5 in the second, two points away from victory, the drama began. Serena was called for a foot fault on the very next serve and found herself match point down. Irate, she turned to the line judge and launched into a tirade against her, pointing her racket in the official's direction. 'If I could, I would take this fucking ball and shove it down your fucking throat,' she reportedly said. The line judge conferred with the umpire and, as this was Serena's second unsportsmanlike conduct warning of the match, she was docked a point and lost the match 6–4 7–5. Though she protested for a few minutes, eventually she saw there was no turning the decision. Serena marched to the other side of the net where Clijsters was right at the back of the court, trying to remain focused. Once she realised what was happening, Clijsters looked dejected at the victory being taken out of her control. But she gamely shook Serena's hand to seal her place in a Grand Slam final. This was one of the great upsets and performances of Clijsters' career. She was also only the third woman to ever beat both Williams sisters during a major tournament, after Justine Henin and Martina Hingis.

She had outpowered and outmanoeuvred Serena for much of the match. But afterwards, the headlines were all about Serena.

'Clijsters wins as Serena erupts,' so went the BBC's take. 'Clijsters wins on penalty assessed on Williams,' the *New York Times* wrote. The *Guardian* did not even mention Clijsters in theirs: 'Serena Williams blows her top, and her chance, at the US Open'. Williams issued an apology and was fined $10,000 for the offence, while Clijsters moved into the championship match, against teenager Caroline Wozniacki. It was a mind-blowing result for Clijsters, in her first major appearance since her comeback. It also marked the first moment where she officially became the tournament favourite. Clijsters had played in five major finals before, while Wozniacki was making her debut at this stage of a major. That experience for Clijsters was valuable, but it also came with baggage. In her 'first career', she lost the first four major finals she played – including three against her great rival, Henin. This run in New York so far was about overcoming the odds, but now she was tipped to lift the trophy against an inexperienced Wozniacki. Coping with that shift would be a new test.

*

In the end, the final was nerve-riddled and not as high calibre as previous rounds. But Clijsters made it work. Winning when not quite at your best is a skill in itself, and one champions often need to push through. She did just that in what turned out to be a messy match, where error counts far outweighed winners on both her and Wozniacki's rackets. But Clijsters crucially won the important points and kept plugging away against Wozniacki's defensive, percentage game. She showed her nerve when serving for the match, after she went 0-30 down to Wozniacki. Next she stormed the net to force an error from her opponent, hit an unreturned serve and then a forehand winner to set up championship point. The cameras panned to her daughter Jada up in the rafters, who cheered on her mother gleefully. When she finally hit the smash at the net to seal the greatest win of her career, Jada's angelic face appeared on screens around the world as she clapped for her mother. Clijsters collapsed to the ground in disbelief, and still looked dazed when the trophy was brought out for her to lift.

The photo of her crouched on the court with open arms as Jada tottered towards her inspired mothers across the world. Clijsters recently shared that she still receives messages on social media from women who refer to that moment as a seismic influence in their sport-watching lives. 'This is something in my wildest dreams I couldn't have imagined happening,' she said speaking at her press conference. 'As a woman who has a family and being an athlete, I think it's possible for other athletes out there. To win a Grand Slam now is a big deal in women's tennis and in the history of women's tennis. I'm glad I'm part of that history.'

The best part? This was the start of a renaissance in Clijsters' career. The following year, she successfully defended her title, extending her winning streak in New York to 21 matches. Then in 2011, she won her fourth and final major trophy in Melbourne, at the Australian Open. In 2012 she called time on her career again, when she was still only 28. She had a brief shot at a third career in 2020, but the pandemic and injury scuppered her plans. The memories of 2009 remain sharp for those who lived it with her. Verslegers is still close friends with Clijsters, and says hindsight has given him better appreciation of all she achieved. 'Sometimes I don't hear from her for one or two months, but then she'll call me twice a week. When I speak to Kim now, we go over things, like: "Do you remember this," and "Yeah, that was something." At that time, it felt quite normal. At the moment you don't 100 per cent realise how special it is – it's only looking back that you really know that something special happened.'

*

At the 2024 US Open final between Aryna Sabalenka and Jessica Pegula, Clijsters returned to the Arthur Ashe Stadium to present the coin toss with a special guest – her 16 year-old daughter Jada. To mark 15 years since her iconic win, the pair had their photo taken on the stadium court, just as they had back in 2009. It was the perfect tribute in a sense, but when Kim Clijsters is asked about being held up as a trailblazer for mothers in tennis, she seems to almost cringe. 'There's so many women on the tour who leave their families behind to help the athletes,' she says. 'Then there's my grandmother, mother, aunts, they're all super hard-working women [in other fields], right? Yes, I was a mother but that didn't mean that I became more vulnerable or sometimes made it look like I became Superwoman. Just because I'm an athlete it doesn't mean that I'm doing something better than a mum going to work nine to five. So I never really put a lot of energy into the attention that I got for being a mum on tour.'

Regardless of Clijsters' own feelings, fellow players now view her as living proof that it is possible to be a mother and the best tennis player in the world. Former world No.1 Victoria Azarenka, of Belarus, cites Clijsters as a role model. Azarenka gave birth to her son in 2016, three years after becoming a two-time Australian Open champion. She did so in the full belief that she could make it back to the top of the tour post-partum. If Kim could do it, she thought, so can I. 'Kim was one of the really prime examples for me,' Azarenka says. 'She retired early, then had a family, then decided to come back. It was my goal to break that stereotype that you can't do that. For it not to be an exception what Kim did, but more of actually, that's the way our tour is. The changes still need to happen more, progress needs to happen more. But I definitely feel like we've started a very good path for women.' Though Azarenka, 35, is yet to win a Grand Slam since the birth of her son, she clawed her way back to the top 15 and reached the US Open final in 2020.

That was all in spite of the ranking system failing to specifically cater for pregnancy allowances until 2019.

When Azarenka returned to the tour, new mothers' pregnancies were treated like injury absences: it gave players licence to enter 12 tournaments based on their ranking prior to leaving the tour for maternity leave, but without any seeding protections. It meant that new mothers were effectively returning to the tour at a disadvantage – without their well-earned seedings, they were at risk of being drawn against top-ranked opponents in the first rounds of tournaments. It was the equivalent of a working mother returning to employment after maternity leave in a less senior position, the type of treatment that would give women grounds to sue in most developed economies. The unfairness was brought into the spotlight when Serena Williams started her tennis comeback after giving birth, in the spring of 2018. When Williams had left the tour for pregnancy, she was world No. 1 and had just won the Australian Open (remarkably, when she was seven weeks pregnant). In her first major tournament back, eight months after nearly dying in childbirth due to a pulmonary embolism, Williams was allowed to enter the French Open on a protected ranking in the same way any injured player might. But it was at the discretion of organisers whether she would be seeded or not, as her real ranking had plummeted to No. 453. Ultimately, the French Tennis Federation (FFT) decided against it. With all eyes on Williams's comeback, in that now famous black and red Wakanda-inspired catsuit, the ridiculous rule book came under intense scrutiny. Even Maria Sharapova, Williams's long-time rival on the court, spoke up ahead of that French Open, to support the calls for a rule change. 'I would like to see that [rule] change,' Sharapova said at the Italian Open that year. 'It's such an incredible effort for a woman to come back from physically, emotionally . . . There's just another whole dimension to the travel, to the experiences, to the emotions to the physicality of every single day.'

By the end of the year, the WTA brought in specific protocols for pregnancy that applied across every tournament. It means that now, if a player's protected ranking would have placed them as a seed, they can enter their first eight tournaments as an 'additional seed' – so are not at risk of playing another seeded player in the opening round of a tournament. It also does not push any seeded players out of those coveted positions. Since its introduction six years ago, 50 players have benefitted from the special ranking. The tour also set up a women's health taskforce in 2023, and are working on developing standardised international protocols for athletes returning post-childbirth. The most seismic change came in March 2025, when the WTA announced players will now receive maternity pay for the first time, with more than 300 players elegible for up to 12 months' paid leave, plus grants available for fertility treatment. Azarenka, who is a member of the WTA Player Council, was a pivotal voice in helping to push for changes like this. 'I was like, me having my son is not an injury,' she says, with a slight scoff. 'It cannot be treated in the same category. Now the rules are much clearer; we needed to adapt them to give people more opportunity to maybe stay home longer, to be ready to come back. Somebody might not be ready to come back after five or six months like I did. I don't think of myself as a pioneer in that way [like Clijsters], but I do believe that change has started to happen. Myself, with the help of my colleagues, we drove that change to what it is now. It is not any more, can I do it or not? There's more and more women who feel comfortable and confident to see that it's been done. They think: "Why can't it be me?" I feel like it also had an impact on other sports. We hear a lot more stories with track and field, soccer and other sports. It definitely became a much bigger conversation, and it's a very cool thing to see.'

To Azarenka, one of the main changes has been the perception of female athletes who also happen to be mothers. A huge part of that was Williams's impact, but so too was it the success of Clijsters, which has become a touchstone of sorts. 'I wouldn't call it as far as celebrated, but I would say uplifted and highlighted,' Azarenka says. 'I love that it gets attention because it is hard. It's not easy.' Azarenka was very comfortable with taking the baton from the likes of Clijsters and Williams. More so than her own needs as a leading mother in the sport, now she wants more provisions to help players without the means of a former world No. 1 like her. While she and Clijsters travelled on tour with full-time nannies or family help, other players lower down the rankings do not have that kind of luxury. Top of Azarenka's wish list: more consistent childcare at tournaments (beyond the slams and combined tour events). 'I do feel like there is more accommodation for children at the events, as our mothers' club is still growing. That's the next component we have to improve, to have proper care while we are at the tournaments. Our sport deserves that. Things take a little bit more time than we probably want or have patience for, but it took a bit of time to even change people's perspective on motherhood. Everybody who knows me, knows that if I have my eyes on something I'm going to make it happen one way or another.'

She adds: 'I didn't really care if I was going to be the one benefitting from these rule changes. I wanted to make sure that other people after me have that. Tennis is generational; we have amazing athletes and people like Billie Jean King and the Original Nine who started the tour for us to have certain benefits that they didn't have. And I really see this the same way. It's about growing our sport and making it better – and that's what I want to be part of my legacy.'

As Azarenka references, each player's experience is different. She, like Clijsters and Osaka, had the privilege of better financial security and help to guide them. Clijsters' age when she had her daughter (24) meant she was really in no rush. Compare that to Williams, who was nearly 36, and their experiences would be vastly different.

Clijsters had the luxury of time and took an extended break. It was not until Jada turned one that Clijsters began exercising properly. Compare that with Lindsay Davenport who was competing a few weeks after childbirth in 2008 and, more recently, Osaka was already back on tour barely six months after the birth of her daughter. She only had a three-month training block as preparation. That could be for any number of reasons, but mostly because Clijsters never expected to make her U-turn on retirement, so approached her pregnancy like the average person would, rather than as an athlete. The obvious disadvantage was that Clijsters was truly starting from zero, with no level of base fitness. But it also meant all of her pre-existing injuries had time to heal and she has described beginning again with a 'clean slate'. She spent six full months exclusively on the practice courts and in the gym.

Fissette worked with both Clijsters and Osaka in their first seasons back after giving birth. He says Osaka took inspiration from Clijsters' story, and was certainly frustrated that her return did not have as swift a climax. 'Players were probably thinking, it's easy, I just come back, and then I'm just gonna be back where I was at the top of women's tennis. Naomi definitely asked questions like how Kim's schedule looked, and maybe thought it was a little bit easier than [it has been]. The first conversation I had with Naomi, around September 2023, I said: "Well, it's going to be difficult, and you have to be a lot better than you've ever been, but I believe in you." In her mind, there was still an extreme belief in herself. It's a great thing, that's why she's a champion and will be a champion in the future. For sure, Naomi was thinking: "Wim, you're right, but I'm just gonna come back and win."' That has not been the case so far. Osaka is a four-time Grand Slam champion and one of the stars of the game. But her 22-18 record for the 2024 season was her worst winning rate in 10 years, and she suffered from a couple of injuries that put her progress on hold too. Fissette worked with her for nearly a year up to September 2024, and her impatience grew over the months. 'Of course, there were some questions [from Naomi]: "Why did someone like Kim come back and just win? Why was Serena immediately back in the finals?" In life, you cannot compare, right? Everyone's different. Everyone has a different pace, a different journey to success. With Kim, it was a huge success from the beginning. Others will need a little bit more time. If I compare Naomi with Kim, Kim took seven months to train, Naomi took three months. Kim did not need much match rhythm like others. Kim was really at the top of women's tennis when she left in 2007, Naomi was not in 2023 – her last good tennis she brought was Australia 2021. She had like three years to catch up. Serena as well, she had a baby at a much later stage of her life. But I still think of her comeback as a big success. I mean, four Grand Slam finals? We cannot say that that comeback was a failure.'

His point on what counts as a successful comeback is a good one. In sport, winning is the ultimate goal. Clijsters' comeback is remembered all these years later because of the great success she gained. But the mere fact that this path is being seen as an option for more and more players on tour is the key factor. Clijsters contributed hugely to that. So did Serena and Azarenka, even though Grand Slam titles have not materialised for them. The same applies to Osaka – though Fissette envisages more trophies in her future. 'Someone like Naomi, I have zero doubts that she will be very successful in the next years, the way she has developed herself and has become really the best version of herself. There is just a little bit of confidence missing to make that big, big run in a big tournament. Plus, tennis has evolved a lot. The depth in women's tennis is much different than if you compare it to 2009. Everyone is physically strong, has a good serve. The margins are way smaller. It's definitely a little bit more difficult now.'

There is no one formula, but Clijsters proved it was possible in the modern era. With the added advantages that Azarenka and fellow advocates on tour – including within the WTA itself – plan to secure for other mothers, someone may finally follow in her footsteps with the trophy to match.

CHAPTER 7

Ash Barty:
The all-rounder

WHEN Ash Barty stepped into the nets at Allan Border Field for the first time in 2015, there was no heavy weight of expectation. Borrowed pads were strapped on her shins, she had a Queensland Cricket helmet on her head and she clutched the handle of a borrowed cricket bat in her hands. This was a casual hit, nothing more, nothing less. Allan Border Field in Brisbane was a 30-minute drive from her home town, Springfield. For an athlete who had become accustomed to flying thousands of miles overseas to play tennis tournaments, that proximity to home might have been the first mental tick in her box. There was not a tennis racket in sight either, the tool she had spent her whole life adoring and deploying with such skill, but which had also been the source of so much frustration and anxiety in recent years. Instead, the wooden bat in her hand felt heavy, unfamiliar, new. Another mental tick.

Barty was a former world No. 2 junior tennis player and one of Australia's top sporting prospects. But after suffering from burnout aged just 18, she stepped away from the sport. That day in the nets, she was 11 months into her tennis hiatus and nearly five years away from reaching world No. 1 in the WTA rankings. She had shocked sports fans in Australia the previous August when she announced her decision to spend time at home with her family and consider her next steps. Tipped to be the best of her generation, Barty had already reached three Grand Slam finals in doubles and had won the Wimbledon girls' title when she was just 15, so the news was received with confusion. She had just started, so how could she already be stepping away? But in private, Barty was grappling with her mental health. She was spending her time coaching young children and even elderly women at her home club, West Brisbane Tennis Centre. Just £68 would have bought a local school child eight lessons with her.

She now had time to spare, coupled with a competitive inclination that meant she was still curious about what she could achieve in sport. That's why she found herself in the cricket nets that day, with an opportunity to start afresh. Crucially, there was no huge risk of failure attached. If it went well, great, there might be an opportunity to learn a new sport and stoke the competitive fires in her. If it didn't, then it was a fun way to spend the afternoon. Andy Richards was the women's head coach at Queensland Cricket, in charge of the Queensland Fire and soon-to-be-launched Women's Big Bash League team, the Brisbane Heat. He had heard of Barty's interest via a few of his players. Barty had been an invited speaker at a recent Cricket Australia event at the national centre, where she shared her experience of playing professional sport. Domestic women's cricketers were due to make the transition to full-time contracts later that year, and Cricket Australia wanted a well-known female athlete to share what it was like. That day she mentioned to a couple of players, including Australia captain and Queensland cricketer Jodie Fields, that she might fancy trying cricket. Fields excitedly relayed the information to Richards, so he invited Barty to coffee and asked her, 'Well, what do you want to do?'

At the time, he may not have known what a loaded question that was for Barty, who was still very much figuring it out and in her own personal limbo. 'Look, I really don't know,' she said. 'I'm having a break from tennis as I hit a bit of a wall.' That was no secret, Richards had seen the press coverage of her decision to leave the tennis tour indefinitely. 'She hadn't been happy for a while and she was up front and honest about that,' Richards says. 'She said: "You know, I'm dealing with a bit of stuff." And I said: "That's okay. Most of us are."' She also admitted to him that she had never played any formal type of cricket, and she had only ever had a hit in her back garden with her dad and the rest of the family. He was intrigued enough to invite her down to the field though. 'We did it quietly,' he says, remembering that day. There was no fanfare, no other players, just him, Barty and a ball machine. He fired it up, sending hardballs Barty's way at about 105 kph. 'She might have faced 150 balls,' he says, 'and without a word of a lie, she might have missed three.' Richards' incredulity grew as the session wore on. Towards the backend of the hour, he asked Barty to hit straight, leg side or off side. She did it all, and at the first time of asking. He found himself asking her multiple times: 'Are you sure you haven't played this before.' Each time she shook her head. 'I was fairly blown away,' he says, reflecting on it now. 'And I don't think I masked it well.' After her batting session she bowled a few off-spinners and he thought, we can work with that. He immediately asked her to come down to training with his team. But Barty was cautious. 'She didn't feel she was good enough initially; she wanted to have a few more hits. The reality, from my perspective, was that she was already better than the bottom third of my squad,' Richards says.

That reaction is exactly a measure of Barty's character, as told by those closest to her: pure humility. After a few sessions, she felt comfortable enough to join the group. As good as he believed she already was, Richards says he wanted her to spend time with the team from a selfish perspective too. 'The benefits for my group was that they could train with an athlete who had been professional – there were mutual benefits, and that was the case all the way through.' As an athlete who had only ever played an individual sport, Richards was unsure how she would slot in, especially in a group of players who were vying for the first professional contracts in domestic women's cricket history. She might have been seen as someone trying to take their spot. Instead he saw that she slotted in just fine, on account of her ability to laugh at herself, as her new teammates were immediately 'taking the piss'. Barty was initially slightly 'timid' but after she copped some stick during her very first session for turning up with a designer handbag to put her kit in, that broke the ice. 'She gave some back,' Richards says, laughing at the memory. 'It worked straight away.'

Soon after, she was invited to the three-day pre-season training camp, where they did mud-soaked obstacle courses, with rope tasks and endurance tests. 'She looked like she belonged there all the time; she loved the team thing,' Richards says. 'As the season went on, the dressing room became a pretty wonderful place for her, because you know, she could have a bad day herself, but still enjoy the results of the team, or if the team lost, still enjoy crying on each other's shoulders. She always belonged in a team. There is no doubt about that. I think it was really beneficial for her.' As Richards saw, and anyone who knew her could have told you, Barty was a natural team member who had found herself locked into one of the most punishing and isolating individual professional sports in existence. Tennis gave her very few opportunities to be part of something bigger than herself and, on some level, that had always been the disconnect for her. She spent months at a time travelling away from her close-knit family, and it made her feel adrift. Losses cut deeper as she shouldered them entirely on her own. In cricket, she finally found a way to be a cog in a wider machine. This was the starting point of a cricket career that ultimately only lasted a year, but it helped to change the entire trajectory of her tennis life.

*

Ash Barty was born in Ipswich, Queensland, and lived on a quiet, suburban cul-de-sac with her parents and two older sisters in nearby Springfield. Her dad, Rob, was a talented golfer, who represented Australia and played at state level in his younger years. He went on to have a career in the State Library and her mum Josie was a radiographer. Barty first played tennis at the age of four. She was not keen on netball like her sisters (in her mind, it was a girls' sport), and instead just wanted to play tennis. Her father took her to Jim Joyce's West Brisbane Tennis Centre one Saturday morning. Joyce almost turned her away because he only coached players from age eight and above, as he did not believe in children specialising early, but that they should try a range of sports. But he was immediately impressed by her hand-eye coordination and her enthusiasm.

In her autobiography *Dream Time*, Barty described hitting the ball against her parents' garage door any spare moment she got, and she never missed an opportunity to head over to Joyce's courts, come rain or shine. Joyce saw that commitment and encouraged her to have fun playing tennis. 'He challenged me to be the most complete player I could be,' Barty has said of her years under his tutelage. He instilled in her the fundamentals on the court and even sternly chastised her in a rare moment when she might have started to believe her own hype. When she started picking up trophies like another child might collect stickers, at the end of each year she and her family would donate them to the tennis centre, so Joyce could repurpose them for club tournaments for younger children. He was keen to keep her grounded and advised her parents against joining the national squads until she was 13, despite Tennis Australia coming calling when she was just 10. Barty's parents listened to Joyce as they saw he had her best interests at heart. It is a rare story in tennis in which neither of her parents were pushy or too hands-on. They put their trust in Joyce from an early age, and it paid off in the long run. But influential people within the sport took notice of this tiny girl who had every shot in her arsenal.

Alicia Molik, a former top 10 player, remembers being told by a friend that she needed to watch this 11-year-old at the clay court national championships. 'She could hit a heavy topspin ball, drop shots, lobs – she had the full array and still has it,' Molik says. 'She did it better in her senior career than when she was that little up-starter grasshopper, but even then she could do a bit of everything which the rest of the field couldn't. She set herself apart in her playing style very early.' Eventually though, she needed to join national teams to access Tennis Australia's funding towards her coaching and development. Interestingly, it's at this point that Barty refers in her book to David Epstein's notable work *Range: Why Generalists Triumph in a Specialised World*. It has a section that looks at the benefits of children developing in sport through a range of activities. Epstein refers primarily to Tiger Woods (who played only golf from his formative years) to Roger Federer (who juggled football, ping pong, skateboarding and swimming alongside tennis, which he didn't play competitively until he was a teenager). 'Both methods can produce a champion, clearly, but which one is healthier for the individual? Jim felt he knew the answer,' Barty writes.

This note comes at a fascinating juncture in her own story: when she joined Tennis Australia's national programme. In what felt at the time like an inevitable development, aged 14, Barty switched to the intense specialisation route. It's just the way it was for Barty, the best route she and her family could take if she wanted to become a professional tennis player. She left school to do 'distance learning' provided by Tennis Australia, which she hated, saying 'curiosity was sucked out of me'. Her first trip to Europe with Tennis Australia was with fellow top prospects, including Nick Kyrgios, and lasted seven weeks. She hated every moment of that too, and even admitted to throwing one match so that she did not get left behind, as the rest of the group were moving on to another city and tournament the next day. The trip sparked her long-term anxieties around the extensive travel, a requirement in this sport that she loved. 'That was when I knew I wasn't meant for this life,' she writes in her autobiography.

Alongside all of these negative feelings though, her on-court results were building her prodigious status. When she was 15 she started working with former player Jason Stoltenberg, and later that year she won junior Wimbledon (the youngest ever to do so) and the under-18 national title. It made her the only person in Australian tennis history to win the under-12, 14, 16 and 18 titles by the time she was 15. In early 2012, when she was still only 15, she was given a wildcard to the Australian Open main draw. While most young players might have felt excited by their future prospects, Barty began to feel the walls closing in. In her own words: 'I feared failure: what if I don't achieve these things that people think I should? But I also feared success: what if I do well enough that this lonely way of living becomes my life? I was trapped in the game – this sport, this industry of winning – cornered by my own ability.'

Barty is very candid about her mental health challenges. The first mention of her early experiences of depression come at page 18 in her book. It was at 16 years old, while competing far from home in the US, that she first reached out for help from a family member, who was a doctor. Barely a year later, she was announcing her decision to leave tennis. She had risen to world No. 129 and was having big success in doubles with Casey Dellacqua, but that could not stop her from feeling suffocated by tennis. When she quit, no one in her circle was surprised; the pressure was too much for her to handle. Dellacqua has known her since she was 13. At the time, Dellacqua was a top 10 doubles player and Barty approached her to ask if she wanted to play doubles with her at the Brisbane International. It was a bold proposal, and Dellacqua thought she would 'take a punt on someone young and give her an opportunity'.

'From the moment we started playing together it was pretty obvious how talented she was, how knowledgeable, skilful and how she anticipated the game so well for such a young person,' Dellacqua says. 'We made the final in Brisbane and have kind of been best friends ever since.' That team dynamic was where Barty thrived, and they finished runners-up at no less than three major tournaments in 2013. Dellacqua took her under her wing on tour, so when Barty decided to leave tennis in August 2014, her friend could see it coming. 'Knowing her at that time, how she needed to take a step back from the game, I really respected that from someone so young. I had never been in her shoes, in terms of winning junior Wimbledon at 15. Her experience was very different to mine, but I could see she needed that. I respected her for that, as I did when she wanted to come back and I was there for her. She was there for me too.'

A fellow former Australian tennis player, Mark Philippoussis, believes those years may have been challenging but her doubles experience was the key to how she performed later in her career in singles. 'I think that doubles helped her in singles as well, helped her develop that all-court game as far as with the slice, the serve, coming into the net. The doubles in her early career, that success, just completed her game.' Barty's future mindset coach, Ben Crowe, agrees that it is an underrated element to her story, but for different reasons. To him, the team dynamic Barty created with Dellacqua was the biggest source of development for a young Barty and a precursor to cricket. 'Prior to cricket, she loved playing doubles. Her best friend Casey, even today, you see them together and it's hilarious, they're like two little kids mucking around. How they ever got to take it seriously on the tennis court is beyond me. But doubles tennis and cricket is where she experienced the joy. That beautiful quote, 'happiness is best shared', I think it relates very much to Ash.

Rather than just feeling alone on this journey, you can celebrate it with others and have fun, take the piss, and so forth. It makes the whole journey so much more enjoyable.' Barty was still three years away from beginning her work with Crowe, whom she credits much of her success to, but even as a 19-year-old she was figuring out for herself that a team game was where she thrived. She just did not know how tennis would ultimately fit into that.

*

There have been ample examples of professional athletes switching sports – some more successfully than others. Michael Jordan is perhaps the most famous example, when he abruptly left the NBA at his peak in 1993 to fulfil his childhood dream and join the Chicago White Sox, a Major League Baseball team. It lasted all of a year, and by 1995 he was back playing NBA basketball with the Chicago Bulls. He won three more Championships, and three more NBA Finals Most Valuable Player awards. Record-breaking Jamaican sprinter Usain Bolt tried to make it as a footballer after retiring from athletics and had a brief professional spell at Australian club Central Coast Mariners. It never really worked and he was accused of doing it for publicity. Dame Sarah Storey is perhaps one of sport's best switch stories. She was a double Paralympic champion swimmer in the 1990s, before winning a further 17 golds in cycling, to become Britain's greatest ever Paralympian at the Paris 2024 Games.

Ash Barty's foray into cricket could well have been a permanent switch, if she had wanted it. She was the 'perfect' example of an all-round sporting talent, says her former coach Andy Richards, and a complete natural as a batter. 'In ball-striking sports, all really good athletes know where their body has to be to access the ball, and she was perfect at it. My coaching of her was limited, she didn't need it; it was more about the nuances of the game – and she picked those up quicker than most. I just asked her to hit it somewhere and she put her body in the right place to hit the ball where it needed to be hit. It was quite remarkable from that point of view, going from a cross-bat sport to a straight bat. From a coaching perspective, she was a pleasure to coach.' Richards recalls using some tennis comparisons to give her tips about fielding, getting low and in a similar athletic power stance to how she might receive a serve, for example. When he talked about hitting over cover, he said the position of her hands on the bat should be similar to how she would try to generate topspin with her racket.

Speaking to Richards now, after moving on from the professional game to coach cricket at a co-educational private school in Brisbane, his time working with Barty remains fresh in his mind. That's partly because of how often he is asked about it, he admits, but also because of the impression she left. Away from her performances, he says she was also the model team player: 'She's as humble as they come; what you see is what you get. She's the most generous, extraordinary human being, and that humbleness . . . She was not accepting a free ride at all, and that she made really clear. She was about wanting to earn her place. Yes, she is a perfectionist. But in the training sort of things, she never, never stood on anybody's toes at all. She made an effort to get along with everybody.'

Richards took the bold step of awarding Barty a much-coveted and rare full-time state contract during that inaugural WBBL season, along with the league contract she was awarded. Barty had earned a few hundred thousand dollars playing tennis over the previous two years. Her total salary in cricket would have been shy of $50,000, but that was a non-issue. 'I said: "Look, it only pays so much." And she didn't care,' Richards says. 'She said: "That's not what I'm here for." I think she was just happy to be doing something that wasn't tennis.' Richards only had 15 or 16 contracts to give out, but Barty's selection was a 'no-brainer' for him. It came with scrutiny, both from outside voices and even those within the franchise who worried about being accused of choosing her for publicity. 'There was a bit of flak, we're always going to cop that, but at the end of the day, anybody who'd seen her hit for the first time was blown away.'

One person who backed him was Belinda Clark, a former national team player who at the time was managing team performance at Cricket Australia. 'She was in the nets next door and I asked her to come and have a look,' Richards says. 'I said, "I think Ash can play for Australia in a year," and she said: "I have no doubt."' The outside noise built during her first three trial matches, when Barty scored just one run. 'She wondered what the hell she was doing there,' Richards says. But it wasn't long before she found her stride. At her third T20 game in club cricket, she scored a century. On the way home, she shouted out of the car window at her mum Josie, to tell her the news. That spark in her had returned. The chairman of selectors, who had questioned Richards about the decision to sign her initially, watched Barty that day. 'He rang me up straight away, and he said: "That's the best call you've ever made in your life,"' says Richards. 'I told him it was an easy call to make.'

Barty played in the first ever WBBL match at the Junction Oval in Melbourne, which attracted 2,000 fans – a decent crowd at the time for women's cricket. Barty was one of the only players on her team used to an audience like that, and she was the first Heat player to clear the boundary and score a six, hitting 39 off 27 balls in the opening match. If Barty was trying to escape the pressure of expectation she had felt in tennis, it soon became clear that would be impossible. The media lapped up the story. 'It was a bit hard; it was a bit of a travelling circus from the press perspective, and she's not a fan of the press; she probably got burned a little bit and became a little wary,' Richards says. 'She wanted to make as little fanfare as possible, but that probably wasn't ever going to be the case.' The team did their best to shield her, even running dummy team buses which Barty wasn't travelling in. She made a decent contribution that season, averaging 11 runs across nine matches. But by the time the season was drawing to a close in January 2016, she was already being lured back to the tennis court. Richards knew it was coming, and Barty was honest about her continuing contact with Tennis Australia too. 'We enjoyed the ride. At that stage, you think, that's what she's done since she was five years old, and she loves it; you're not going to take that away from her. Her mind was really clear: she had a good 12 months to wind down and find out what life was about, I think. She enjoyed being closer to her family, and Mum and Dad were tremendously supportive along the way. When she told me [she was leaving] she was crying, I said don't be sorry, we were lucky to have you for the time we did and that she had a place with us anytime she wanted to, if the whole tennis thing didn't work out. It was bittersweet for us, but she certainly made the right decision.' Cricket was the first turning point in Barty's career. Taking a meeting with Ben Crowe just over two years later was the second one.

CHAPTER 8

Ash Barty:
Tennis reimagined

BEN Crowe remembers his first meeting with Ash Barty well. She had just crashed out of Wimbledon in the summer of 2018, in a 24-unforced error loss to Daria Kasatkina. She had been back on tour for two years. Though she had the option of a protected ranking of 186 when she returned, she rejected it and instead started from scratch. Again, Barty did not want any freebies. Nor maybe did she want any part of her mostly unhappy first couple of years on tour to mar her return. So she built herself up from unranked to top 20 in the space of two seasons. But her progress had been stalling for about nine months by the time she lost this match at Wimbledon and, at the majors, she was making no impact; at that stage she had never made it to the second week. It was not so much the loss to Kasatkina that struck such a chord; she was a solid opponent. It was the way she lost. In her frustration, Barty directed an out-of-character tantrum towards members of her team in the player box. Afterwards she felt deep shame, but she was not sure what to do next.

The person in charge of her team was head coach Craig Tyzzer. He is the first character we meet in her autobiography, and she writes that he is 'the person I trust most'. Tyzzer led a team that included Barty's long-time manager, Nikki Craig, and strength and conditioning coach, Mark Taylor, plus physiotherapists Adam Schumacher and Melanie Omizzolo. The previous year, strength and conditioning coach Narelle Sibte had got her back to fitness after her hiatus, through running, bike riding, boxing sessions on the beach and rope courses. But there was a missing piece. Tyzzer called up Ben Crowe, a mindset coach who had previously worked wonders with Australian Football League player Trent Cotchin, a close friend of Barty's. Cotchin spoke to Crowe about Barty too, as did her manager Craig. When he sat down to that first coffee with Barty not long after Wimbledon, his first impression was her ability to maintain eye contact. 'Which is quite rare; athletes are typically looking down or at their phones or away,' Crowe says. 'It meant she was genuinely engaged in learning and growing and understanding herself, and her perspective on things. I guess she was just really keen to connect with herself first and foremost as a human being, rather than a tennis player initially. Just to understand her emotions a lot more. Don't get me wrong, she was shitting herself – as most people are, right? Here's this bloke: 'what's he going to do?' type of thing. Very, very quickly she relaxed and was incredibly curious, but also incredibly vulnerable and opened up. She literally poured her heart out and told her story for the first time ever. I quickly realised, wow, this is one of the most humble humans I think I've met, given she was an elite athlete dealing with the spotlight.'

Crowe had previous experience in tennis. During his former role as Nike's international director of sports marketing, he worked closely with seven-time major champion Andre Agassi. He also worked closely with Australian sprint icon Cathy Freeman. Barty was about to put her complete trust into him. As he did with any athlete or individual he worked with, he asked her her backstory, unlocking stories she had kept buried, to 'find that connection'. 'Most athletes come to us for performance confidence, but what they actually need is self-confidence,' he says. 'It's what holds us back – not confidence in our skills, but confidence in ourselves. Learning about ourselves, finding that authenticity, and being vulnerable to that in a counter-intuitive way actually gives you permission to then have the courage and resilience to follow your dreams, knowing it's a goal, not an expectation. The expectation is to be true to yourself, not necessarily to win the match or live up to someone else's expectations, which is often the biggest distraction for athletes today.' The work he did with Barty was centred on a couple of key pillars: the first was separating 'the human being and the human doing', or the person from the persona, and the second was identifying things she couldn't control in her tennis or her life, and helping her learn the power of acceptance and what she could control, namely, being the best version of herself. Crowe's work is put into practice via a three-step framework: getting an athlete to connect with their authentic story and tackling their inner fan and critic with mantras and affirmations; developing a purpose mindset, which for Barty was about recognising tennis was 'just a chapter in her life' and looking to the impact and fulfilment she could find beyond her own career; and performance mindset, where you learn how to identify distractions beyond your control.

It all sounds straightforward in principle, but harder to put into practice, especially when so much of a sporting career is geared around rankings, prize money and trophies. Barty took to his principles quite naturally. 'Ash not only understood but then practised maybe harder than any athlete I've ever worked with,' he says. 'She did a very good thing of separating goals from expectations.' Incorporating a team mindset was key to this. She had learned the power of the collective in a very real way through her year of cricket, and she wanted that to be a big part of her future. 'That was something very much born out of Ash, in Ash Barty version 2.0. She very much wanted to do things differently and her way. In conjunction with Craig Tyzzer, she was of the philosophy that no one in the world can do anything on their own; they all need people around them. She devoted herself to creating a world-class team where everyone knew what their roles were and would help each other out. That was deliberate on Ash's part, to really focus on getting the right people supporting her. She even developed team rules, like a "no dickhead" policy, or "work hard and have fun", "compete, have fun, play". It's amazing what can be achieved when no one cares who gets the credit, right?'

Listen to any interview Barty ever gave after she began working with Crowe, and the language she used was always plural. There was no 'I', it was always 'we'. This was about fostering a positive team environment, and Crowe describes her as someone who had 'an incredible leadership philosophy'. The other thing it helped do was remove 'ego and fear', says Crowe, and that became integral to removing the pressure she had previously experienced in her career. For someone who had literally quit the sport because of the loneliness she felt on tour and on the court, this was really powerful. 'That sense of team and connection was so important to her success I think,' Crowe says. 'It means you're never alone.' It has to be said, sometimes those collective nouns and platitudes sounded trite when they came out of Barty's mouth during interviews and press conferences. In general, she kept her cards close to her chest, spoke in what, from the outside, seemed like clichés. But many of the words were literally mantras she repeated to herself, like how she wanted to be a good person, beyond wanting to be a good tennis player. 'Each match is an opportunity to do the best that I can on that given day,' she told the *New York Times* in 2021. 'Whether that's a win or a loss is quite irrelevant. It's more about going out there with the right attitude regardless of the result.' That messaging can and did induce an eye roll from the cynical press packs that cover world sport. This is an elite athlete saying it is 'irrelevant' whether they win or lose. Surely that could not be genuine. But in saying those words, Barty was not saying she did not care about the result – in private she would often cry after losses – she was saying that her worth was not tied up in a W or an L. It doesn't necessarily make for good copy, but it made for a champion's mindset.

She credited these new mindset techniques and Crowe with the trophies that followed. In January 2019, she finally made her breakthrough to a Grand Slam quarter-final, after a thrilling three-set victory over five-time major champion Maria Sharapova. What was sweeter is that it happened on Rod Laver Arena in front of a home crowd at the Australian Open. She was the first Australian woman to do so in a decade. A couple of months later she won her first WTA 1000 title in Miami to make her top 10 debut. That was the goal she had set herself for the season, and one which had eluded her for over a year. When she entered the clay court season, everything felt possible – and it was. She played well in Madrid, and subsequently ploughed through the Roland Garros draw. Marketa Vondrousova, the Czech teen, did not stand a chance against the Barty that stood before her in the final, the final score a very one-sided 6-1 6-3. When Barty won, her first look was to her team box. She mouthed the words, 'What the fuck just happened.' It was classic Barty, down-to-earth to a tee. Later, more words that just about summed up the person and player: 'Mate,' she told Tyzzer while posing for photos with the trophy, 'can I retire now?'

It was meant as a joke, but it was also telling of how – for all of Barty's mindset improvements – she remained a player constantly grappling between two things: her love for the sport and her desire to live a 'simple life' close by to her family, her dogs and at home. Where other champions describe winning their first Grand Slam title as only feeling briefly fulfilling before they moved on to the next goal, Barty already had the perspective to really know that, although she wanted to win more, that was not the key to happiness for her. Luckily for tennis fans, she didn't stop just yet.

Not long after her Roland Garros win, before she even got to the next slam at Wimbledon, she rose to world No. 1. She had spent only 12 weeks in the top 10 before reaching that milestone. According to her subsequent results, the bump in profile seemed to throw her. She lost in the fourth round at both Wimbledon and the US Open. Crowe said she tried to keep her sense of play, even as the attention on her built and more people seemed to focus on every result she had. During press conferences that year at Wimbledon, she set herself the task of getting Disney movie quotes into her answers to questions. It was bizarre, but it helped her to keep things light when people were expecting more and more from her. She fed her curiosity off the court too, by being a voracious reader. As well as spy thrillers, she read self-help genre on stoicism and vulner-ability, and was particularly a fan of Brené Brown on those topics. 'If you can tap into curiosity and imagination, which I believe is a superpower of Ash Barty's, you are constantly learning to be the best version of yourself,' says Crowe.

This curiosity translated on to the court too. It helped her to recapture the sense of playfulness and fun that tennis had always been to her, at least at the start, before tournaments and travel got in the way. Joyce had helped Barty tap into her creativity as a child and moulded a game built around variety. That was always what set her apart. While the WTA Tour was full of baseline grinders coming up against first-strike tennis connoisseurs, Barty was a maverick. Her game was a tribute to more traditional styles from the 1970s and '80s. Billie Jean King was delighted to see a player like her start to make her mark. Serena Williams once said of Barty: 'She has the most beautiful game. Her technique is, like, flawless.' Barty's signature was her killer backhand slice. It was the shot that got her back into tennis when Casey Dellacqua invited her to have a hit at Homebush, where the Sydney International was being played. Barty was still playing cricket, but her head was turned by a particular moment during their session: 'It was the slice backhand that got me, hook, line and sinker.' She could slice and dice her way to wins, just as soon as she could also send heavy groundstrokes into positions that made her opponents uncomfortable. Her serve was precise and bouncy too. Barty could deploy these shots at will, but it was her ability to rise to the moment at key stages in her second career which drove her success. 'When you're in the play state, as Ash did so wonderfully, having fun and taking your sport seriously but not taking yourself so seriously, you can compete without constantly getting angry, judging yourself,' Crowe says. 'Ash can accept it, have some self-compassion, and get back to the play state. That attitude is a superpower. It creates freedom on the tennis court, and also to live a life true to herself and not the expectations of others.'

At the end of the year, she won the WTA Finals, picking up the $4.42 million winner's cheque which, at the time, was the most money won by a (male or female) tennis player for a single tournament. A few weeks later, she and her Aussie teammates came agonisingly close to winning the Fed Cup, losing to France in the final, in what would turn out to be one of the toughest results to take of her career – in no small part because it was a team competition. As much as Barty was finally at the pinnacle of her sport, she was not always well understood. Crowe saw this first-hand when, in early 2020, she got a lot of criticism in her home country after losing her Australian Open semi-final 7-6 7-5 to eventual champion Sofia Kenin. She had set points in both sets, and seemed to buckle under Kenin's firepower. In her press conference, she brought her infant niece Olivia with her. 'Perspective is a beautiful thing,' Barty said. 'She brought a smile to my face as soon as I came off the court. It's all good.' She was later accused of trying to deflect criticism, and some even wondered if she was upset enough about falling short. Crowe laughed at that. That is exactly the kind of attitude he had tried to build in Barty, someone capable of failing in their sport without falling apart off it as a result. 'It scares people,' he says. 'It gets them off guard when you see someone so comfortable in their own skin that they're not defined by whether or not they lose a game of sport. Don't get me wrong, she was devastated she lost the match, and shed a tear. She still wanted to win, be No. 1 and win Grand Slams. But when you redefine success as Ash did, it's not from an extrinsic point of view. The rest of us are living in this gap mentality: I need that win, that prize money, then I'll feel validated or happy or successful. But when you measure backwards, and you redefine success differently, and create that internal scorecard, you don't have to wait any longer. But that scares the hell out of the rest of us.'

It can all sound a bit virtuous but Barty never wavered from that way of thinking. When the pandemic threw the world into disarray in March 2020, she hunkered down at home in Queensland. Even when the tour made its tentative first steps back to competition, she opted out of travelling to the US Open or defending her French Open title, when the delayed tournament was played in October. A few days before the tournament began, she was instead competing at her local golf club, Brookwater, and ended up winning the women's club championship. Golf runs deep in her family, with her father playing as an amateur for Australia and her partner Garry Kissick working in the sport. The pair even met on the Brookwater course. The previous year at an exhibition event, golfing great Tiger Woods had complimented Barty's swing.

Tennis was very much off the agenda at that point, beyond the practice courts. So on the day of the French Open final, Barty was instead pictured watching her beloved AFL team, the Richmond Tigers, with a pint of beer in hand. In all she spent 11 months out of competition. When she got back on tour in 2021, it turned out to be her last full season. It represented a big sacrifice for Barty, along with many players who hailed from countries with stricter Covid travel protocols. After a disappointing loss in the Australian Open quarter-final, she packed her bags to head abroad, knowing she and her team would be embarking on a six-month trip, with no visits home for the duration. As a self-confessed homebody, it was a tough call to make. But Barty clearly had goals she still wanted to achieve. She won the Miami Open again, picked up another clay title in Stuttgart and reached the final in Madrid too. She was struck down by injury in Paris though, pulling out of the French Open during her second-round match.

The bad news was she had a 10cm adductor tear. The good news was that she had nearly three weeks to fix it before Wimbledon. In her book she describes those weeks as full of uncertainty, but also immeasurably fun. She and her team shared a large house in leafy west London where she tried to rest and recover. They had barbecue evenings, and she made her way around the house on a small scooter where she could rest her leg and everyone kept their spirits up. Even as the tournament rolled around, she should not have strictly been playing. She could barely serve for most of the week ahead of it. 'The work her team did was absolutely extraordinary,' Crowe says of Adam Schumacher and Melanie Omizzolo, who managed the injury with care but did not tell Barty the extent of it. This was the first Wimbledon since 2019, on account of the tournament being cancelled due to the pandemic. Barty was desperate to play. In the previous few months she had let her guard down somewhat in saying publicly that winning Wimbledon was a dream of hers. It sounds like an obvious statement to make for a tennis player, but for her it felt like a big step, to put that out into the world. 'There were a lot of people asking me: "Ben, how could you let Ash do that? She's putting all this pressure on herself,"' Crowe says. 'I said no she's not; quite the opposite. Ash did a great job of putting these goals and dreams out into the universe and chasing them down, knowing that there's no guarantees, promises or expectations that she'll actually achieve those. Success wasn't winning

Wimbledon, success was when she believed she was worthy of winning Wimbledon.'

There was more motivation behind this particular Wimbledon too. It was the 50th anniversary of Evonne Goolagong Cawley's first Grand Slam victory, a fellow Australian and Indigenous woman who had inspired Barty throughout her career. The pair had struck up a strong friendship too, and Barty was paying tribute to Goolagong Cawley by wearing a skirt reminiscent of the scalloped dress from her famous 1980 Wimbledon victory – which remains the only time a mother has won the tournament in the Open Era. 'Evonne has guided the way,' Barty said on the eve of Wimbledon. 'She's created a path for all of us as Australians, but as a family and for our heritage to know that there is an opportunity to chase after your dreams and to do what you love. She's created a legacy like no other in Australia. I think I'm exceptionally proud to be able to call her a friend and a mentor, to be able to share heritage.'

This was not a regular Grand Slam for other reasons. Due to the ongoing challenges of the pandemic, Wimbledon was being played within a bubble. Whereas in most years players will rent large homes on quiet suburban streets within walking distance of the All England Club, this year players and their teams were required to stay at a hotel in central London. It was another obstacle for a player like Barty who so tried to replicate home comforts during tournaments. Her team even jokingly dubbed her the 'travelling house' because of how she packed her own coffee devices with her, for example. When they moved from their rental property in Wimbledon to the hotel that year, Barty ordered tea towels, dishwashing liquid, a frying pan and toaster to cook some simple meals on the stove in her room.

While on the court, she looked right at home too. As the world No. 1, she had the honour of opening play on Centre Court on day two of the championships, usually reserved for the reigning champion, but Simona Halep was injured. It turned out to be a good omen for Barty. She swept through the draw, losing only one set on her way to the final, defeating two Grand Slam champions in Barbora Krejcikova and Angelique Kerber. In her press conference, she paid tribute to her team. 'I'm pretty excited that I could repay them the favour in a way, of giving us the opportunity as a collective, as a whole, to do something pretty special this week.' She also said it was all the sweeter that she had finally reached a final at Wimbledon, when it was the place in 2018 that she had suffered what turned out to be a career-changing loss.

Ahead of the final, she and her team kept things light. The cameras captured her at Aorangi Park, the practice courts and warm-up area at the All England Club, playing a makeshift cricket game with her team using a broomstick as a bat. Back in Australia, her former Brisbane Heat coach Andy Richards saw that clip. 'I told her she needed to pack a small bat,' he says now, laughing, but adds: 'I'm quite sure that that was a reflection back to when she was having some fun and enjoying herself. That's when most of us play our best sport. I was really very excited when I saw it. I spoke to her a bit after and she says, "Yeah, it's always there."'

Not long after, when she and her opponent, the Czech Republic's Karolina Pliskova, walked out on to Centre Court, they did so to a full-capacity 15,000 crowd. It was the first at an outdoor sporting event in the United Kingdom since the pandemic began more than a year prior. They were rewarded with a thriller, but the first 10 minutes threatened for this to be a complete walkover. Barty won the first 12 points of the match, so in the zone was she. Pliskova eventually worked her way into it, digging in and forcing this match to a deciding set. But as much as Pliskova lifted herself out of trouble, Barty rose to the biggest of occasions to win 6-3 6-7 6-3. It was the first time a top seed had won a women's major title since Wimbledon 2016, Serena Williams's final victory at the All England Club.

Individual achievements were far from Barty's mind though. After match point, she was more overcome with emotion than she had ever been in victory. The sacrifices her team, including Tyzzer and her soon-to-be husband Garry Kissick, had made to commit to travelling the world for six consecutive months with her came into sharp focus. Also, just how unlikely this win was, considering her injury trouble: 'Being able to play here at Wimbledon was nothing short of a miracle.' As had been the case when she won the French Open, not long afterwards her thoughts already were considering retirement. She suffered a shock first-round loss at the Tokyo Olympics that summer, and despite lifting the trophy in Cincinnati, she then crashed out in the US Open third round to 43rd-ranked Shelby Rogers. It was an uninspiring end to her season, but when she returned home to Queensland, it became clearer to her that there was still unfinished business at the Australian Open. As much as Barty was described as one of the sport's most complete players, she had still not won a slam on a hard court. Melbourne was where she had always come closest at the slams. Apart from winning her titles in Paris and at Wimbledon, she had never had any great runs there. But at the Australian Open from 2019 to 2021, Barty had made the quarter-final twice and a semi-final.

She was about to embark on the dream Australian summer, winning the Adelaide International and finally clinching the elusive Australian Open too. She dropped only one set in that 11-match streak (incidentally, it was the first one she played, against Coco Gauff in Adelaide). She made light work of nearly every opponent, and possessed a levity despite being the home favourite with the hopes of ending a 44-year wait for an Australian champion. The final, a 6-3 7-6 win over fiery American Danielle Collins, was watched by 4.2 million people in Australia – the biggest ever television audience for a women's final. When it was over, the usually reserved Barty let out a full throttle roar. In Rod Laver Arena, every crowd member lived each point with Barty and that included Rod Laver himself. It made her one of only seven women to win Grand Slams on all three surfaces, joining Serena Williams and Maria Sharapova as the only women who have achieved that this century. She did so in the space of three and a half glorious seasons. As the celebrations began in Melbourne, Laver called her 'the complete player'. Higher praise, perhaps, could not exist in Barty's mind.

That stadium had everyone behind her, but it felt apt that every person who influenced her career was present too. As soon as she hit the winning passing shot, she grabbed her best friend and former doubles partner Casey Dellacqua for a hug, as she was courtside working for a national broadcaster. Then Evonne Goolagong Cawley surprised Barty by presenting her with the trophy. In her on-court speech, she paid tribute to her team. 'We started right together, right from the start, in this second part of our career. We did it all together; no one has changed from our team. I love you guys to death.' In the stands that day were the family that raised her, her ever-present Fed Cup captain Alicia Molik, Crowe, and the three men that shaped her tennis game: Jim Joyce, Jason Stoltenberg and Tyzzer. All three had remained mentors for her throughout her career. Joyce could often be seen in Barty's player box over the years, but this was the first time he had seen her lift such an important trophy. 'In the foyer after, Ash saw me, came over and gave me a big hug, a lovely smile and said: "Jimbo, you finally made it to one [Grand Slam victory]." And that just meant the world to me,' Joyce said in an interview afterwards. 'It would have been the biggest tragedy in tennis in Australia, if not sport, if she hadn't come back and just never played again.'

When you look at Barty's Grand Slam record, what is quite remarkable is that – apart from at the Australian Open – she never had any runs beyond the fourth round at the majors except for when she won them. It is almost like she set her mind to winning them the one time, and was satisfied with those victories in a way that is rarely seen. That Australian Open final was the last match of her career. She announced her retirement in March 2022, at the ripe old age of just 25. Just as soon as Barty was being anointed as the queen of women's tennis, as the rightful world No. 1, with the magical game, consistency and demeanour of a worthy champion, she was stepping away. We were being denied a potential era-defining rivalry with Osaka and a future in which Barty may establish herself as a repeat champion at multiple slams. It rattled the tennis world and sparked widespread debate about the state of the women's game. Over the previous season, Naomi Osaka had brought to the fore how players' mental health was being impacted by both the brutal schedule and the spotlight placed on its stars, and had taken long breaks from competing. People pondered whether Barty's retirement was further evidence of women's tennis proving to be an unsustainable career path, at least for the top players.

But this was as individual and predictable a decision as any, if you knew Barty personally. Very few within her circle were surprised by her retirement. It was hard for her to break up the team, but she was content in her decision. That did not make it easy to swallow for those around her. 'It was really, really, hard,' Crowe says of the day Barty delivered the news. 'I was genuinely sad because I literally just loved to watch her play. Forget my role, she was like a ballet dancer and problem-solver on the tennis court. It was literally incredible to watch live. I wanted to also make sure she was doing the right thing for the right reason, in the right way, at the right time, with the right people. That was one of Ash's strengths.' Still he found himself challenging her decision, pushing her buttons a bit to make sure she had definitely thought it all through. 'When your career doesn't define you and you've got so many other goals and dreams you want to pursue – her foundation, a family – it's quite liberating. It's also scary for the rest of us. Don't get me wrong, it was stressful, because it was an incredible anthropological experiment. I thought, is she going to get attacked here from the classic clickbait Twitter people going, "Get back to work, girl; you're only 25 years old?" I care so much for Ash, so I was concerned about that. But it was quite the opposite. When you see someone do that, it's like "Woah, God I'd love to have a bit of that." It was that courage to live life on her terms.'

For Molik, Barty's Fed Cup captain for many years, she understands why some fans might have felt short-changed by her abrupt career end. But she sees it the opposite way. 'A lot of people craved more of Ash, but on the flip side we're probably fortunate she stayed in it as long as she did too. Ash had a great team, great coach and great support network. She was really clever at having sound minds around her that really grounded her, helped her success and helped her stay in the game as long as she did in the end.' Most of all, her career was a lesson in reframing individual sport. She stepped away from an environment that did not serve her, and returned with the tools and the team she needed to make it work. 'Times have changed,' Molik says. 'I think when you look at careers as a whole, a year or two out of the game as a teenager is nothing. It's not that she didn't love the sport, she had all those things; it just became incredibly difficult. But careers are long, and if people take that long-term viewpoint early on, other players may just have success later on or hang on a bit longer. I think it's just a really good example that there are so many different pathways to be successful. Ash had hers.'

CHAPTER 9

Barbora Krejcikova:
The state project

BARBORA Krejcikova turns the key in the front door and steps into the warmth. On the streets outside, thousands of tennis fans are walking up the hill on Church Road towards Wimbledon Village, maybe stopping at the Dog & Fox for a pint on the way home after an epic women's semi-final day at the All England Club. Krejcikova sparked the biggest upset that Thursday by defeating tournament favourite and former champion Elena Rybakina in three riveting sets of tennis. On Saturday she will be a Wimbledon finalist for the very first time. But for now, she is greeted by the dog. Not her dog, but the one that belongs to the couple whom she lodges with each year at Wimbledon, ever since her first appearance in 2015. That year, she lost in the first qualifying round at Roehampton. In 2024, she is in with a chance of holding the Venus Rosewater Dish in her hands, just as her idol and mentor Jana Novotna did in 1998. It is all quite difficult to wrap her mind around.

Instead of obsessively percolating on what could happen in Saturday's final, she tries to distract herself by keeping to her routine. She drops her bags in her room and then curls up on the sofa in the lounge. Her adoptive Wimbledon family, an American-British couple who have three grown-up children of their own, don't dwell on the tennis with her either. They know her as Barbora the person rather than just the tennis player, she says. It has become their tradition to spend post-match binge-watching television together. Previous nights included watching a hospital drama and even BBC coverage of Coldplay live at Glastonbury on the eve of the tournament. Tonight it's a detective series followed by a card game. Krejcikova can pretend, if only for a couple of hours, that this is just a normal night.

This is the ninth year Krejcikova and her team have moved in for the Wimbledon fortnight. It is not uncommon for residents that share the same postcode with the All England Club to rent a room or two to players at Wimbledon each year. The top-ranked talent tend to rent out entire properties in the area. Owners can stand to make up to £15,000 per week if they give up their home to a player and their entourage, so they happily book a two-week holiday and welcome the tennis circus in. Usually if a player is bunking with a family, they're lower-ranked or a junior – not a former Grand Slam champion. But 2021 French Open champion Krejcikova has few airs or graces, and she has continued her tradition of staying with the same family she always has done. 'Since 2015 it's the same house, with the same people. I feel very at home,' she says. 'They're actually my second family, I love them so much, and they've been through the whole journey with me. They also had the opportunity to meet Jana. So I feel like those people, they understand me. They really know me.'

The All England Club is wedged within the most suburban area of all the major events. The affluent surrounding streets offer quiet residential roads and cul-de-sacs with some mega homes. There are parks and green spaces all around. But within the tournament grounds the pressure is perhaps higher than any other tournament of the year. The buzz within the club is palpable, the space smaller than other Grand Slam sites, hundreds of players milling around, the media coverage more acute than anywhere else. And that can get in your head, Krejcikova says, so an escape from it is necessary. 'I go to tennis and everything is very stressed out and a lot of pressure, and you feel it, it's just there. Especially at the beginning of the tournament, when it's the full event. When there are fewer people it's getting a little bit easier and easier. But then you get into the house, it's quiet, it's warm, you can cook, you can order in. You can watch TV; we were sitting on a sofa and having a good time. It's different. It's just more familiar. I was feeling very nice in that environment.'

In 2024, this home provided the perfect backdrop to her surprise run to the title as the 31st seed. Her adopted Wimbledon family were in her box cheering her on, as were members of her extended family, who flew over from the Czech Republic for the seismic occasion. This was a hugely personal achievement for the unassuming Krejcikova, but she was also carrying the torch for a great Czech tennis tradition. The 1973 Wimbledon champion and compatriot Jan Kodes watched her win alongside her family in her player box. In her speech, Krejcikova referred to Novotna, the 1998 champion, as one of the most inspiring people to have influenced her life. In the rankings, she was one of seven fellow Czech women in the top 50. Few countries can boast the same Grand Slam success and depth of talent as the Czech Republic. Krejcikova's win was further evidence of a nation that consistently punches above its weight on the tennis circuit, especially in the women's draw. But what makes them so good?

*

There must be something in the water, so goes the saying. It has perhaps never applied more to a tennis nation than to the Czech Republic. Nestled between Poland, Slovakia, Germany and Austria, the eastern European country has a population of 10.5 million people. Compare that to three tennis powerhouses like Great Britain (68.4m), France (68.2m), Italy (58.8m), and they are a relatively small country. But in tennis, they are heavy hitters. They consistently outshine countries of similar size as well as those much larger. Czech tennis (including when previously known as Czechoslovakia) has produced eight major champions in the Open Era. France has four, Great Britain has five and Italy has four. Belgium (population 11.8 million) has two.

That tally of eight champions does not include Martina Navratilova either, the all-time great and winner of 18 Grand Slam singles titles. She was born in Czechoslovakia but defected from communist rule to the US as an 18-year-old. She now has dual citizenship, but competed under the American flag throughout most of her career. The first two major finals she played in 1975 were under the Czech flag. But by 1978, when she lifted the Venus Rosewater Dish for the first of nine times, she was competing as an American. Her father Miroslav, who continued to coach her over the phone despite her defection, was denied the opportunity to travel to England to watch her win. Instead, her family was back home in Czechoslovakia, where state network television opted not to broadcast the match (but did broadcast the men's final the following day). 'I will always be Czech down in my heart,' Navratilova said after clinching the trophy. 'I hope the Czech people will be proud of me.'

Navratilova remains the star of women's tennis that so many of the current crop of Czech players still refer to as a source of inspiration. As well as her 18 major titles in singles, she won 31 in doubles, and remarkably continued to compete up until she was a month shy of her 50th birthday. She won her final singles title on the tour in 2006, when she was 49. She followed in the footsteps of three-time major champion Jaroslav Drobny, a Czech-born top player who defected midway through his career, competing under the Egyptian flag when he won his titles in the 1950s. Then Kodes was the first of the (officially) Czech champions in the Open Era, who emulated Drobny's record with back-to-back titles at the French

Open in 1970 and 1971, before his win in 1973 on the Wimbledon lawns (the year in which 80 top male players boycotted over a dispute between Nikola Pilic and the ITF). Later, Ivan Lendl held the No. 1 spot for 270 weeks, winning eight major titles in the 1980s and early 1990s. On the women's side, Hana Mandlikova won four majors in the 1980s, while Petr Korda picked up his sole trophy in 1998 at the Australian Open. Earlier that year, Jana Novotna pulled at the heartstrings of the British public by winning Wimbledon five years after her famous tears on the Duchess of Kent's shoulder when she lost in the 1993 final.

'It reaches the point where it's self-perpetuating,' Catherine Whitaker, of *The Tennis Podcast*, says. 'You've got the role models and icons on screen to inspire people, the culture and the coaches.' Each country experiences different challenges. In the USA, tennis is only the eighth most popular participation sport and trying to attract the best athletes away from baseball, basketball or American football can prove difficult. The picture is similar in Britain, with the added issue of poor weather, considering that only 12 per cent of courts are indoor. Spain may be comparably sunny and have more than 13,000 courts across the country, but tennis is only the 12th most popular sport there too. Canada has had good results at the top level in recent years and ranks top on gender parity for players, but the number of clubs has dropped by two thirds in the last five years. Tunisia has not got a particularly strong history in tennis – it only has 56 clubs and just 19,000 people who actually play tennis – but having a built-in role model like Grand Slam finalist Ons Jabeur is expected to help boost a new generation. In the Czech Republic, cold winters and smaller budgets than richer tennis nations should, on paper, limit their success, but they have created a system that somehow churns out talent to rival almost any other country.

Just as when it comes to individuals, there seems to be no set way or combination to build a group of champions. 'Being a Grand

Slam nation, with the money and profile that it provides to the sport helps, but I actually think that's quite a small piece in the jigsaw overall,' Whitaker says. 'For example, over the years the LTA have tried a bit of everything. They saw Canada having big success and brought in the head of Canadian tennis and said, "Do what you did there here." It wasn't a spectacular failure, but it didn't work to build wholesale another country's plan and build it here. It's also always really striking to me how in France they have such a good club system, a really accessible network of your quintessential tennis court or club in every village or town. But then France has its own problems with not producing any male champions. There doesn't seem to be a perfect formula of how to create a successful tennis nation.'

It appears, for women's tennis at least, the Czech Republic have found a version of the formula that works a charm. Alongside the individual champions who led the way, the Czech Republic's success as a nation has been solidified in team competition too. They won three Davis Cup titles, first in 1980, plus 2012 and 2013, right in the midst of the Big Three's most dominant period. In the women's version of the team event (previously known as the Fed Cup and now the Billie Jean King Cup), they won it a whopping 11 times – including six titles between 2011 and 2018. It makes them the second most successful nation, behind the USA, who have 18 titles. Long-time captain of the Czech women's team Petr Pala has had top players to pick from each year. In the last 15 seasons, at least one Czech woman has featured in the end-of-year top 10 all but twice. A Czech woman has ranked in the top 10 of doubles for each of the last 15 years too. Krejcikova, Marketa Vondrousova and Petra Kvitova are the three women with Grand Slam singles titles to their name this century, while their compatriots Karolina Pliskova, Karolina Muchova and Lucie Safarova have all finished runners-up at major tournaments too.

At the end of 2024, along with Krejcikova's Wimbledon title, seven Czech women finished in the top 100. Only the USA and Russia had more. Remarkably, when Vondrousova won Wimbledon in 2023, she was only the seventh ranked player from her country (at 42nd in the world). That level of depth is unprecedented, when some countries with rich tennis histories can barely manage two top 50 players. So what on earth is creating such a production line of top female players from the Czech Republic? Some cite the numbers. According to the International Tennis Federation Global Tennis Report for 2024, the Czech Republic's sporting infrastructure may just be what sets them apart. There are more tennis clubs (1,251) in the country than other top nations like Spain or Switzerland, and even the ever-growing mammoth tennis project ongoing in China. There are more tennis coaches in the Czech Republic (9,493) than in Spain and Switzerland, or even Grand Slam nations like Britain and Australia. The Czech Republic ranks sixth in the world on that front, trailing only the USA, Germany, Italy, Turkey and France. In the junior ranks in 2023, 5.3 per cent of boys to make the top 100 were from Czechia, and that rose to 7.5 per cent for girls. It put Czechia third across all nations. The World Junior Tennis title has been claimed by the Czech under-14 girls' team five times in the last seven years. It does not automatically mean that will translate to success at professional level, not to mention actually winning majors, but the more players doing well at junior level suggests more are likely to compete well in the big leagues. Perhaps most pertinent are the ratios though. There are 5.9 players for every coach in the Czech Republic, and 11.2 players for every court. By comparison, in Great Britain there are 1,387.2 players for every coach and 379.1 players for every court. Based on those numbers, aspiring Czech players can enjoy far more focused attention from coaches as well as easier access to facilities too.

Four-time major champion Hana Mandlikova, who became a coach to Novotna in the 1990s, has cited the quality of coaching as the reason for her country's tennis prowess. 'There is only one reason that so many Czech players have been successful, and it's because the coaches there all teach good technique,' she told the *New York Times* in 2021. 'Sometimes it takes a little longer to develop, but it stays with you for your whole life.' It is not all rosy, though. Amid the success on the court, in February 2024 a fraud investigation was launched into misuse of state funds in the Czech tennis federation, and remains a cloud hanging over the federation.

Krejcikova, who is 29, grew up in Brno (the second largest city in the Czech Republic) in the early noughties. In terms of coaching, she does believe that young tennis players are particularly sound when it comes to technique in her country. Though she had an older coach as a child, who taught her 'the old style, closed stance and old grip' which eventually changed as she levelled up to the national academy, she does believe it gave her a solid foundation which she recognises in her peers too. 'My basics, my roots, are very much the old style. We have a lot of good coaches for the kids, and growing up with other fellow tennis players, I think most of us have really nice technique, very smooth and good-looking.' Krejcikova cannot claim to have picked up a racket because of a specific role model or because she was particularly closely linked to a tennis club. She started playing because her brothers were taking lessons, and she and her mum would hang around the courts, waiting to drive them home. 'My family background is not sporty, like no tennis background. My mum is a doctor and my dad used to be a teacher, so we were more a degree family than a sports family. I have two older brothers, and one of them started to go to tennis with his school friends. I was like three or four years old so I had to go with them.'

Krejcikova was instantly fascinated by this game her older brother played. But she was relegated to hitting against the wall for years before she was 'allowed' on court. 'I think I was very patient for a kid,' she says. 'I was running around the tennis wall trying to hit the ball with a cutting board, because it was the very first thing that I had. Later on, I got my first tennis racket but I was still playing against the wall for quite some time, because it was a privilege to actually go on court. I had to be more developed and skilled before I was allowed. It took maybe a year or two.' Eventually she graduated to actually playing on a tennis court. But Krejcikova still needed to show patience. At eight years old, she played her first tournament. 'The coach that we had, he told us the regular overhand serve you start learning at 11. But I got to the tournament and everybody knew how to serve. I was the only one serving underhand. I loved the game, so I didn't mind. But I lost to every single girl I played.'

As for facilities, having courts or a small club in every town is an accurate representation according to the numbers, as well as champions Navratilova and Kodes, who cite the cheap and readily available courts as one of the big reasons the sport is so strong among Czech women. But the reality is that Krejcikova still had weather-related access issues. 'During the summer, in my city we had six clay courts. I was allowed to go and play there when I was in the first grade of elementary school. But during winter we didn't have any courts so basically I only played like two times a week in a school gymnasium. That's pretty much how I developed from the age of six to nine.'

Two-time Wimbledon champion Petra Kvitova had a similar experience, except in her tiny home town of Fulnek, which has barely 5,000 inhabitants. Despite how small Fulnek is, there were somehow four tennis courts to work with and her father, a strict former teacher, coached her until she was 16. The harsh winters in her small town, near the border with Poland, meant she also became accustomed to indoor gymnasiums like Krejcikova, playing on creaky wooden flooring where dead bounces came every other ball.

What did make a difference to both of their lives, and the careers of the majority of the top players in the Czech Republic, was the multitude of junior tournaments they could compete in across the country, as well as training camps for each region from the age of 10 up until 14. 'I was not the very best one; I was around number five or six in the year I was born,' Krejcikova says of how she ranked in her area, but she had ample opportunities to pit herself against the best girls in her age group. 'We had many, many tournaments, categories from A to D and we played in singles and doubles. I think this was nice from the Czech tennis association to do this. I was gradually getting better and better.'

The player pathway to the regional club system was a massive stepping stone after that. Krejcikova was 15 when she was selected to train in the facility in Prostejov with a fully funded place. The indoor facility was a huge bonus, but so was having a coach assigned to her and travelling to tournaments abroad without her parents needing to contribute financially. It was a massive commitment of course. An hour's drive from her home, for the first year she would complete an 8 a.m. to 1.30 p.m. school day, and then her father would drive her to the Prostejov tennis centre. After a few hours of training, they would drive home, she would start her homework that night, wake up early before school to complete it, and then continue the cycle again: 'I remember I was falling asleep in my third class, around 10.30 a.m., because I was so tired.'

When she was 16, she was offered an apartment in Prostejov where she and her father moved to, and she continued her schooling remotely. Her story is similar to all of the other Czech women who have grown to establish themselves on the WTA Tour to great success. Kvitova also came through the Prostejov system, while the Pliskova twins, Karolina and Kristyna, were based in the capital at Sparta Prague and Karolina Muchova and Marketa Vondrousova both came through neighbouring club, CLTK Prague. Vondrousova was born in Sokolov, a town of 22,000, but was ferried the two-hour car journey to the club by her grandfather from the time she was 12 years old. At 15, she was put up in a flat in Prague, moving there without her family to pursue her tennis career.

For Krejcikova, the time at Prostejov was transformative and she rose to No. 3 in the junior world rankings by the time she was 17 in 2013, the same year she won three junior doubles titles at Grand Slams with partner Katerina Siniakova. It was only then that she seriously started to consider tennis as a career option. Krejcikova was not a big-hitting power player; her serve was reliable but not outstanding and her weapons were more understated. She had guile, a varied toolbox, and the potential for a creative game, but she had never been singled out as the one to watch, especially in the crowded Czech talent pool. 'Definitely, I was quite a successful junior. It was quite a big thing. But on the other hand, before that, I never had where people would see something in me or would say that I will make it. It was good, because I could just enjoy tennis and I didn't have that target or that heavy pack on my back. But I didn't have self-confidence, and to be honest, I'm still fighting with that today. I was never told that I'd be a top player. Even back home, I didn't really have big dreams because that was the communist development that my parents had. They pretty much raised me in this way. Even now, I have so much success, but still it's tough for me to actually have the self-belief that I actually belong there. Inside, the self-esteem or something, I just still see myself as a regular player. I'm not really seeing myself as one of the top 10 and one of the players that has two Grand Slams. I'm really working on it right now, very hard, as I need to improve that.'

The moment that changed Krejcikova's life came when she was 18 in January 2014. She was at a crossroads, considering whether going professional was really for her and trying to map out her future. She was unsure, as struggles with illness had scuppered the last few months of her junior career. 'I didn't really know if I should turn pro and try to play the little tournaments to really work my ranking to actually be part of the top 100 and make a living with tennis, or if I should go and study to the US, play college tennis and start like that. I just didn't know at the beginning.' She needed guidance, and her mother Hana figured the best person to give them advice was someone who had been in their very shoes. She knew 1998 Wimbledon champion Jana Novotna lived in their city, so she sought her out. 'To be honest, I didn't have the guts to do it, it was more my mum, she is a little bit like that,' Krejcikova says. 'She was very ambitious and wanted always the best for me. I was never really pushed, but she was really trying to help me with everything to get me to the place where I wanted to be.'

Hana told her daughter to write a letter to Novotna, and she would find out where to deliver it. With the letter in hand, Krejcikova and her mother asked around town if anyone knew where Novotna lived and found out her address. It was a bold move, but in a moment of serendipity, when they pulled up at the house to put the letter in her postbox, Novotna was walking up her driveway with her dog. 'I was shy and I was feeling weird that we shouldn't go there, that we should wait until she enters the door and then put it in the postbox,' Krejcikova says. 'But my mom got out of the car straight away.' 'Mrs Novotna,' Krejcikova's mother called out, striding towards Novotna and waving the letter in her hand. Krejcikova was mortified, but she reluctantly trudged behind her mother. 'My mum started talking, saying that I'm playing tennis and I'm finishing juniors and we don't know what to do,' Krejcikova says, now laughing at her mother's brazenness. 'Jana, she offered us a try-out, that I can go with her and practise, and that she can see how I play and she can maybe help me. She was very, very nice from the very first day. Very polite and just warm. In the next couple of days, I went to hit with her, and that's how the whole story started.'

CHAPTER 10

Barbora Krejcikova:
The power of a mentor

JANA Novotna became the coach and mentor Barbora Krejcikova had desperately been hoping for. The irony is that for all Czech tennis's golden history and the role models available to aspiring players in the country, Krejcikova says she had to google who exactly Novotna was. 'I don't like to say it out loud, because . . . I don't know, it's not very nice,' Krejcikova says. 'But to be honest, when I was growing up, I was not really aware of the players that were there. I knew the name Jana Novotna, but I didn't know the face. For me, I was actually thinking that Jana is Martina Navratilova. I wasn't really aware. Even back then, I was ashamed by that because I should know about it, but because I didn't have the tennis background, I don't know, I just wasn't that interested in the history of tennis. When I was growing up, there was already Petra Kvitova playing, players that were there from Czech Republic on TV. So I was more aware of these players than actually of the previous players.'

Kvitova was front and centre in Czech tennis at the time. She first emerged on tour in 2008 as a gangly left-handed teenager, beating Venus Williams in Memphis when she was a week shy of her 18th birthday and then reaching the fourth round in her Grand Slam debut in Paris. She broke into the top 50 later that year and picked up her first title in Hobart in January 2009. The following year she got to the Wimbledon semi-finals, despite never having previously won a match on grass, ousting Victoria Azarenka and third seed Caroline Wozniacki before falling to Serena Williams. Three titles in the first half of 2011 – including the Madrid Open – plus a run to the quarter-final in Melbourne tipped Kvitova as a player to watch out for, and she quickly pushed herself into the top 10. No one was expecting her to do what she did at Wimbledon, aged just 21, but she overcame the odds to beat the favourite, Maria Sharapova, in a one-sided 6-3 6-4 final. At 6ft tall, Kvitova outhit the famously powerful Sharapova, and concluded with an ice-cold ace, her only one of the match. With a bona fide superstar across the net, Kvitova was full of poise during the match, but she was endearingly humble and shocked upon clinching the biggest prize in world tennis. Navratilova anointed Kvitova as the future of women's tennis, even saying she believed she could get close to her own tally of titles.

She has admitted to struggling with those expectations, but in 2014, Kvitova backed that up with her second Wimbledon victory, beating Venus Williams and three fellow Czech players on her way to a final victory over Canada's Eugenie Bouchard. The 6-3 6-0 scoreline and crushing performance saw Bouchard blown out of the water by Kvitova. But in December 2016, her tennis career and life was threatened when a burglar stabbed her in the neck in her home. She wrestled away a knife from her attacker, but by doing so cut through every single finger in her left hand, causing extensive nerve damage. She survived, and her attacker was later jailed, but doctors were unsure whether she would ever hold a tennis racket again – not to mention the huge psychological impact of the harrowing incident. Remarkably, she made her comeback at Roland Garros in May 2017, and won her first title upon her return in Birmingham the following month. 'It is like a dream or fairy tale,' she said. 'It wasn't about tennis, but to come back healthy and alive.'

The following season she won five titles, returning to the top 10 and then reached the 2019 Australian Open final, losing in a tight battle 7-6 5-7 6-4 to Naomi Osaka. In the trophy ceremony, there was not a dry eye in the house on Rod Laver Arena. 'Mostly thank you for sticking with me even when we didn't know if I was able to hold a racket again,' she said to her team, tears falling from her eyes. 'You were there every single day supporting me and staying positive when I needed it; it probably wasn't easy so thank you so much.'

Kvitova's career served as a leading source of inspiration for the current crop of Czech players. Her 2014 Wimbledon win was the backdrop to Krejcikova transitioning into her professional career. There was a very real example of a player, who had literally trained (and continued to train) at her club who had gone on to achieve two Wimbledon titles. In training every day, Krejcikova was learning from a Czech legend in Novotna too. Novotna put together a schedule for her, beginning at $10,000 and $25,000 tournaments on the ITF tour, moving beyond just the European circuit. In the first year, she nearly halved her ranking, rising to 185. They trained together, with Novotna joining her for fitness sessions as well as tennis. But the physical aspect came second to what Novotna offered Krejcikova in mentorship.

'It was more the mental guide that I got from her,' Krejcikova says. 'It was just the way she guided me and how she tried to put me on the right path as a tennis player, but not really just that. With the tennis, you just keep hitting, hitting, hitting and – at some point if you keep working hard – it's going to click and come together. But I think more of the mental part is what she gave me: how to talk to people, how to behave to the fans, how to talk to the tournaments, how to talk with the journalists and all this. This was kind of something that she was trying to prepare me for. I was too young, I couldn't really fully understand, but I understand it now better, what she wanted to give to me. This is something I appreciate more than the hours on the court hitting the balls and doing the slices and volleys and serving and all this. It was more this other part because, if it wasn't for her, I wouldn't have anybody that would help me with this kind of stuff. She had the experience and she knew how to transfer this experience to a younger player. This was the very important part for the development when I'm entering the bigger courts and I'm playing the biggest matches, because that's something that we talked about earlier.'

That faith Novotna showed in Krejcikova so early in her career was not based on results as such. Her first real run at a WTA level event was not until in May 2017 when she reached the Nuremberg Cup final after coming through qualifying. That week she was ranked 254, but scored her third and fourth wins over top 100 players. Krejcikova spent years on the cusp of breaking into the top 100, but it never actually became a reality until 2020. That is six years after she started working with Novotna, and three years on from her untimely death. Novotna sadly passed away at the age of 49 in November 2017, having been diagnosed with cancer. It was a huge loss to Krejcikova and one she continues to feel, but she kept plugging away at her tennis career, as Novotna would have wanted.

Between 2014 and 2019, Krejcikova tried to qualify for a major 16 times, and only succeeded once (at Roland Garros, in 2018, where she lost her first round match). Her singles career, for a long time, was very much secondary to her doubles. In 2018, while she dipped outside the top 200 in singles, she became the world No. 1 doubles player thanks in large part to her and Siniakova's victory at the French Open and Wimbledon that year. The real switch came during the pandemic, when she had an opportunity to slow down and focus on improving her singles game. 'I think the Covid break really helped me. The season stopped. When I was playing singles on ITF and playing doubles on the top level, trying to split the time in between, I did not have much time for practising; I was constantly just going, going, going, going. It's difficult. Doubles was funding my whole career. I remember many times I played very well in doubles, but I missed the qualies [qualifiers] of the singles the next week. Covid meant I finally had the time to do the physical preparation, be more consistent.'

She was also lucky to be in the Czech Republic during the pandemic, where a few interim tournaments were set up once facilities began reopening but travel remained limited. Whereas usually she would have been apart from most top Czech talent in Brno, she opted to play exhibition events in Prague and, because of the depth in Czech tennis, had fellow top 100 players to practise with. It was a benefit that other players dotted around the world did not have. 'I got so much match experience that other players didn't, and playing other top players. In a charity exhibition I was part of the group with Petra Kvitova, Barbora Strycova and Siniakova. Against us, there was Vondrousova, both Pliskovas, Muchova. It was a little bit of a rivalry. But I could play with them, practise with them, play some points. That part was so important in my singles transition, and I didn't have that before.'

That October, once the tour started up again, she had her first meaningful run at a major at the delayed French Open, reaching the fourth round. For a player who had never previously won a match at a slam, and only qualified for one once before, it was significant. It saw her jump into the top 100, and opened up opportunities for her in singles that she had never been able to enjoy based on her ranking. In Melbourne, at the Australian Open tune-up event, she scored the first top 20 win of her career by beating Elena Rybakina on her way to the quarter-final. In March she reached the Dubai final too, but her true breakthrough came on the clay. It is the surface she and most Czech players grow up on, so it felt most appropriate. She beat world No. 5 Sofia Kenin on her way to the Italian Open third round, and then landed her first ever WTA title in Strasbourg. It put her on the radar of other players, and on the cusp of the top 30 too. 'I never actually knew that I can win one WTA tournament. I was so excited and so happy about it. I went to Roland Garros that night, and I was like I don't care how I'm gonna play here. I'm sorry for that, but I don't give a shit about it.' Two weeks later, she was lifting the trophy in Paris.

That outcome seemed unimaginable when she was a set and a break down to compatriot Krystina Pliskova, someone she had never beaten, in the first round. 'I was super happy that I won a match in Paris – like, winning a match at the slam at that point was a huge achievement for me. Out of nowhere, I was sailing through the draw, and I don't even know how.' She beat world No. 6 Elina Svitolina and former US Open champion Sloane Stephens to reach the quarter-finals, before taking out teen sensation Coco Gauff next. An epic, messy semi-final against Maria Sakkari followed, which she won 9-7 in the deciding set despite being match point down. It put her on course for her first major final against Anastasia Pavlyuchenkova of Russia. Pavlyuchenkova was far more experienced. She was the first woman to reach her first final after playing more than 50 slam tournaments. By comparison, this was only Krejcikova's fifth.

The unseeded 25-year-old had shown ample grit to get to the final, and she needed it in the championship match too which went to a decider. At 3-3 she hit two winners off both wings, taking the match by the scruff of the neck to break Pavlyuchenkova's serve and put her in a winning position. After holding her nerve to serve it out, she made sure to pay tribute to Novotna in an emotional on-court speech. 'All of this that happened the past two weeks has happened because she is looking out for me somewhere,' she said. 'I was going through a really hard time when Jana was passing away. I was with her most of the time and I really [wanted to] experience this because I thought she was going to make me really strong.

Pretty much her last words were: "Just enjoy, and try to win a Grand Slam." I know all of this that happened, these two weeks, is because she's pretty much looking after me.' Fittingly, Martina Navratilova presented her with the trophy. The next day, she became the first woman since Mary Pierce 21 years prior to do the double in Paris, by teaming up with Siniakova to win the women's doubles event too. 'I like to memorise that,' Krejcikova says. 'I like to go back and just try to understand what actually happened and how much I achieved by winning singles and doubles during one year.'

For all that success, Krejcikova did not feel like life changed that significantly for her away from the tennis court. 'I thought that things would change, and it will be kind of like crazy because that's what I saw in other players winning a slam. But I felt like in my case, it didn't happen like that.' Perhaps because she was the sixth consecutive first-time Grand Slam champion to be crowned in Paris. People might have written off her win as some kind of fluke, in a tournament that saw the top seeds tumbling throughout the early rounds. But the months preceding her win in Paris had shown her growth, her ability to compete at the top level. That she has not wavered from the top 30 ever since is a testament to that. Regardless, write off Czech talent at your own peril.

Some might have seen Marketa Vondrousova as a flash in the pan after she too made a relatively surprising surge to the final in Paris two years prior. Her story was very different to Krejcikova's as she was only 19 years old when it happened, not a player who had toiled away on the ITF circuit for years at that point. Vondrousova by comparison was the top junior in the world, and quickly transitioned to success on tour. She went into the French Open that year with a 22-6 record for the season, including quarter-finals in Indian Wells, Miami and Rome. But she was absolutely dismantled by Ash Barty in their Roland Garros final 6-1 6-3, a match where she looked overawed by the occasion. She never got the chance to push on either, suffering a wrist injury that sidelined her for the rest of the season, before the pandemic ended her comeback chances in 2020 too. A silver medal at the Tokyo Olympics was further evidence of her talent, but more injury in 2022 proved fatal to her season and even saw her lose her Nike endorsement deal when it expired that year.

She made the Nike executives live to regret that in 2023. Vondrousova was known for her delicate drop shots, lefty game that rattled opponents and her sketchbook collection of tattoos on her arms, but was not exactly considered a grass court maestro. She had a played a total of 19 career matches on the green stuff heading into Wimbledon, and had just three main draw wins (one of which was a retirement). At Wimbledon, she had only one match win to her name, a 2021 victory over Anett Kontaveit. Unseeded and inexperienced, she walked into the All England Club in 2023 with little to no expectations. But how wrong she and everyone else was.

All but two of her opponents that fortnight were ranked ahead of her, including fourth seed Jessica Pegula, whom she trailed 4-1 in the deciding set before clinching a startling win. With four seeds in her pocket, she then ended Elina Svitolina's feel-good post-baby comeback before overcoming all of the odds to defeat fan favourite Ons Jabeur 6-4 6-4 in the final. Not only was Vondrousova, 24, the first unseeded Wimbledon champion of the Open Era, but she was the lowest ranked (42) too. 'I feel like everybody is playing such great tennis that it doesn't matter whether you are [ranked] 70 or 20; anyone can beat anyone,' she said.

That especially seems to apply to the Czechs, often regardless of form. Her clubmate Muchova had been causing upsets all over the shop in recent years, using her slice and dice, inventive game to knock the likes of major champions Ash Barty and Garbiñe Muguruza out of Grand Slams. At the 2021 Australian Open, she beat home favourite Barty to reach the semi-final and the month before Vondrousova's Wimbledon victory, Muchova reached the French Open final by beating world No. 2 Aryna Sabalenka. She then ran heavy favourite Iga Swiatek incredibly close in the championship match, leading by a break in the deciding set before suffering a crushing loss. Injury has ravaged much of her career but, when fit, Muchova can compete with the best in the world.

By Vondrousova's win, Czech women had reached nine major finals within the previous decade. Krejcikova would make it 10 the following year. She arrived at the All England Club with a 7-8 win-loss record for the season. Even after Wimbledon, she only managed seven more wins in 2024. They are not exactly results worthy of a Grand Slam champion. 'Quite a disaster,' she says on reflection. That fortnight in SW19, Krejcikova experienced a purple patch for the ages. 'The rest of the season, it just sucked. It's a little bittersweet, but I believe anyone would exchange their year with mine right now. I got the cherry on top and two weeks changed my perspective. It would be a really nice movie, those two weeks. Everything that I went through, people would not believe how things changed within 20 days of my life. I went from below the ground to being on top of an 8,000-metre mountain.'

As the 31st seed, she beat in-form player Danielle Collins, swept past major champion Jelena Ostapenko and then forged a comeback against the former Wimbledon queen Elena Rybakina 3-6 6-3 6-4, who was the heavy favourite for the title. 'Nobody had any expectations. I was pretty much the underdog in every match that I played. I was just able to play free. That's something that fits me. I can produce my best tennis. Against Elena, she was kicking my butt the first set and a half. I was basically hanging in there and just trying to stay there and enjoying playing. I wanted to prolong the match as it was my first time on Centre Court in singles. My doubles experience definitely helped me mentally, but it was a different pressure.'

Again, Novotna's figure loomed large for Krejcikova as parallels were drawn between the former Wimbledon champion and her mentee. 'Did you ever dream of reaching the Wimbledon final?' Annabel Croft asked her in her on-court interview. 'No, never. I mean, a few years ago I was working with Jana Novotna; she won it here in 1998. And I mean at that point she was telling me a lot of stories about her journeys here and how she was trying to win Wimbledon. I was so far when we had this talk. Now I'm here, and wow, I'm in the finals. Definitely, I'm thinking about Jana a lot. I have so many beautiful memories. When I step on the court here, I'm just fighting for every single ball because that's what I think she'd want me to do.' She paused then, stepping away from the microphone and wiping her tears with a towel. As the Centre Court crowd applauded her, she managed to add. 'I just miss her very much.'

Krejcikova admits that a very small part of her had started dreaming about lifting the Venus Rosewater Dish at Wimbledon in the months before she did so. 'After winning the French Open I ticked all the boxes that I wanted to achieve in my career, and I didn't really know what to do next. I was looking for the next goal and, because I was attached to Jana and to Wimbledon, it was very, very personal to me. Very deep inside of myself, I started a little bit dreaming that it would be nice to be able to win Wimbledon and be part of the All England Club forever.' The only person she had really told was her sport psychologist. It was not something she would ever have shared with Novotna as it seemed so unrealistic considering she was barely able to keep herself in the world's top 200 at that time. Novotna always had it in her mind though. 'She was trying to guide me somewhere; I didn't understand back then,' Krejcikova says. Now with that goal within reach, the pressure was back on her for the final. She was the more experienced player in the match, facing Jasmine Paolini of Italy, who had also reached the French Open final the previous month. 'That Friday was difficult, very difficult,' Krejcikova says of the preparations. 'I just really wanted to win a lot. But you have one day to over-analyse everything.'

It was her third three-setter of the week, but she managed to quash Paolini's revival to take the match 6-2 2-6 6-4. She held her arms aloft, her mouth formed in an 'O' shape as the shock of the moment hit her. 'I always dreamed that once I win something big, I'm gonna have some crazy celebration, that I fell on the grass or something. But it happens and it kind of paralyses me. I do remember sitting on my chair and telling myself, "Oh shit, I won Wimbledon."' She grins. People saw the powerful symmetry of her winning the title, continuing not only the Czech tradition but also doing so 26 years after Novotna.

Since her first WTA title in Strasbourg in 2021, she has won seven of her 10 finals. That steeliness in the most important moments is a feature of her game, something she cultivated through her doubles career too, as the winner of seven major titles, plus seven more in mixed doubles. That winning formula under pressure is a feature of Kvitova's record too (38-14 in career finals) and Vondrousova (10-7). For all the extra coaches, accessible courts and a junior system to rival any other nation's, most of the women who have emerged at the top of Czech tennis have very different ways of playing the game. Krejcikova has her guile and solidity, Kvitova her clean, forceful groundstrokes, Pliskova her serving prowess, Muchova her inventiveness and Vondrousova the lefty, drop-shotting nightmare to play against. What most Czech players refer to as a trait they all possess though is an inner fire – often referring to the communist regime, that lasted from 1948 to 1989, which informed their upbringings.

Navratilova, perhaps the greatest symbol of sporting defiance against that regime, has said the Czech players are 'born with it', and even those born after the Iron Curtain fell feel similar. 'We have something inside that makes us want to be better,' Kvitova said in a 2019 *Guardian* interview. 'It makes us work harder. Maybe it's because our parents had a harsh life before us.' Krejcikova nods in recognition: 'I'm trying to find a way to describe it. The big part, especially for me, is how I was raised. I never had anything for free. I really had to work for that. It's this constant fight for something. I'm not gonna say it's like survival fight, but if I wanted to beat the other girl, only in Czech Republic, I really had to dig deep. It was something that helped me learn to get through the tough situations. And if I can get through like, the tough situation and not be in my comfort zone, I can just improve with that.'

Krejcikova's career has been informed by the experience of existing as one of many fish in a big old pond. She was never the fastest, the most skilled, the best, growing up. And though she has her name printed alongside fellow Czech greats on the All England Club's champions board, she remains lacking in self-esteem. 'I still feel like I am that little kid sometimes,' she says. 'Patience was important. Everything clicked not when I was 18 or 19. Nobody was expecting me, as someone who entered the top 100 at 25, to win a slam. It's very unusual. If I could talk to myself then, I would say to try not to stress about it too much. Maybe try and enjoy it a little bit more. I think the inner voice is something I'm trying to even listen to more. That voice is authentic, real.' She has learned to live without the guiding voice Novotna offered her in those early years. Even now, she continues to have vivid dreams about her. They could be in a shopping mall or on the court, simply spending time together. Novotna does not speak, but she is 'giving the energy' that Krejcikova came to know so well. 'It's very lifelike for me,' Krejcikova says, emotion cutting through her voice. 'Sometimes I just feel like she's never gone.'

CHAPTER 11

Emma Raducanu:
The bolt from the blue

ON A chilly January morning in 2020, I found myself at the Queen's Club watching Emma Raducanu get her photo taken. At the time, that was still a novelty for the 17-year-old. Queen's Club in Barons Court, west London, is pitched between charming rows of Edwardian and Victorian terraced homes on leafy, affluent streets. It is a site laced with history, with a clubhouse that has stood since 1886 and claims to be the first ever purpose-built multi-sports venue in the world. Queen's is usually known for its green lawns, exclusive membership list and the Wimbledon tune-up event it hosts in June each year, dating back more than a century. But on this day, I'm warming my hands and standing inside a synthetic bubble structure that houses one of the rarest things in British tennis: a clay court. I don't know it yet, but I'm also waiting to meet a rare talent, a young woman destined to join the list of British Grand Slam champions. This is the first time I've seen Raducanu hit a tennis ball. Unfortunately for me, the session is mostly fun drills with her British Fed Cup teammates for the cameras. Her angular shot-making and aggressive style will be something I'll watch closely for years to come. But on this day she spends more time on court posing for the snappers, an easy, relaxed smile painted across her face, betraying little in the way of teen self-consciousness.

Raducanu moonlighted as a practice partner for the squad the previous season, 2019, but this time she is a rookie member of the British Fed Cup team (the global women's tennis team event, since rebranded the Billie Jean King Cup). We're a week out from Britain's qualifier against Slovakia and, though Raducanu's chances of making her debut are a long shot, it is still notable that the 17-year-old got the call-up to join Anne Keothavong's squad. Raducanu would not have had the opportunity, if not for top-ranked Brits Johanna Konta and Katie Boulter ruling themselves out of selection, on account of injury and scheduling preferences. It put captain Keothavong in a pickle really. Like many in British tennis, she had known of Raducanu's potential for years and predicted she had the most promise of the up-and-coming prospects in the country. That weight of expectation is not always an easy one to carry for juniors. Putting Raducanu in a squad at her age might be premature pressure but, really, Keothavong had few other options available.

So I jumped on the District line from the *Daily Telegraph*'s Victoria offices to make the short trip to Barons Court to meet the rookie. Setting up the interview with Raducanu was vaguely challenging. Her parents were sceptical about drawing too much attention to her. Keen to shield her from the limelight for as long as possible, they only agreed to the interview after requesting – via the Lawn Tennis Association – that the article's lead image be of Raducanu with a teammate, rather than on her own. They did not want the interview to be a one-to-one either, which is why veteran squad member Heather Watson joined us too. These were not the kinds of requests that sports desks at national newspapers usually accommodated, especially for a relative nobody. But it was decided that these were small and fair concessions to make considering Raducanu's age and inexperience. She was still in her first year of A levels and not a regular on the Challenger circuit yet, let alone the WTA Tour. At the time of our meeting, she was ranked 363, a couple of months after she won her first ITF 25k Challenger title.

This was her first interview with a national newspaper, and easing her in was probably wise. Besides, having a buffer like the permanently congenial Watson during such interviews can be helpful. Getting any kind of usable quotes from a teenager can be tricky. They can be prone to very short answers (even one word) due to nerves and lack of experience. Getting a meaningful conversation going can feel like you're gently coaxing the words out of them. Having Watson on hand to make Raducanu feel more comfortable – and also to fill in the gaps – would be helpful, I thought. But Raducanu was different from most young athletes I've ever met. While Watson described feeling like 'Bambi on ice' on the clay in her first session, Raducanu already had that measured confidence about her. 'The first day I definitely didn't know where my feet were, but after that I felt a lot more confident,' she said. 'I've always loved moving on clay. So I'm feeling pretty good.'

Sitting around a small coffee table in the club, I remember feeling struck by that cool demeanour. Firstly because it is commonplace for British tennis players to detest clay. Unlike mainland Europeans growing up in the Mediterranean sunshine, Brits have few opportunities to play clay-court tennis at all in the United Kingdom. They tend to feel ill at ease, and some never make much effort to master it. But Raducanu's response suggested immediately that she was not like the rest. Nor was she prone to a quintessentially British sensibility: self-deprecation. That may well stem from her upbringing. Since the age of two, Raducanu grew up primarily in England, specifically Bromley on the outskirts of south-east London. But she could have represented three other nations: Canada (owing to being born in Toronto), Romania (where her father, Ian, is from), or China (where her mother, Renee, is from).

I've interviewed young, up-and-coming athletes before across a range of sports, from football to climbing to cricket. Though they were elite at what they did, many often found it more daunting to talk about their potential or achievements, or took some warming up. But I recall Raducanu as laser-focused during that first discussion and very self-assured. Sure, she laughed easily with Watson and even blushed momentarily when her teammate praised her awesome ability to hip thrust 200kg aged 16. But she was weighing up questions seriously and I could even sense her sizing me up. Her answers were concise, delivered with precision, and she was not easily drawn to expand. She was guarded in a way I had never known such a young interviewee to be. The one revealing moment came when she described her parents' influence on her. 'They definitely have very high expectations,' she said, letting a small laugh escape her lips. 'In anything, not even just tennis, any task. I have to be the best, do the best I can. I definitely feel it's made me push myself harder.' She added: 'When I was younger it was to please them, and satisfy them, but now I actually realise it's great for me to do it on my own and actually push myself. That's where I think I see the best results – when it's me driving it.'

No one could predict how Raducanu would go on to prove that in the next 18 months, in becoming the first qualifier to ever win a Grand Slam title at the US Open. But I do remember leaving Queen's Club feeling impressed. This was not your average teenager, excited about making up the numbers or getting a thrill out of being profiled by a national newspaper. There was no sense of over-awe. This was exactly where she expected to be. That mindset does not make Raducanu's journey particularly unique though, not when you pit her against the other champions in this book. Two other things differentiated her development. First, that she prioritised her education above her tennis. Second, and more controversially, that – by some accounts – her game was crafted using a 'coach-per-shot' method.

A few weeks before I met Raducanu that February, Belgian coach Philippe Dehaes had started working with her. She had a primary coach at the time, Matt James, but Dehaes had been hand-picked after a gruelling selection process to earn the invite into her circle. His main task was to hone a new forehand grip with Raducanu. While he was bemused by the fragmented approach to developing a teenager, he understood that he was not the first nor would he be the last coach to consult on her game in this way. The Raducanu camp's penchant for bringing in multiple coaches at one time was unconventional and primarily orchestrated by her father, Ian. 'Nobody is doing that,' Dehaes says, reflecting on it now. 'We have to understand how Ian is working; he analysed everything. He doesn't see the player as her entirety. He sees it like a puzzle, you know, and every piece of the puzzle has to have the best fit. That's why he likes to look left, right, top, bottom, to find a lot of coaches.' Did Dehaes think it worked? 'If you are the main coach, you'd be completely desperate with it,' he says flatly. 'But we have to respect one thing: Emma Raducanu won the US Open at 18 because Ian did an amazing job with her. That's the reality.'

*

Emma Raducanu was born in Toronto on 13 November 2002. Her family moved to England when she was two years old, and she grew up mostly in Bromley, in the deepest corner of south-east London, bordering on Kent. She started playing tennis when she was at The Parklangley Club, a two-mile drive from her home, where she was coached by Harry Bushnell. She had a precocious athletic ability from the start. Her primary school teacher in reception grade, Rebecca Rodgers, told me that she remembered a tennis coach join-ing their PE session, and that Raducanu was 'just on a completely different level to everyone else'. Rodgers went home and presciently told her family that she had a future Wimbledon champion in her class. By the time she was eight years old, Raducanu was working with strength and conditioning coach Suzanne Williams. She challenged Raducanu to see how many press-ups she could muster within 60 seconds, and watched as the tiny girl delivered 48 reps. 'No knees, feet on the floor, the flattest back plank . . . she just smashed it,' Williams said, when I spoke with her in 2021 for the *Telegraph.*

Raducanu had all the early hallmarks of a player with potential. Her parents encouraged their only child to do her very best, and quickly took the sport seriously. But that is not to say they approached it with blinkers on. Alongside her tennis, Raducanu tried ballet, horse riding, swimming, tap dancing, basketball and motocross – the latter being a passion she would pursue for the longest time, making regular trips to a Streatham bus garage where she would zoom around a makeshift track on her bike. To this day, Formula One remains one of Raducanu's favourite sports to follow. By the time she was nearly 11 though, things ramped up a gear on the tennis front.

She moved from Parklangley to Bromley Tennis Centre, an LTA regional player development centre (RPDC), where New Zealander Clint Harris was the head of tennis. He remembers her being 'the absolute standout' among the players he had worked with, throughout his decades-long career. 'If you'd seen Emma play at 11, you would have thought this girl is going places – you wouldn't need to be a tennis coach to actually recognise that, to say there's something different with this young lady. In the office with the rest of the coaches, the manager said: "Would you put your mortgage on her becoming a success?" And I think all of us said yes. You don't normally get that sort of agreement with everybody. We had had three or four players prior to that who were national junior champions and went on to play at Wimbledon, but the sheer enjoyment and ferociousness of Emma's racket-head speed, her athleticism and

Venus and Serena Williams broke boundaries and made history with their rivalry –
but never lost their close sisterhood. *Pictorial Press / Alamy Stock Photo*

29 January 2017 marked the last Grand Slam final contested between this historic pair
of sisters. *Frank Molter / Alamy Stock Phot*

The mother of all champions: Kim Clijsters celebrates with daughter Jada in New York. *PCN Photography / Alamy Stock Photo*

Ash Barty's Australian Open win capped off her career.

Ash Barty with her Brisbane Heat coach Andy Richards.

Barbora Krejcikova with Czech tennis royalty and mentor Jana Novotna.
CTK / Alamy Stock Photo

Barbora Krejcikova joining a long line of Czech women champions at Wimbledon.
PA Images

The summer of Emma Raducanu began at Wimbledon in 2021.

Paul Marriott / Alamy Stock Photo

Emma Raducanu's fairytale in New York. *UPI / Alamy Stock Photo*

Iga Swiatek with her close confidante, sports psychologist Daria Abramowicz.
Zuma Press / Alamy Stock Photo

Fifteen-year-old Coco Gauff announces herself to the world at Wimbledon in 2019.
PA Images / Alamy Stock Photo

A serve fix changed the course of Aryna Sabalenka's career.

competitiveness, and just sheer intelligence and joy for the game was a standout at 11.'

The Bromley Tennis Centre was also the perfect fit as she was starting at the highly regarded selective grammar school, Newstead Wood School, which shared the same grounds. To get to her tennis court, she quite literally had to walk through her school gates. It was the ideal set-up. With six indoor and four outdoor courts, Bromley Tennis Centre was equipped with some of the best facilities in London and she was quite possibly living in the best part of suburbia – and maybe even the entire country – to become a tennis player alongside remaining in traditional state schooling. The Raducanus had no intention of following the path laid out by most tennis prodigies, who dropped out or cut down their schooling to the bare bones. She was to stay in school and complete her GCSEs and A levels like any other teenager, by attending lessons as normal, and missing as few days as possible – while also crafting a tennis career. This made her different from her peers in British tennis, many of whom opt for homeschooling or remote learning, in order to be near the National Tennis Centre or another top RPDC, as well as travel to competitions as early as possible. Many decide to leave school as soon as they finish their GCSEs aged 15 or 16 too.

Clint Harris often worked as the middleman between Raducanu's school and the LTA, negotiating time off for certain tournaments and adjusting her programme according to the exams she had coming up. 'She could literally walk three minutes and she was in the club, and that made it easier for her to do her 15 to 16 hours a week training,' Harris says. 'Although her peer group were playing full-time [by the age of 15], there's no one right way. The game's an individual sport and any structure is only made to be broken by individuals. But she was probably more an exception to the rule in terms of the academic side of what she was doing. She's a very clever, intellectual girl as well. I think having a conventional school gave

Emma a really good rounding and she enjoyed the social side of the school, albeit sometimes you get a little bit isolated because you are so committed to a passion, you're so much involved in a sport. Skipping out, you miss this and that, but being very academic, she did very well with the GCSEs and A levels as well.'

During her years at Bromley, she had various coaches working closely with her day to day. In her early days there she worked with Andrew Richardson (whom she would enlist for her US Open debut) as well as Nick Cavaday (whom she later called upon in 2023 after an injury-plagued couple of years). When Cavaday left to head up the LTA's Loughborough Academy, she then was paired with Alastair Filmer for nearly three years. Her reputation preceded her. 'You get them in juniors sometimes, this mythological player that's supposedly so good,' Filmer says. 'You're thinking, they can't be that good, they're 10 or something. I'm from Kent too. Emma and I lived like five minutes apart, and in my mind no one from Bromley could be that good, surely.' But while at a tournament she was playing at in the Midlands, Filmer went over to the court she was on to see what all the fuss was about. His reaction: 'My goodness, she *is* good.'

When it came to coaching her, Filmer remembers being the 'default' option, after Cavaday and Richardson's earlier exits. 'I was the only coach left,' he says, laughing at the memory. Despite that, as he had never coached a top talent at that stage in his career, Filmer was put through a 'vetting process' by Ian Raducanu. It was the first of many well-meaning 'grillings' the coach received from his charge's father over the years. 'Super-intense, a lot of questions,' he says. 'He'd always say: "Blue sky thinking, if you had an ideal week, what would her week look like? How much tennis? How much fitness? Can you put it on an Excel? Can you tell me what development plans you would do if you had to decide today?" There's a lot of that side of things. He's the strategist, looking at her game and going, what does she need? It was fair enough, but I'm thinking, wow, all of this to coach an 11-year-old girl.'

Raducanu herself was comparably reserved and unfailingly polite. During their first few sessions, he was struck by her 'unbelievable balance', timing and how she just absorbed information 'like a sponge'. He realised that his job was going to be a case of tweaking and maintaining what was already there. They would do two sessions a day, one before school started and one after. Filmer remembers her scurrying over to the courts after her lessons and doing a serving session while still in her uniform, such was her dedication. She pushed him more than any player had before or since. 'Her ability to learn quickly and want more and more and more – the best players, they're kind of squeezing the coach. If you give her something and she trusts it, she'll do it. A lot of players, you spend like hours trying to teach a skill. You'll try one thing, another thing, another thing, and maybe the fifth or sixth thing will be the thing that clicks with them. With Emma, it's more like the first thing; she doesn't take long to build up the skill.' He said Ian Raducanu was not so much of a physical presence in his experience, as he did not attend many sessions. But he set targets to meet. 'Make her the best returner in the world,' was one of the things Ian told Filmer. 'Don't worry about the serve, she can learn that later.'

Filmer followed the instructions, mostly because they 'made sense'. In this case, her timing was great and she liked taking the ball early, so putting effort into honing her naturally good return game was a no-brainer. Sometimes, the father's inquisitiveness missed the mark though. 'Because he doesn't play, he sees the game not like a tennis player,' Filmer says. 'He'd be like: "Why can't she just return down the line all the time? Or hit every rally ball down the line, it seems like they're more effective?"' Raducanu's dynamic with her father, on the tennis court at least, was all about how to get better. Even when she was beating opponents 6-0 6-0, there was always room for improvement in his book. Filmer recalls it like this: 'She would win a match comfortably and he would go: "Yeah, but you didn't have that girl's footwork, it was unbelievable on a pivot backhand she hit." I'm like, that's your feedback? A lot of players would probably crack, but she could withstand quite a lot of "you need to be better at this" or "that's not good enough". She's eating it up; she's fine with it.'

Though her training regime was always very serious, there was never too much pressure on Raducanu in terms of competition results. Though she still did well. In 2014, she came fifth at the U12 Orange Bowl in California, one of junior tennis's most prestigious events. After losing her opening match, Raducanu had another shot in the repêchage and won 10 matches in a row thereafter. It was the kind of run that Filmer says became somewhat of her trademark as a junior, where she could get in the zone and decide she was not losing. That is why her US Open title charge was not a total surprise to those who understood her mindset from a young age. 'When she won the US, I was like, she's got so much precedent for that,' he says. Two years later, she bettered her result at the Orange Bowl U14s by coming third. Later in 2014, when she had just turned 13, she made a splash when she became the youngest winner of an ITF U18 event at the Nike Junior International in Liverpool.

'In coaching you talk about high performance all the time, but until you really experience what high performance people are like, it's hard to explain,' Filmer says of the Raducanus. 'I always used to think, I'm just a normal person in the middle of this, because I'm thinking this is absurd what he's asking here. For them it's totally normal. This is where we're going, this is what she needs to be able to do, this would be the amount of hours it'll take to do it. It's that entrenchment of those habits early, those unbelievable things to have. I didn't have them before Emma. I think that's an important thing to know about Ian. Because he gets a bit of a bad rap, but I always got on with him pretty well, to be honest. With any coach that doesn't understand what the mission is, it could be a little bit more difficult, potentially. But once you understood that this is what we're aiming for, don't mess with it, he's fine. You get on board.'

Once Raducanu was nearly 15, Filmer was given his leave by her father, as the partnership had run its course: 'It was disappointing but also fair enough. At that time, I wasn't really experienced enough for the next part. By the end of the three years, I was like: "Oh my God, I'm actually exhausted – I don't know if I've got much left to offer here."' Clint Harris took the reins thereafter for a few months, until Matt James entered the picture. Harris managed her schedule, alongside the guidance of the LTA's Jane O'Donoghue and Jeremy Bates. The Raducanus did not want their daughter competing too much though, especially as school came first. She did not play national junior events, and only dabbled occasionally in international tournaments and the junior Grand Slams. 'Lots of parents want to go through the ITF juniors, under-18s, play all the Grand Slams and then build up that way,' Harris says. 'Whereas, actually, I think Ian just had a longer-term philosophy of it's just a vehicle of learning at the under-18s and ITFs, because the ultimate goal is to play senior tennis. Let's dabble in that earlier, but not to an extent where you're getting beaten up there.'

Harris got a real sense of Ian's influence when he began working with Raducanu one-on-one. 'Ian's very much the driver,' he says. 'He does ask a lot of questions, but he's very knowledgeable and very insightful – and challenging in the right sense. I actually found him really, in many respects, a joy to work with, because he asked the pertinent questions.' Ian asked Harris to give a fair assessment of her game, without speaking to her former coaches, but just by watching. Harris delivered a three-page report, where he would prioritise four things: adjusting her knee on her backhand, as her weight was transferring outwards instead of forward into the court, and that could result in injury long-term; changing her serve from an abbreviated action to a full swing, to gain more fluidity; improving her forehand lag, to gain racket speed; and working on her tactical side, as he thought she lacked a plan B during matches.

The comprehensive plan was dissected in detail by Ian, and adjustments were made, as well as to the strength and conditioning and the tournament plans presented to him. It was a full-on approach from the Raducanu patriarch, but Harris says he always understood Ian as a father intent on getting the best outcomes for his daughter. 'He was cross-examining my thoughts on what she should be doing, but only to get more information and understanding of the rationale behind my thinking, which I think is a good thing,' Harris says. 'I think the business that he's in (Ian was trained as a civil engineer and worked in finance), it dictates that he's always finding those tricky questions to ensure that people know what they're doing. He doesn't take things by reputation, like "Clint Harris is a great coach", he will actually find that out for himself.' As much as Raducanu's father grew to trust Harris's expertise, he still hovered close to training sessions, and often offered his own input. Harris put the brakes on that because of the impact it had on Raducanu herself. 'The dynamics didn't work for a while with us, because you've got the dynamic of a parent that really wants the best for their child, who wants to optimise potential, but you've also got the player. That got to a stage where it became a disruption. It's not untypical, you know; a parent comes on court and the player gets a little bit disgruntled because they think they're encroaching upon their court time.'

He implemented a four-week trial period where Ian was not to step on to the court at all. 'Emma became more relaxed, more free, expressed her view a bit more without having Ian cross-examining what she was thinking and reprioritising what she should be doing.

I think he learned that sometimes he needs to step back and just let Emma experiment and enjoy tennis.' Harris may have worked closely on project Raducanu for years, but had never been working with her one-to-one, so he had to establish those boundaries. He was also her fourth primary coach in the last five years. That was largely on account of individuals leaving Bromley unexpectedly. But this coaching merry-go-round also became a feature of her development, because Ian was often seeking out new voices, with specific expertise to help shape her talent. Even this past year, Ian texted Harris to ask what he thought, after Raducanu's fourth round loss at Wimbledon to New Zealand's Lulu Sun. Harris had not been involved for years, but Ian was keen to get a debrief from her former coach. It gives a glimpse into their approach, which has always figured around gaining as much input and knowledge as possible from multiple coaching influences that they either trust or respect.

CHAPTER 12

Emma Raducanu:
The coach buffet

MATT James saw the Team Raducanu methods close up, working with her for two years. He met Emma Raducanu when she was 15 and a half. At the time, he was working as a tennis coach at Millfield School in Somerset, and spending the summer holidays employed at Wimbledon as a hitting partner during the championships. While there, he ran into prominent British coach Nigel Sears (Andy Murray's father-in-law). He was working on a consultancy basis with Raducanu, who was playing in the junior Wimbledon event, while also coaching top 20 player Anett Kontaveit. 'I didn't really know who Emma was to be honest,' James says. 'I wasn't really involved with high-level potential at the time. Then I went to watch her match, ironically against Leylah Fernandez.'

Three short years later, Raducanu would be beating Fernandez in front of 23,000 people on Arthur Ashe Stadium, in the most remarkable US Open result in recent memory. The day James mentions in 2018, the pair played on an outside court at the All England Club, where Raducanu also got the win. But James remembers her next match, in the third round, more vividly: a hard-fought 7-5 6-4 win against Joanna Garland of Chinese Taipei. 'She was playing on Court 18 and it was incredible,' James recalls. 'Nothing was different [to now] with Emma. She was fearless, aggressive, it didn't matter what the score was, and she enjoyed playing in front of a crowd. She's 15 years old, the scoreline is absolutely nip and tuck, Garland smoked a return to her and Emma got down on one knee and leathered a backhand cross. I think at that point she used the crowd to her advantage, to put pressure on the opponent. It was almost that maturity. This girl probably hasn't been in this situation before, but she knows what to do. The score's close, but it doesn't change how she's playing – if anything she's probably being more aggressive than before. It was qualities like that which showed she was different. She could have lost that match but it wouldn't have made any difference to how I viewed her. There were a couple of people who said to me later on: "This girl is a little bit different. You don't see many Brits like her, on that stage and wanting to be on that stage."'

After her win over Garland, James was invited by Sears to hit with Raducanu at Aorangi Park, the practice courts at the All England Club. Sears was keen to find a coach to work closely with Raducanu, and he was being primed as a candidate. After she lost to Iga Swiatek in the quarter-finals, he went down to Brighton to hit with Raducanu and Sears again. 'It was right place, right time,' James says. Next was a trial with Raducanu and her father, Ian, in Bromley: 'She didn't ask too many questions, but it wasn't a normal trial like you'd expect. The dad asked a lot of questions. I think they wanted to know what my level of understanding was. They said: "We want to hear your feedback. It's a chance to see what your thoughts are." [Ian and I] had a two-hour lunch between sessions too. There were lots of questions. It felt like verbal diarrhoea, they just wanted me to talk the whole time: about what I'm seeing, commentating on the tennis, constant feedback – more so than you would do in a normal coaching role. Plenty of questions at the end of the session too, lots of thoughts, just to get into my brain I think, to get an understanding of what my thoughts and views were and if I can help her.'

After getting the green light from Camp Raducanu that he was the man they wanted, James quickly left his job at the school and stepped into a two-year contract with the LTA in an apprenticeship coaching role. He moved nearby to Sutton, and his primary responsibility was to work with Raducanu in Bromley. James was only in his late twenties, quite early in his career and a fairly low-key kind of guy. It quickly dawned on him that he was being entrusted with developing one of the most promising tennis players in Britain. 'I had trained some good players at Millfield, one lad made junior Wimbledon, we had some good ITF players. But to be thrown into Bromley suddenly with Emma, on her own, in a bubble, and I'm just cracking on . . . at times it was a bit daunting. Like, flipping heck, because they're putting a lot of time and effort into her. But it was also quite nice because I had free rein to work with her, whereas some might have too many influences from above. That's why I think we worked quite well.'

Like Harris, James saw first-hand the school-tennis juggle that Raducanu was committed to each and every day. In the same way as she knew there were tennis rivals competing and practising for more hours than she was, she was also very aware of fellow students who had more time to dedicate to their studies. Throughout most of the year they would 'lean more towards the tennis side', but when exams rolled around the tennis 'certainly took a back seat,' according to James. 'You could feel that on the court during that time,' he adds of exam season in May and June. She skipped French Open juniors and was 'completely undercooked' going into the grass court season and Wimbledon qualifiers – otherwise known as the most important, high-profile portion of the tennis season for any aspiring young Brit. But the Raducanus were playing the long game.

'The thing that stood out with her was that they were going to do it their own way in a sense,' James says. 'School and education was a massive part for her parents. I think even if the parents had wanted her to leave school she wouldn't. She was so keen to do well academically and a very, very bright girl and put a lot of work into it. She got top marks. I think the education side is still a huge part of her. She needs it alongside tennis. You see now, she's learning musical instruments, languages and keeping things going. I wouldn't be surprised if she goes and does a degree one day. She's so bright and that complements the tennis really well.' During trips James took with Raducanu to India and Belarus, she would spend most of her spare moments studying for exams or doing homework. Even in the occasional downtime she would allow herself, they would play Sporcle online trivia quizzes about topics as varied as geography, history or music. 'She would try to keep her brain engaged.'

The start of James's tenure with Raducanu coincided with her being promoted to the LTA Pro Scholarship Programme that same summer, worth around £80,000 in annual funding. Top agency IMG also signed her later that year. While James was the day-to-day grounding force for Raducanu in Bromley, there were plenty of other influences. In an interview with the *Evening Standard* after her US Open win, he acknowledged that Raducanu always liked to have 'multiple voices' involved. Those included Sears, who would check in a few days a month to track her progress, as well as Jane O'Donoghue, who was James's line manager at the LTA. O'Donoghue had worked with Raducanu since she was at least 13. A former top 200 player, O'Donoghue spent a decade working for the LTA from 2009 before switching to a high-flying job in finance.

I spoke with her former LTA colleague and doubles partner Claire Curran in 2022, when O'Donoghue first cropped up at Wimbledon with Raducanu when she was newly coachless. Many were surprised by O'Donoghue's sudden (and brief) appearance on tour, especially as she was still working full-time in her finance sector job. But Curran knew better. 'Jane's never not been on Emma's team,' she shared with me, adding, 'She's always been an invisible mentor to Emma; she's a friend of the family, and very much been part of her inner circle.' James remembers O'Donoghue's influence similarly, when Raducanu was still plugging away in obscurity as a junior: 'She was brilliant to have, someone who knew Emma really well, someone whom Emma trusted, knew the women's game, and whom I got on really well with. Jane was a big part of it. She was a case manager for Emma, who oversaw the project almost.'

With O'Donoghue and James as the constants, during those two years there were others who contributed to the Raducanu camp more sporadically. Louis Cayer briefly stepped in to help on a few technical adjustments. Iain Bates was also involved in the overall picture, as the LTA's head of women's tennis. So too did Keothavong keep an eye on things, as the British Fed Cup team captain. When Filmer was still in the picture, a couple of years prior, there was also a two-week trip to the Netherlands, where she was assessed by Laura Robson's former coach, Martijn Bok. But neither James nor Filmer are convinced by the interpretation that Raducanu's father Ian had a 'coach-per-shot' plan. It was more organic than that, James says, and about maximising the resources they had available to them, in terms of coaches. 'There was certainly never a conversation around either forehand, backhand, serve or needing different coaches,' James says. 'We had trials with other coaches. That coach might specialise in a certain shot but it wasn't 'let's go see this guy because he specialises in the forehand'. It was almost filling gaps. 'For example, there was an opportunity to see Louis Cayer, who is very well regarded at the LTA. He worked on the men's side so it didn't quite work, but they knew he'd be good for more momentum on the groundstrokes or volleying. But it was never discussed as: "Her volley needs to get better, let's go and see Louis." It was more: "Actually we know we've got Louis down the road it would be great to tap into his expertise." Certainly when those trials were happening it was more about finding out where their strengths were. It almost happened naturally I think.'

The search for that resource went further afield when Philippe Dehaes was added to the mix in early 2020, when Raducanu was 17 and still working with James. In late 2019, Dehaes was at home in Belgium, plotting his next steps after a coaching stint with tour player Daria Kasatkina ended. He got a call from Raducanu's IMG agent at the time, John Morris, about a potential opportunity to coach Britain's next big thing. The only catch: he had to make a pitch for the job, and would have a few days of testing to compete alongside a handful of other coaches. Dehaes raised an eyebrow at that, but he was intrigued enough to hop on the Eurostar to London. 'I thought, why not? I love the idea to be in competition with other guys, you know? So let's see if I'm strong enough to have the expertise,' he says, a little tongue-in-cheek. He arrived in Bromley soon after ('Shitty hotel, but very nice tennis club'), and was blown away by Raducanu. 'The moment she started to hit the ball, I say: "What the hell, what the hell." I was so impressed about her ability to pay attention, to be focused, to ask questions. She was on a mission. She was already practising with the intensity of a pro player.'

Dehaes qualified his giddiness with some trepidation though as he had seen plenty of standout juniors completely tank during competitive matches. In the end, he only had the chance to travel to two tournaments with Raducanu in February 2020. The most memorable was an ITF 25k in Sunderland. Raducanu blitzed through the first four rounds without dropping a set, including in the semi-final, against the equally hyped Danish teenager Clara Tauson. In the final, she lost to the more experienced Bulgarian Viktoriya Tomova, who was ranked around 150, more than 200 places above Raducanu. But Dehaes had seen enough to convince him to go all-in on this project. 'We arrived there, boom, final. She was playing like drinking an espresso, drinking the pressure like this. I thought: "Okay, now, this girl, she's made in another wood – she's extraordinary, yes." Emma Raducanu, she's a pure talent, pure talent.'

A few short weeks later, the pandemic brought the world to a crunching halt, marking a premature end to Dehaes's involvement as he hastily returned to lockdown in Belgium. But those three months or so spent in Bromley had a lasting impact. What he remembers most was Ian Raducanu's influence. Within an hour of first arriving that January, it became clear to him that this was all about impressing the maestro of the Raducanu machine. He describes Ian as a 'very nice man' and also learned very quickly how his analytical brain worked. Like coaches before him, Dehaes was struck by the questions Ian rattled off during their first meeting. He agrees Ian was an ever-present figure, but not imposing by any means, describing him as 'very low profile, very humble – but with a clear idea of what he wants'. Ian was specifically looking for someone with a development plan to fit into his 'vision' for his daughter, and that suited Dehaes just fine. He had never been one to chase the finished product, top-ranked players, but rather had spent the last couple of years working with up-and-comers like the hot-and-cold Monica Puig and future top 10 Russian player Kasatkina.

Armed with his two-year proposal, Dehaes said he would focus primarily on changing her forehand grip, how to transition fully to the professional ITF tour, and finding that balance between playing and practising. 'The main idea is not going too fast,' Dehaes says. 'If you go too fast, you forget to improve.' He immediately saw that, despite Ian's clinically hands-on approach, he was also very open to new ideas and amenable to change. 'At this time, she had a very weak forehand,' Dehaes says. 'She had this extreme grip. And I remember when I arrived, we had a discussion concerning this grip. And actually, her father was completely agreeing with me to change this forehand, because it was not good enough on a very high level. On a very high level, the ball is coming quite flat, very fast, and with this kind of grip it's tough. So we worked a lot on that. The philosophy was take the time, develop physically, technically, tactically, go to competition, come back, but not going too fast.'

Dehaes's glimpse into the Raducanu world coincided with her first year of A levels. He had seen plenty of talented tennis players give up every notion of a proper education in the pursuit of a career in the professional game. He admired the Raducanus for not bowing to those pressures, and instead putting their daughter's development on and off the court above anything else. 'For me, it was very healthy to hear that I had in front of me parents who were not thinking about money, about winning matches, but who kept talking about the development of their daughter,' he says. 'All the time as coaches, the parents we face normally – and especially from Eastern Europe and even Central Europe – have only one goal: making money as fast as possible. I always had the feeling that Emma's dad and mum were worried about her development, not about winning some tennis competition. And now, she's a super clever girl and had a very good education, thanks to her parents. They did an amazing job with her – I mean, a parent's job.'

He acknowledges that Ian's reputation is not always positive, considering the knee-jerk coaching changes she made post-US Open and how she has struggled to settle into tour life. The role he played as protective and very involved parent served her well as an adolescent, but as a professional that appears to have created friction behind the scenes. The ruthless way the Raducanus dismissed Andrew Richardson after he guided her to the US Open title was enough to make coaches wary. 'Thank you, bro, good job, you won the US Open – now you can stay home,' Dehaes says, imagining how that conversation went. 'You'd become depressed after – that's so tough!' He adds: 'This is the negative thing; Ian believed that with an engineer's mind, you can solve everything. In tennis, one plus one can be three, right? It's like this. You cannot control every parameter. Many things can happen and without you understanding why. The match can turn for any reason. But Ian, he believes that if you control every parameter, you can really reach the super high level, because it's a mathematical way of thinking. And sports, it's not mathematics. That, for me, is the reason why he has very tough relations with coaches [now], because he believes that he's a little bit more clever than anybody around the table, and that makes the discussion very, very, very difficult.'

One particular moment from his testing stage with Raducanu revealed this perfectly to Dehaes. He was called to a boardroom with Iain Bates, Ian Raducanu and Emma herself to review some in-match footage to explain what she was doing tactically and how he would improve her game in those scenarios. The person controlling the video was her father Ian. 'Suddenly, the father stopped the video, and he says: "Philippe, why did Emma play this ball on the right side of the court?" Me, I'm a funny guy, you know, so I say: "Ian, because she decided not to play on the left side of the court."' After that failed to get a laugh, Dehaes played ball, but said Ian was relentless. Every answer he gave had a follow-up question, asking for him to be more specific or challenging his assessment of grainy one-camera video footage from an ITF 25k match. 'With this camera, it's not easy to be precise, but I said: "It doesn't matter where the ball is. The ball is short, in the middle of the point, and she has a huge forehand – if she hits it like hell, it's gonna be a winner." Ian replies: "But Philippe, don't you think that the backhand of the opponent is a little bit weaker?" I say: "Yeah, maybe." And he says: "So she can play the short ball to the forehand, even if the backhand is weak?" I say: "Yes, if the ball is fast enough." He says: "What do you mean fast, which speed?" We had a discussion around this one point, but it was from another planet, the discussion.' The questions were incessant: why did she miss this ball? Was this about footwork or her forehand grip? What could Emma have done differently? Why did this ball end up in the net? Dehaes says he has never experienced a meeting like it.

But Ian is not the only one. Dehaes, as well as plenty of other coaches and people who have worked with Raducanu herself, says she is her father's daughter in many ways. 'Emma is like this also,' he says. At the start of each coaching relationship, Dehaes always asks his player to complete an extensive personality test. It is his way of understanding more about who they are and how best to adapt his teaching style to their sessions. With Raducanu, she scored incredibly high from an analytical standpoint. 'I will not give you the full profile, because it's a little bit too personal, but I can tell you that she's super, super analytic. It means she is not easy to practise with because if you give her basic advice, she will say, "What's the reason to do that?" And only if you explain this is the reason, you can improve this or it will help you for that, then, boom, she's a machine and she goes for it. For example, you cannot send her to play a match without giving her a lot of information about the opponent. I knew it, because it was in her profile. But if you started the job and you don't know that she loves to know a lot of info, after three weeks you'll be fired, that's for sure,' he says laughing. 'No chance.'

Harris remembers Raducanu similarly. 'She won't take things on face value, even then, aged say 15 or 16. She would ask the question, why? I think once you get to know her, then the trust of your knowledge is as important, and the data just backs up that trust. An example would be on her backhand drive. That was always her best, most explosive, exciting shot. There's some technical things there that still could be improved, but if she thought: "I'm hitting the ball so well, why do I need to change it?" she would need some stats on that and some video footage to ensure that she trusts in what you're doing, really. Once she's bought into it, she'll go at it like anything she wants to accomplish.'

James says this also stemmed from the fact she was so academic. 'Her memory was unbelievable; how quickly she learned things was impressive. She probably wouldn't have enjoyed coaches who maybe said the same things or didn't push her, more from an intellectual kind of way. It was always wanting someone to work her hard, but she almost needed her brain to work hard as well. There wasn't anyone at that time that I'd seen work harder on a tennis court. Even if she was slightly injured, we'd still be watching matches, discussing tactics, talking about players, making notes, watching practice. It almost felt like no stone unturned at times. When you're talking about a teenage girl, a young mind, that was super impressive to see that she was always thinking about the long game.'

Raducanu was not necessarily a fan of watching tennis or specific players in so much as she was a student of the game: she would watch back matches for analytical purposes, looking at how it could inform her own game, rather than because she loved to follow the tour. James recalls watching footage of Garbiñe Muguruza closely for the footwork and backhand, Ash Barty for the hand skills and in particular Bianca Andreescu, who had recently won the US Open in 2019. As well as Andreescu and Raducanu sharing Romanian heritage and being born in the same Toronto hospital, they both prefer first-strike tennis tactics. James remembers focusing a lot of time on unpicking what the Canadian player did, and Raducanu soaking up the information. 'She'd have had certain players she looked up,' he says. 'But predominantly watching matches was about trying to steal ideas, learn visually and watch players that suited her game style, rather than players she probably just had a liking for.' James's time coaching Raducanu came to an end in the summer of 2020. A year later, she would be emulating the videos of Andreescu that he and she had studied.

CHAPTER 13

Emma Raducanu:
A run (and debut) like no other

THERE is no doubt 2021 will be remembered by all tennis fans as the year of Emma Raducanu. She still had Nigel Sears in her camp, and he took a more hands-on approach as she made her WTA Tour debut at the Nottingham Open that June. It was a wildcard entry, and she lost in straight sets to fellow Briton Harriet Dart. Probably to be expected, after completing her A levels in maths and economics a few weeks prior. Next, she won two rounds at a Nottingham Challenger tournament against two top 150 opponents. At the time she was still ranked 361, so it was good going and great preparation for Wimbledon, which was only a fortnight away.

In a genius move by the All England Club, with more than a touch of influence from former British No. 1 and committee member Tim Henman, Raducanu was awarded the wildcard that changed her young life. She was drawn in the first round at Wimbledon against qualifier and world No. 150 Vitalia Diatchenko of Russia, and sailed through 7-6 6-0. She was the only British woman to make it into the second round. Next up was a rain-delayed evening fixture, switched from Court 18 to Court 12 in front of 1,700 eager Wimbledon punters. Raducanu scored the first top 50 win of her career, winning 6-2 6-4 against future Wimbledon champion

Marketa Vondrousova, even overcoming a 3-0 deficit in the second set. Andy Murray tweeted "Let's go Emma Raducanu", complete with a fire emoji, and her winning smile was printed across the national sports pages. True to form, she betrayed no hint of pressure, despite becoming an overnight national treasure at her home tournament. 'I feel like I'm on holiday,' she told reporters of her surprising run. 'It's unbelievable.'

A couple of days later, the calls for her to make her show court debut were answered by the Wimbledon scheduling team: she walked on to No. 1 Court, where 12,000 expectant fans held their breath as she romped to another straight sets win. This time, it was over Romania's Sorana Cirstea, ranked 45th in the world (293 places above Raducanu). It made Raducanu the youngest British woman to reach the second week of Wimbledon since 1959. This was a Grand Slam debut like no other, at a Wimbledon tournament like no other too. After the third round win, Raducanu spoke about being thankful for the bubble that the players were living in, on account of Covid-19 protocols in place. She and the rest of the 128-player draw, plus their teams, were confined to the All England Club grounds and the Park Plaza Westminster Bridge Hotel in Central London. There was no eating out at Wimbledon village, or grabbing a coffee in Southfields, so no real opportunity for Raducanu to feel the extent of her new-found fame, as she fast became the most recognisable woman in British sport.

On the rare occasions she asked her osteopath for her phone though (she said she gave it to him for safekeeping, to avoid getting distracted by it), the reality hit through her screen. Matt James was in the bubble with Raducanu, and recalls her scrolling through her notifications in amazement, as messages from the most famous names in world sport clogged her DMs on Instagram. She had 2,000 followers before she started the tournament and her count grew to a whopping 255,000 by the end of her run. Instagram even locked her out of her account, suspecting she might be a robot.

Though she bossed her third-round foray on No. 1 Court, the huge expectations caught up with her during the fourth round on that same court, albeit under the roof. After going behind against Australia's Ajla Tomljanovic, Raducanu struggled with breathing difficulties and retired from the match. It was a sorry end to what had been a dream-like week. On social media and television coverage, prominent personalities chimed in with criticism, broadcasting it to their millions of followers. Piers Morgan said she "couldn't handle the pressure and quit when she was losing badly", while Kevin Pietersen told her to just "deal with it". Even in the midst of her disappointment, and after skipping her post-match press conference, she appeared on the BBC via a recorded interview the following day. As Sue Barker gently probed Raducanu on the details around her withdrawal, the 18-year-old explained that she had struggled to regulate her breathing and was advised by the tournament's medical team to retire. 'I think that it was a combination of everything that has gone on behind the scenes in the last week, the accumulation of the excitement, the buzz and I think it's a great learning experience for me going forward. Hopefully next time I'll be better prepared.' Asked what the biggest crowd she had previously played in front of had been? 'I'm not sure, maybe 100 people,' Raducanu replied with a shy smile. In a savvy PR move, she wore an England shirt in support of the men's national football team, who were due to play the Euro semi-final against Denmark the following day. 'It's coming home, isn't it,' she said, before predicting the 2-1 winning score. Raducanu's breakthrough was eclipsed by the England team reaching the first men's major tournament final in 55 years. That should have been the biggest British sporting story of the year, but her season was far from over.

*

After Wimbledon, Raducanu set her sights stateside. She won 13 of 16 matches she played ahead of the US Open in late August, including two positive Challenger tournament runs in Pennsylvania and Chicago. At the latter, she reached the final. It meant that she arrived in New York ranked 150th in the world and brimming with confidence. Dehaes was at Flushing Meadows and spotted her on the practice courts ahead of qualifying starting. 'I crossed paths with her, and I said: "Emma, you're playing this girl, forehand a bit weak so *allez*, you should be all right,"' he says. When she went through all three qualifying matches, without dropping a set, Dehaes was impressed. 'I thought, hmm, not too bad,' he adds, laughing at the memory now. Knowing what we know now, those three qualifying matches seem like a given. But it truly is impressive to win three qualifying matches. Only three of the six British women in the qualifying that year, including Raducanu, reached the main draw. 'I'm really proud of myself,' Raducanu said at the time. 'Maximising every single opportunity I get is what I want to do.'

When Ella Ling arrived at Flushing Meadows the day before the main draw began, pandemic travel restrictions meant she was the only British photographer on the grounds. The grounds were a ghost town that Sunday afternoon, and she was the only snapper on court to cover Raducanu's final practice session before the tournament opened its gates to the public. 'I was shocked that I was the only one. As I was the only British photographer, it felt like it was just me stalking her. It was bizarre, but very good for me. As a result I got some really lovely pictures; she gave me some nice smiles. It was really low key. It was empty, the site, and she was just carrying her phone and rackets in hand. You could tell she was just so happy to be there, carefree and just innocent.'

It was probably the last time Raducanu ever experienced a solo walk around the grounds at any major tennis tournament. As the next fortnight played out, everything fell into place in her draw.

Her first round opponent, world No. 13 American Jennifer Brady, pulled out on the eve of the tournament through injury. Instead, Raducanu faced a lucky loser, Stefanie Vögele of Switzerland who, like her, was ranked outside the top 100. When she won in straight sets, finally converting on her seventh match point, it effectively meant she had taken the place of seeded player Brady in the draw. That guaranteed she would not face another seed until at least the third round. Next she beat top 50 player Zhang Shuai on Court 10. At the beginning of that August, Zhang had blitzed past Raducanu in San Jose, but the teen had learned from her mistakes and was clinical in the 6-2 6-4 rout. Again, it was her first-strike tennis and ability to take the ball early that helped her sweep past opponents who, on paper, should have been superior. She won 49 per cent of return points, fulfilling her father's early aims to make her a brutal returner of the ball.

Her form only improved as she progressed. The third round opponent was a tricky Spaniard, Sara Sorribes Tormo, who had just beaten world No. 1 Ash Barty at the Olympics in Tokyo. She is known for hanging in and drawing out matches, sometimes for hours on end, but Raducanu did not give her a chance in a 6-0 6-1 annihilation. Next up: Arthur Ashe Stadium, but against a surprising opponent. American Shelby Rogers scored the shock of the tournament (at least at that stage) by beating Barty in the third round. With the best player on the planet slain, Raducanu seized her opportunity. In the biggest cauldron in world tennis and against a big ball striker like Rogers, she shrugged off any doubters' opinions about her Wimbledon stage fright, and steamrollered to a 6-2 6-1 victory. With Virginia Wade, the last British woman to win the US Open in 1968, watching on from the stands, Raducanu won 12 of the last 13 games. She had completely rattled her more experienced opponent yet again, and was into her first Grand Slam quarter-final at only her second attempt. She was doing it by playing fearless tennis.

Her first top 40 opponent ever, Belinda Bencic, stood in her way. Bencic had just won Olympic gold for Switzerland earlier that summer and was arguably in the best shape of her life. She was ranked 12th in the world – more than 100 places above Raducanu. This was where everyone expected Raducanu's dream run to falter. It was a significant step up. But somehow, she took control again. Grit and composure got her through the 6-3 6-4 win, and made her the first qualifier to reach the last four at Flushing Meadows ever. While the world watched in utter awe, and even Raducanu was in some disbelief during those winning moments, her childhood coaches were less surprised. These were the kind of steely performances that Alastair Filmer had watched her display as a 12-year-old and that Matt James had coached her through during her mid-teens. It was always the case that once Raducanu was in the zone, they say, few could ever stop her. It was remarkable that she was doing this in front of millions of people, but that ability was always within her grasp. The win put Raducanu on the brink of breaking into the top 50 and earned her £490,000. Martina Navratilova, an 18-time Grand Slam singles champion, described her as 'almost like a finished product when she is just getting started'.

Again, her next opponent turned out to be a surprise package, as 17th seed Maria Sakkari beat Karolina Pliskova, a Wimbledon finalist earlier that summer and the world No. 5, in their quarter-final. Sakkari is one of the most athletic players on the WTA Tour and could certainly outpower Raducanu, especially on the serve and forehand. But she was also prone to choking in the big moments. Earlier that season she lost her only other Grand Slam semi-final at the French Open, despite being the favourite and having match point. By contrast, Raducanu's mental fortitude was seemingly impenetrable in New York, and she proved that on Arthur Ashe Stadium by romping to a 6-1 6-4 victory over an error-strewn Sakkari. Raducanu's reaction once again gave a glimpse of her disbelief as she beamed up at her box. 'Is there any expectation?' she said during the post-match interview, looking ahead to the final. 'I'm a qualifier, so technically there's no pressure on me.'

It did not matter whom she faced next in the final, she was guaranteed to be the underdog once again. Yet again, a twist of fate ensured Raducanu's opponent was not a top seed, but rather another young, surprise package who had blasted her way through the other half of the draw: Leylah Fernandez. In her own semi-final, Fernandez overcame Aryna Sabalenka, the second seed, who had been the tournament favourite ever since Barty's early exit. This trophy was considered hers to lose by anyone's measure but she bottled it against an inspired Fernandez, hitting two double faults and spraying two errors in the decisive final game of their marathon semi-final.

Sabalenka may have thrown away a huge opportunity, but this was no fluke from Fernandez. Standing at 5ft 6in and of a slight build, Canada's Fernandez was previously left out of her federation's funding programme as she was considered too small, but she proved herself to be a giant-killer in New York. Using her surprising power game, she eliminated four seeds: Sabalenka, fifth seed Elina Svitolina, and two former champions in Angelique Kerber and Naomi Osaka. All of those wins were nail-biting three-setters too, where Fernandez showed plucky determination and nerve. It was an astonishing feat and, up until Raducanu joined her in the final, Fernandez was the youngest woman to reach the championship match at a Grand Slam since Maria Sharapova's own fairy tale at Wimbledon 2004. 'It's magical,' Fernandez said of her run.

No one could quite believe that after two weeks of Grand Slam tennis (or three, if you count Raducanu's qualifying efforts), two young guns were about to contest the greatest prize in tennis. This was the first Grand Slam final between two teenagers since 1999, when Serena Williams won her maiden major title against Martina

Hingis in New York, and between two women whom no one had really heard of until that summer. Fernandez was ranked 73rd going into the US Open, and had been quietly building her way up the rankings that season. Her previous best performance at a major was reaching the third round at the French Open earlier that year. Like Raducanu, she was an unknown quantity in many senses and this match was near-impossible to call – but one that everyone was keen to watch play out.

In the end, nine million people tuned into Channel 4 to watch in Britain. That included her old coaches, Clint Harris, Alastair Filmer and Matt James. Harris remembers being told to pipe down by a friend whom he was watching the final with. 'I was like the fourth commentator,' he says, chuckling. 'They were saying just shut up, let us enjoy the match.' In another living room not far from Harris, Raducanu's parents Ian and Renee watched on as their daughter achieved the impossible. They remained in Bromley on account of travel restrictions that still blocked entry to the US, and braced for their lives to officially change forever as their daughter recorded another straight sets win in the biggest moment of her life, pocketing a $2.5 million cheque in the process.

Raducanu was in the driving seat for the majority of her final over Fernandez, but it briefly got complicated. While serving for the match at 5-3 up in the second set, she faced break point but forced a stoppage after cutting her knee. She kept her composure, staved off another break point and then closed out the match on her third championship point with an ace. It ended Britain's 44-year wait for a female Grand Slam champion. She also became the first ever qualifier to win a major title in the Open Era. There were not enough superlatives to describe her achievement. This was only the fourth tour-level event Raducanu had ever played. And it was a Grand Slam, and she was a champion. As she lay on her back in the middle of the Arthur Ashe Stadium court, covering her eyes from the flash of the cameras capturing history in motion, she would have been forgiven for being unable to even muster any semblance of a sentence.

Speaking at her victory press conference, though, she was as charming as ever. She also referred almost immediately to the guiding forces in her life, her parents, whom she had spoken to by phone call. 'My dad said to me: "You're even better than your dad thought," so that was reassurance,' Raducanu said. 'My dad is definitely very tough to please. But I managed to today.' Knowing what we know now about the specific blueprint the Raducanus laid out for their daughter, it was an apt reaction. When she returned home to Bromley, where a gaggle of paparazzi were stationed on her street, her father Ian greeted her and lifted her arms aloft to pose for the cameras, pride etched across his face.

Life was never going to be the same again, but Raducanu was not about to play it safe. She had jovially presented her coach Andrew Richardson with a 'coach of the tournament' trophy during her victory press conference in New York but, within three weeks, she had opted against renewing their partnership. It was a shock decision which made an impression on those looking on: Raducanu may have the world watching now, but she was going to continue to carve out her own way of doing things, regardless of what those on the outside thought.

*

Raducanu's win catapulted her into a different stratosphere of fame, fortune and national treasure status. She attended the Met Gala, personally invited by *Vogue* editor Anna Wintour. She won BBC Sports Personality of the Year that December too. She also began collecting six-figure sponsorship deals. Dior, Evian, Tiffany & Co, HSBC, Vodafone, Porsche and British Airways were among those that came calling. Unfortunately, her results on the court could not match up to the success she had in those dazzling first three months of her WTA career. And unsurprisingly so. Her body struggled with the new rigours of the unrelenting professional tour and her off-court decision-making baffled the pundits.

Her 74 per cent winning record in 2021 was replaced by a 47 per cent record in 2022. Her reality check was delivered in the first match of the season in Sydney by Elena Rybakina, who thrashed her 6-0 6-1. The main issue has been injuries though. Raducanu has been hampered by acute blisters on her hands, a troublesome hip, and had surgery on both wrists and her ankle in 2023, in a season where she was only able to play 10 times. From 2021 up until 2024, she was forced to retire from seven matches through injury.

She also had to adapt to some of the downsides of becoming one of Britain's most famous athletes. In 2022, a man was given a five-year restraining order after showing up at Raducanu's family home three times, including walking 23 miles to get there and even stealing her father's shoe as a souvenir. The court heard that Raducanu was 'constantly looking over her shoulder' and no longer felt 'safe in her own home' as a result of this harassment. Stalking is unfortunately a grim reality for many women athletes, and a more recent incident in 2025 saw Raducanu fearfully crying on court at the Dubai Championships after spotting a man in the crowd with whom she said she had had an 'unsettling encounter' a couple of days earlier. Considering these experiences, it's any wonder how Raducanu manages to step onto the court at all.

Alongside her physical and off-court troubles, Raducanu's coaching situation has been pored over since the US Open. It was referred to as a one-woman merry-go-around in the papers, and her every decision tracked as she chopped and changed at will. One coach who dabbled in a trial period with team Raducanu was Dmitry Tursunov. A former top 30 player on the ATP tour and a seasoned tour coach, Tursunov had worked with the likes of world

No. 2 Aryna Sabalenka. After Raducanu had navigated the clay and grass-court season without a full-time coach, she was in the market for someone to steer her through her title defence in New York. Tursunov saw Raducanu's talent, but mostly saw the scope for improvement. 'It's kind of like someone who comes in, puts a coin into a slot machine and gets a jackpot. You're a winner, but you don't know how it happened and so you can't repeat it. In that sense, it was interesting because I felt that she had a lot of room to improve. It's kind of an interesting puzzle to solve.' After a week of training at the IMG Academy in Florida, Tursunov agreed to a six-week trial. He saw a disciplined, hands-on hard-worker in Raducanu, but felt she lacked weight on her shots. He felt like she could 'turn into someone like Ash Barty', owing to her court movement and coordination.

Immediately he sensed her 'obsessive' approach to tennis. 'The way she was making decisions on court, the problems weren't coming from her being stupid, it was maybe coming from her being too intelligent, or overthinking quite often,' he says. 'I felt like she was very professional, almost on the borderline of obsessively professional – a lot more professional than many players on the tour. She carried a lot of pressure [into the 2022 US Open]. That's the other side of the coin: by being such a perfectionist, you can drive yourself mad with the same qualities that can get you far.' He liked how inquisitive Raducanu was, how she challenged his coaching methods and also noted it was a trait he saw in her father, in the handful of times they met. But he also sensed that it was a case of information overload when she stepped on to the court. 'Imagine if while you're dancing, you have to think where your foot is pointing, where your hand is pointing, you wouldn't be able to hear the music, right? So it's a bit of a process of learning how to apply that information sparingly.'

This extended beyond the court. Tursunov recalls heading out for ice-cream with Raducanu in Florida, where she dragged them around four different shops to try to find the perfect gelato she had researched online. 'I don't think we ended up getting one,' he says. 'That's fine, it's just gelato, but now if you're trying to hit a forehand and you're thinking shall I hit down the line, should I hit cross court, what type of speed, how much spin, what type of trajectory to apply – it's like paralysis by analysis.' In the end, Tursunov never agreed to a permanent contract with Raducanu. He liked her, and felt that if given the time to work with her, within two years she would have been contesting at Grand Slams again. But he sensed he would not survive that long, nor did he think he would be able to have the impact he would have wanted. 'Sometimes as a coach it's tough to change and navigate the boundaries that already exist there. Do I feel relevant in this environment, or do I feel like I'm going to lose this fight? That's the feeling I was getting with her, not because of her on the court, but things I felt I would not be able to control. It was a gut feeling.' Reports also suggested that he could not agree contract terms with her team. Either way, it was a fair prediction from Tursunov, considering how quickly she has moved through coaches so far in her career.

After Richardson, she worked with Torben Beltz (November 2021 to April 2022), Tursunov (August to October 2022) and Sebastian Sachs (December 2022 to June 2023). In between those stints, she had time consulting with LTA coaches as well as guiding her own career. In an interview in 2023 with the BBC's *Today* show, she raised eyebrows for saying: 'I ask my coaches a lot of questions. I think on certain occasions they haven't been able to keep up with the questions I've asked, so maybe that's why it ended.' Her agent, Max Eisenbud, told *The Tennis Podcast* that same year that he predicted that this constant changing it up behind the scenes was likely to continue for the rest of her career due to the 'philosophy' her father Ian had instilled in her.

In 2024, she found some stability finally. Returning to her childhood coach Nick Cavaday, Raducanu's results improved (20-13 win-loss ratio), and she had a particularly positive run to the fourth round at Wimbledon. Dehaes sees why people criticise the methods, but also says that the Raducanus may simply be following the wisdom they gleaned during her development years: she did well with multiple voices in her camp as a child, so why not as a pro? The difference though is that she now lacked the stability and grounding that her Bromley base provided back then. 'Coaches, they say: "Ah, the parents, they don't know nothing about tennis, they want to be involved, blah, blah, blah." But Ian, he was the guy who gave her the passion for tennis,' Dehaes says. 'I know that it's quite easy to make some critiques, because he's too much involved, because he's the guy making all the decisions. But the decisions he made, we can see it was not too bad, no? That's the reality of the ranking and the reality of the results.' Alistair Filmer agrees: 'When you see the coach situation after Andrew, she's so demanding – and it's nothing on those coaches. She literally will be going, right I've got everything I need out of that one, let's move on. Or they didn't have as much as I thought they had, and move on. She will always be looking for that feedback again and again; she is forensic like that.' He adds: 'The number one thing is high standards and a highly demanding culture, of herself and of others. And if you're not going to get on that level, see you later. There's a ruthlessness to that as well. Her PR is unbelievable, how she comes across, but she's a killer. She's a stone-cold killer. There's no way you can win a Grand Slam without dropping a set if you're not a killer. In all the right ways, she is ruthless.'

The question is whether that ruthlessness will lead to another Grand Slam title. At the moment, Raducanu is one of 15 so-called one-hit wonders to have claimed one solitary major title since the turn of the century (up to the end of 2024). There is absolutely no shame in that. We will always have the pure joy of Flushing Meadows in 2021, as the late summer saw this teenager bloom before our very eyes. If that remains the peak of her tennis career, what a peak it was. She has plenty to fall back on, thanks to the education she worked so hard for and the scores of business opportunities that will continue to be available to her. Her teammate Fran Jones even suggested last summer that they were both contemplating enrolling at Oxford University, during a pre-Wimbledon day trip to the city. Somehow, though, it feels unlikely that there won't be more glory for Raducanu. A formidably impressive woman, who followed a forensically formulated path to glory, will surely have another good crack at things.

CHAPTER 14

Iga Swiatek:
The mentality monster

DARIA Abramowicz was preparing to get into bed on the eve of the Miami Open in March 2022 when her phone started buzzing furiously. There were messages from dozens of people connected with the player she works for, Iga Swiatek. Emails and texts from Swiatek's management and those within their tight-knit tennis circle. 'Have you heard?' one asked urgently. 'Barty's done,' another said. Amid the flurry of messages were links to a news article with the headline: 'World No. 1 Ash Barty retires from tennis at 25.' Abramowicz's head started spinning. She had heard rumours about Barty potentially stepping away, after her win six weeks prior at the Australian Open. But her intel suggested it might come later in the season and that it was unlikely to be permanent. The words 'retire' had a permanency to them that surprised Abramowicz. She watched the clip of Barty being interviewed by her friend, player-turned-broadcaster Casey Dellacqua, and understood this was no short hiatus. Barty was really going for good and with immediate effect. There was no last hurrah planned, no final tournament to say goodbye, no transition period.

Immediately, Abramowicz's thoughts turned to Swiatek, the player she had been working with as a mindset coach for nearly three years at that stage. Swiatek had only been the world No. 2 for a few days, but she was about to get the most monumental, unexpected promotion of her life. Down the corridor of their team's rental apartment, Abramowicz could hear Swiatek laughing loudly. She was watching *Parks and Recreation* on Netflix, a favourite of Swiatek's list of American comedy shows that she often turned to as a way to unwind before a big tournament started. The next day she was due to kick off her Miami Open against Viktorija Golubic. This was a scene of complete calm and relaxation, and total equilibrium. The exact type of environment Swiatek and the team worked hard to create. It was the perfect preparation for a player who relied on keeping routine and stability behind the scenes.

Everything was on track for Swiatek, about 18 months on from winning Roland Garros when she was still a teenager. In fact, things were going better than she could hope: she was on an 11-match winning streak, after winning back-to-back titles in Doha and at Indian Wells – the latter being her biggest title since the French Open in 2020. She also reached her first ever hard-court major semi-final in Melbourne. Her results in the first quarter of the year had seen her climb into the top five for the first time and then up to the No. 2 spot ahead of Miami. She was still only 20 years old though, and more than 2,000 ranking points behind Barty at the top. There was a way to go if she wanted to reach the ultimate goal of world No. 1. At least, that was until Barty decided to abruptly end her career.

Abramowicz listened to Swiatek's carefree chortling, and cursed the timing of the news. 'We were staying in a huge apartment but I could hear Iga laughing hard, so hard,' Abramowicz says. 'I knew that the news will be very tough to swallow, to work through.' She debated with herself for a few minutes: should she wait to tell Swiatek until the morning, ahead of her first-round match, or break the spell now, rip off the Band-Aid? She chose the latter and walked down the corridor, unsure about how this conversation was about to be received. 'Iga just cried for half an hour,' Abramowicz says. 'And you know why? Because she was sorry for Ash. Then everything came into realisation, I remember the next day, when everyone started congratulating her. She needed to win this first-round match to actually get the points to become the No. 1 and she was so over-whelmed with everything. But then she went on court, won the whole thing.'

That moment was maybe the turning point of Swiatek's entire career. Perhaps in years to come, when Swiatek is retired, we will remember Barty's retirement as the event that altered the trajectory of her tennis life and this entire era of women's tennis too. She won the title in Miami without losing a single set, becoming only the fourth woman in history to win the 'Sunshine Double' of Indian Wells and Miami in a single season. Then she won the title on clay in Stuttgart. Another trophy in Rome followed. She kept going, all the way to a second major title at Roland Garros. It ended up being a 135-day, 37-match winning streak – the longest unbeaten stretch the WTA had seen since 1990 – with six consecutive titles to her name.

For some players, the pressure of living up to a title like world No. 1 can throw them into a spin, especially when it was effectively handed to her by default, after Barty's abdication. But Swiatek went out and proved herself to be the best player on earth like it was the most natural thing in the world. That dazzling response to suddenly becoming the 'one to beat' in women's tennis was a measure of just how the Swiatek story usually seems to go: see a challenge, lock in mentally and physically and win. Swiatek won two majors that year, and over the course of two more seasons established herself as a modern great on clay and the most dominant female player since 23-time Grand Slam champion Serena Williams if we're counting Grand Slams and weeks at the top of the rankings. A big aspect to Swiatek's approach, which differs from almost every other person on tour, is that she has done it by prioritising the mental side to tennis.

More than that, she also has a mentality coach in Abramowicz who is on hand and on-site at close to every single tournament she plays. It is a highly unusual set-up, and a quirk to Swiatek's story that makes her all the more interesting.

*

Sport psychology has a long, varied history. The British Psychological Society identifies the late 1800s as when we see the first examples of sport psychology resembling the present-day methods and thinking. In particular, Norman Triplett's 1898 experiment, which found that cyclists tend to produce faster times when riding in with other cyclists rather than alone, is regarded as the first in sport psychology. In the 1920s, various European universities started exploring the psychological benefits of physical activity, while at the University of Illinois they introduced a course entitled 'Psychology and Athletics', where the practice was formalised into teaching by Dr Coleman Roberts Griffith. He even began working with the Chicago Cubs baseball team as a sport psychologist briefly in 1938. The International Society of Sport Psychology met for the first time in 1965, as many Eastern bloc European countries came to acknowledge the importance of mental training alongside elite sporting performance. In football, Professor João Carvalhaes was seen as a pioneer for his work with Brazil's 1958 World Cup-winning team, which included Pelé. It was not until the 1980s that sport psychology began being adopted in European football set-ups. AC Milan introduced its 'Mind Room' in 1986, which had cognitive training and stress relief as its core principles. It is credited with contributing to an unprecedented run of success for the club as Milan won 21 trophies in the 23 seasons the room was operational for. Clubs including Chelsea adopted copycat versions.

As an individual sport, tennis comes with its own unique sets of challenges. Ivan Lendl is considered one of the earliest adopters, and was one of the first top players to speak about his work with a sport psychologist, Alexis Castorri, back in the 1980s. Castorri's methods were designed to help Lendl play more freely, in order to win his first major title. She went on to assist Lendl's charge Andy Murray in breaking his Grand Slam duck in 2012 and also worked closely with Simona Halep, who also lost a string of major finals before being crowned champion. Sport psychology has evolved over time, says Dr Misia Gervis, and performance is not always the core focus now. 'The role of sport psychologists is changing. I always ask my post-grad students: "What do you think the purpose of sport psychology is?" If I asked this 10 years ago, they would focus pretty much on performance. Now, they start with mental health and wellbeing. So the people who are coming into the profession, they've got different rationales and are looking at it in a different way. We have a better understanding of the challenges that are placed on elite athletes, the fact that they're just humans.'

That in turn is filtering down to the athletes themselves: 'If we listen to the narrative from the 2024 Olympics in Paris, many people were talking about things in a very different way. Adam Peaty, for example, was going: "This silver medal, I love it, this means so much to me, this is important." Rather than the old narrative of "second place is nowhere". There were many other people expressing their struggles with grief and their mental health challenges. This was I think the first Olympics where they were very open.'

On the WTA Tour now, there is at least one sport psychologist employed at every tournament, from 250 level and above. Players also have access to mental health professionals via video call if they prefer. Swiatek has embraced the mental side to her sport in a way not previously seen. Abramowicz first met her when Swiatek was only 17 years old. A former sailor for Poland, Abramowicz was in her early thirties and had retrained in sport psychology. She had previously worked with the Polish cycling and swimming teams, when she was sought out by Swiatek's coach Piotr Sierzputowski. Abramowicz had heard of Swiatek, who was working through her first professional season and was already getting significant attention in her homeland.

Swiatek had been playing tennis since the age of six, after her parents wanted to help her burn off some of her overspilling energy. Her father Tomasz was an Olympic rower for Poland at the Seoul Olympics in 1988, so athleticism ran deep in her family. He introduced her to tennis and would put her through her paces in unconventional training sessions away from the court too, even getting her to do volleying drills while balancing on a paddleboard in the water. Tennis suited Swiatek's personality too as she liked to have full control over the outcome of her own sporting endeavours. That sense of control has been a thread that continued to run throughout her life and tennis career.

When Abramowicz was brought in, Swiatek was sitting just inside the top 150, nearly a year on from her junior triumph at Wimbledon. She had already worked with two sport psychologists before, but it had never been a lasting fit. Those around her, including her parents and coaches, were worried about her outbursts. Swiatek would cry openly on court, express her frustration vocally, and she struggled with controlling her emotions during the dead time in a match. She had sobbed into her towel during her Fed Cup matches that week for Poland. 'They said: "There's this girl, she's very young, but she has this temper."' Abramowicz says. 'What I don't like is when coaches, agents, even parents, sometimes describe athletes as "difficult". It's not kind. But anyway, I heard that she's "difficult". I knew Iga had won junior Wimbledon and saw her playing on TV. As someone who watched a lot of sports, you kind of know when you see someone who has potential. You could see that with Iga.'

Abramowicz had space to work with Swiatek, and so she set up a trial. She travelled to Budapest, where the youngster was competing at the Hungarian Ladies Open, the equivalent of a WTA 250. Swiatek was surprised that someone would travel for the sole purpose of meeting her, Abramowicz recalls now. She was also deep into her mathematics homework that week (like Raducanu, she was an outlier in tennis for continuing her schooling up until the age of 18). Abramowicz says it was never a case of convincing her, she saw the value of bringing a sport psychologist on board. 'It is still exceptional about Iga that she is very aware and mindful about all the puzzles that need to fit, in terms of creating a top performer,' she says, 'And also what needs to be done in pursuit of excellence. She was already convinced to put in the work in terms of mental training and sport psychology.'

The source of Swiatek's on-court tantrums had nothing to do with the expectations placed on her shoulders from a young age, Abramowicz discovered. Instead, her latest at the Fed Cup had everything to do with playing at home in front of the fans. She found it 'suffocating' and anxiety-inducing. Swiatek may have been one of the top teenagers in world tennis (at the time, she was ranked sixth for players under 20), but she did not carry herself with that swagger. She was an introvert and those environments were 'challenging for her', according to Abramowicz. There was also an innate 'stubbornness' within Swiatek which needed some direction and figuring out. 'The difficult part was about how that might be processed and transitioned towards grit,' Abramowicz says. 'At the time, she was still 17. There were lots of things she was doing off the court that she was trying to figure out as a young woman who was approaching her career very fast. With Iga's career, it was like pow! It has always been like this because of her athletic potential. I think the difficulty that people would have described was associated more with the stubbornness, with her being a perfectionist, extremely smart and quick-witted. She's very on fire with sarcasm, with being ironic – you need to keep up with her. She remembers everything.

It was, and it still is for so many people, very challenging to engage in conversation, to keep up with this young woman.'

Abramowicz believed she could, so she committed to working with Swiatek. Her first step: travelling to tournaments with her new charge. For those who associate psychology sessions with deep meaningful conversations in a cosy office, like a scene out of *The Sopranos,* that was not it for Abramowicz. She wanted to be in the thick of the action with her athletes. 'I was always working this way – with cyclists, swimmers, sailors, other athletes, I travel. I believe strongly that seeing an athlete on the arena, during practice, during competition, gives me 100 per cent more. When the athlete is very experienced, way older, with life experience as well, it's easier to work remotely, and I do have athletes like this, but I think travelling is very beneficial.' For the first few months, she travelled to certain events, including Toronto that summer, where qualifier Swiatek turned heads with a win over Caroline Wozniacki and by running world No. 2 Naomi Osaka close over two sets. Earlier in the year, Swiatek made a run to the Roland Garros fourth round, which helped her break into the world's top 100. She finished the season inside the top 50 and took that momentum through to Melbourne in the new year, where she got to the fourth round at the Australian Open too.

As well as her swift rise up the rankings, Swiatek's game was eye-catching too. Broad-shouldered and with the biceps to match, she was noticeably strong for someone so young and applied top-spin to her forehand shots. That differentiated her from the flatter groundstrokes usually found at the top of women's tennis. She had variety too, a delicate touch and a consistent game. Her coach Piotr Sierzputowski was relatively inexperienced, but had been with her since January 2016 when she was 15. There was a trust there. What also made Swiatek stand out on tour was Abramowicz's presence. Investing in her mental game so emphatically and openly, particularly when she remained an up-and-comer, was extremely rare. To Swiatek, it felt essential, especially after the pandemic created unexpected travel and competition challenges for the world and her sport. 'We established this team dynamic from that moment, a very specific way of working on tour,' Abramowicz says.

One of the first priorities Abramowicz had was helping Swiatek create coping strategies for what she calls 'the time between'. It may not always be obvious, but tennis players spend an abundance of time during competition not actually competing. In fact, of the hours they can spend on court for each match, only around 20 per cent is spent in play. The rest is dead time: from the 10-minute warm-up; the 25 seconds between each point; the 90 seconds break at each change of ends; the minutes spent between sets too. Then add in medical timeouts and toilet breaks. It is a lot of thinking time, sometimes while standing in arenas with thousands of spectators watching your each and every move. When things are going wrong, it can be overwhelming. Equally, when you're up, your mind can wander to unhelpful memories or feelings.

Even in the macro sense, outside of matches, the thinking time as a professional tennis player is endless. Unlike in other top sports like football, basketball, swimming or rugby, tennis players can never fully predict what time they are going to step out on court. Rain delays and lengthy matches scheduled on the same courts can delay estimated start times by hours, and sometimes days. Players spend copious amounts of time simply sitting around, lying in wait, constantly required to be ready for when their opportunity comes. Oftentimes, that might be spent on-site, in the same spaces as opponents and rivals. Could you imagine Real Madrid and Barcelona players sitting in the same locker room or player lounge ahead of *El Clásico*? You can't, because it would never happen. But tennis players spend their careers awkwardly rubbing shoulders at events. All of that could drive you mad. It could also tire you out and affect how prepared you feel when you finally get on court. Perhaps more than any other sport, and comparable only to golf, tennis players may win or lose based on how they specifically spend their time at the venue when they are *not* playing tennis.

Each player's needs are different in those moments. Some do not feel the need to meticulously manage every element of their preparation. Serena Williams's former coach Patrick Mouratoglou has described his horror at seeing her napping a mere 15 minutes before taking to the court. When she stepped into the arena, she did not skip a beat: she was a different person and brought an unmatched level of intensity. Swiatek falls on the complete other end of the spectrum. She is constantly in search of order in a sport that, off the court, can feel as chaotic as any. That is where Abramowicz comes in. 'Especially in the early stages, we did a lot on court,' Abramowicz says. 'Of course, with tennis being this sport that it's based on pauses and breaks – between points, between games, between sets, between matches and tournaments – I strongly feel that during these breaks, the player can do a lot. So we did cognitive skills training, relaxation imagery, and a lot of breathing training. We did a lot of mindfulness. Now she has that in her toolbox, the early years were definitely about building that up.'

Brain workouts were prioritised in the same way as physical workouts were. Early on, Abramowicz would give Swiatek a device to wear on her ear that measured electrical activity in her brain, and they would do reaction time tests using flash cards and puzzles. They worked on mantras for certain situations and guiding principles, including 'keep expectations low and standards high'. Away from the court, one of the pillars of Abramowicz's philosophy is around 'environmental mastery'. That may seem an impossible aim on the outside. For one, there are all the scheduling uncertainties that come with tennis. Then there is the travel. Tennis players cannot build routine in the way a sprinter who competes five times a year might, or an NFL player who knows the league schedule months in advance. Swiatek cannot count on the exact same meals at every tournament, finds out when she plays the day before an event begins, and might shift her travel plans completely depending on an unexpected loss. On the most basic level, she sleeps in a different bed in a new room nearly every week. Mastering an ever-changing environment seems like a fool's errand. Why not just embrace the chaos? But Abramowicz insists there are ways to do it. 'For most of the time, you travel to the same places every year, so for example you will have your favourite places in these cities; your restaurants, your coffee shops, your parks, lakes, beaches. If you prefer, as Iga does, being connected and close to the nature then you seek that out. You can have your people in those cities too. And the places you stay.'

To fill the time spent between matches, Swiatek became a Lego nut. During the year after Covid, when players were confined to tournament bubbles and mostly spent their time on Netflix or ordering gym gear to their rooms, she would have Lego sets delivered to her hotel. Ahead of matches in the player lounges, she has been known to build elaborate Hogwarts replicas, Pac-Man machines or flower bouquets. The piece-by-piece process requires focus and precision, and she uses it as a way to keep her mind active while staying away from a phone screen. In terms of her wider environment, Swiatek will often avoid tournament hotels if she can too as she prefers to avoid the faces she sees on-site – or across the net – each day. 'There will be people like Petra Kvitova, whom you would see in the hotel lobby engaging in conversation, or others, like Ons [Jabeur], who can be socially engaged all the time,' Abramowicz says. 'But there will be more introverted people as Iga is, so you can have your favourite places to stay – like houses, apartments, you know? Those things become constant. The other constant thing is your team, people that you will be travelling with.' That is where the real environment you exist within is, Abramowicz says. If a team works in harmony for the betterment of the player, giving helpful feedback, communicating well, being assertive and not crossing 'boundaries' in the group, then the outer environmental changes that happen each day for a tennis player will not impact them as much. 'It's not about the tour life itself, but the environment that you live within that will help you, not only achieve great things and perform on the top level, but also would help you with the very challenging life you live, full of sacrifices.'

Her physiotherapist and trainer Maciej Ryszczuk is one of those constants. For the first couple of years on tour, so was her coach Piotr Sierzputowski. Abramowicz became one too. She was an instrumental force in her tennis life. Swiatek trusted Abramowicz's guidance implicitly, and when her biggest wins became a reality, she credited her psychologist. At Roland Garros in 2020, she said Abramowicz made her 'smarter'. 'Daria was the best I could get because she just understands me very well and she can kind of read my mind, which is weird,' Swiatek said, after making it to the quarter-final. 'She was a sailor, so she has experience in sports, and she was a coach so she has the full package. She just made me smarter. I know more about sports and I know more about psychology and I can understand my own feelings and I can say them out loud. She just makes my confidence level higher.'

Her run that week took the tennis world by storm. It was the most unconventional French Open in memory. Due to the Covid pandemic, the tournament was played in October for the very first time. The world No. 1 Ash Barty skipped it, opting not to travel outside of her native Australia where travel rules were stricter, leaving the reigning champion's space in the draw vacant. The conditions were miserable, with cold weather sweeping Paris, making the balls slower and lower-bouncing on the heavier clay. In the final, Swiatek had reigning Australian Open champion Sofia Kenin to compete with. In terms of lightning bolt rises, Kenin had a similar story to Swiatek. She too had never previously reached a major quarter-final on her run to winning the title in Melbourne earlier that year. She was still young too, at 21. In fact, their combined age of 40 was the youngest for a women's Grand Slam final since 2008. They also both bring a startling intensity and focus to their matches, if in slightly different styles. Kenin can appear wired, her eyes bulging as she fights her way through trouble. Swiatek meanwhile has the appearance of someone with blinkers on, methodically and efficiently making her way through points and matches. Swiatek was unstoppable that fortnight, and no amount of fight from Kenin was going to change that. The final score was a smooth 6-4 6-1.

Watching Swiatek seal the victory with a poise beyond her years in that final game, Abramowicz's mind was moving fast. 'It's a very interesting feeling, this last game when you know that your player is going to win. Time stops and you wait for when you can finally burst out. But that time I remember my brain was thinking, what do we need to do now to be able to live through that success? People, especially in sports, would tend to learn how to deal with losses, with failures. But the interesting thing is, when we set the goals, we don't prepare ourselves for what will happen when we do. Athletes dream of winning, of great success, but they are often not prepared for this success.'

For Swiatek, there was not much time to prepare. She was only 19, the youngest singles champion since Rafael Nadal in 2005. On the women's side, you had to go back all the way to Monica Seles in 1992 to find a younger winner. 'It is crazy. Two years ago I won a junior Grand Slam and now I'm here,' said Swiatek in the aftermath, her voice breaking with emotion. 'It feels like such a short time.' Swiatek's winning moment was bizarre for various reasons. You only had to take a look at her, wearing long sleeves and leggings – such was the October chill in the Paris air – to know this

French Open was an anomaly. Her winning moment had only been met by the muted cheers of a few dozen people watching on Court Philippe Chatrier. Most were huddled under blankets. To even plant the customary kiss on the Coupe Suzanne Lenglen trophy for the photographers, Swiatek had to lower her Asics branded face mask which was covering her nose and mouth. This French Open was always going to exist with the asterisk of the circumstances it was played within, and so perhaps it made sense that there was a surprise winner. There was no guarantee or expectation on Swiatek to win another.

But the manner in which she obliterated the rest of the field suggested this was no one-off. The fourth round 6-1 6-2 win over world No. 2 and former champion, Simona Halep – who was on a 17-match winning streak at the time – was the real head-turning result. It was all the more remarkable as 12 months prior, Halep had dispatched of Swiatek at the same tournament in just 45 minutes. Swiatek had come so far in such a short space of time. After the win, another young, newly crowned champion Naomi Osaka tweeted: 'What a star.' The hype train was coming at her fast, the question was inevitably going to be asked: how was Swiatek going to avoid fading out, as other champions had done? No one had been able to keep a firm grip on the mantle at the top of women's tennis since Serena Williams. With every new champion, the chatter came: will this girl be 'the one'? Mats Wilander, a seven-time major champion in his own right, certainly thought Swiatek was it. He immediately predicted that she would win 'so many more'. 'Once she gets control of the rally with her forehand,' he said, 'you just can't get out of the grip. It feels like I'm watching Rafa Nadal.'

It may have been recency bias or the fervour that can take over pundits when trying to big up their sport and its protagonists. But the words 'Rafa Nadal' were just about the highest praise imaginable for Swiatek. She made no secret of idolising Nadal, and her topspin forehand is undoubtedly inspired by him. Few in women's tennis can boast a similar weapon. After winning, her response was Nadal-esque too. She did not refer to the glitzy ways her life might change or what awaited her as a Grand Slam champion. Instead, her mind shifted to a new goal: finding a consistency that had been rare in women's tennis over the past decade or so. She recognised it was not a given, and was perhaps the most difficult goal she could set herself after the thrill of winning a major title. 'That's why we have so many new Grand Slam winners because we are not as consistent as Rafa [Nadal], Roger [Federer] and Novak [Djokovic],' Swiatek said. 'That's why my goal is to be consistent. It's going to be really hard to achieve that.' It was not a sexy answer by any means, but it was a goal that no one had been able to achieve beyond Serena for the past two decades.

Nick Brown flew out to Warsaw that off-season to lend a hand in the Swiatek camp. A former British Davis Cup player, as a coach Brown served as Fed Cup captain for the British team and helped develop the likes of Tim Henman and a young Jack Draper more recently. He also spent a stint in the noughties as the Polish Olympic and Davis Cup team coach. The resources were limited ('a $1 million annual budget, compared to the LTA's $65 million or so,' Brown says), but their ambition was big. Even when his work was over, he kept consulting with them and he was first introduced to Swiatek when she was not yet 17. 'The Polish federation called me in 2018 and said we've got some good young juniors coming up now; they're working with very inexperienced coaches, young coaches who've had no experience on the professional tour. Do you think you could take a look at these players and see if you think you can help them?' Brown was at the French Open commentating for Eurosport anyway, so he met with Swiatek's coach and watched her play through the matches, all the way to the semi-final. The following month, Brown was there when she won junior Wimbledon with the loss of just one set, in a draw that included Coco Gauff, Leylah Fernandez and Emma Raducanu (whom Swiatek pummelled 6-0 6-1 in the quarter-final).

Her parents, at Brown's suggestion, had written to the All England Club to get her entered into the draw as her ranking was too low due to competing sparingly. Remarkably, she had never played on grass before and at the beginning of the tournament she had complained that she hated it. To this day, it remains the surface she has had the least success on, but that week she found her footing. Brown says he set small targets or goals to hit in each match, regardless of the result. 'Watching her play closely, she was totally out of her comfort zone, but it's her ability to try and learn and take things on board. Every match she played, I tried to give her a little goal tactically, what to try and do on the grass, to play better. When she was playing the semi-final against China's Wang Xinyu, the level of tennis was just something else. I knew then that actually she had the potential to win a Grand Slam. She was down 4-2, slightly engaging the wrong tactics to win this match. And I told her coach, try and tell her just to change the direction – she needs to defend a little bit more down the middle, rather than going to the angles – and change the attack to her opponent's forehand. Once the message was delivered, she literally did that within two points. That also told me here's somebody who can take information on board and directly integrate it into a game, without having to complicate the situation. She had an innate way of reading the game, a little bit like Agnieszka Radwanska did.' After she won, Brown pointed to Centre Court and told her coach Piotr that she would be vying for the title there in five years' time. He may have been pointing to the wrong court and have underestimated the timings, but he was on the right track.

Brown remained a mentor and consultant to Swiatek for the next two and a half years. Swiatek, her coach and trainer sometimes stayed with Brown and his wife at their home in Cambridge too. He remembers she was timid and shy, but she also embraced the experience of learning about a new place. One of Brown's lasting memories of those times was Swiatek's glee at being taken out for a hearty lunch at a traditional old pub in a nearby village. At the David Lloyd Club, Brown would get her to train with the men's Cambridge University team which he coached too. He immediately saw some traits in her attitude that he recognised from his playing days, when he spent a lot of time practising in London with champions including Ivan Lendl and Stefan Edberg. 'Sometimes it was difficult to get her off the court, because if you're working on an aspect of a game – say the volley or a slice – she would want to be out there until she felt it had improved. That's a gimme of the great players. They do things slightly differently. They have a different kind of hunger and they're relentless in being the best they can be.'

That work ethic and diligence was clear. Later, he also travelled to Warsaw to train with Swiatek at her base. He was most impressed by her startling focus for someone so young. 'I went on court to play with her, because even now I still like to hit with players just to feel what kind of ball's coming from the other end. We started in the service box and worked backwards to the baseline and consistency wise, just how she was shaping the ball, feeling the ball. She didn't miss a ball for 20 minutes – not one ball. That in itself tells you something right away about somebody. That kind of focus, application, discipline, it is not the norm. I thought, this girl's definitely going to have success on the women's tour. She was driven.' When her sudden success came, that drive kept her on the right track off the court too.

CHAPTER 15

Iga Swiatek:
In pursuit of perfection

WINNING the Roland Garros title meant life changed for Iga Swiatek back in Poland. She was the country's first ever major champion in tennis. Aside from footballer Robert Lewandowski, Swiatek was now the most recognisable sports person back home, and that came with new expectations. On a global front though, her name joined a long list of new champions that tennis fans were still figuring out whether it was worth getting to know. Because of the smaller market she came from, one Grand Slam title was not enough to attract the high-end brands that flocked to Spain's Garbiñe Muguruza or Britain's Emma Raducanu the following year. It meant her feet stayed firmly on the ground.

Brown got a sense of how she would be immune to the trappings of fame when, mere weeks after winning Roland Garros for the first time, 19-year-old Swiatek personally organised a tennis camp at her Warsaw club. There, she workshopped sessions alongside Sierzputowski and Brown for eight of the most talented 14-year-olds in the Polish tennis system, along with their individual coaches. 'It was very thoughtful. It showed the person she is, in terms of wanting to give back and also how she appreciated the support that the Polish federation had given her – limited within their resources, but it's all relative, isn't it? She wanted to inspire the next generation of young players. There are not many Grand Slam champions who would actually do that so soon after their win.'

Speaking with her team, in particular Abramowicz, conversation turned to what next? For Brown, the answer was obvious: go back down the ladder. Swiatek had just skipped a load of grades by achieving a Grand Slam title; she needed to build herself back up to that level. 'She'd never even won a WTA event before,' Brown says. 'The first thing I spoke to Daria about was she's won this, she's created a legacy now for tennis in Poland – never mind women's tennis, because she's the first person to win a Grand Slam at all. When that happens, a bit like you can see what happened to Raducanu, you're kind of thrown into this new world. But what she needed was to go and win a 250, 500 and a Master series because they're the gradual stepping stones. You start winning those events on a regular basis, then you're going to create consistency, what they were looking for.'

Swiatek followed Brown's advice. At the Australian Open she lost in the fourth round to world No. 2 Halep in a tight three-setter, but she started chipping away thereafter. First, she won a WTA 500 title in Adelaide, pushing her into the top 15. Then during the clay season she clinched her first 1000 trophy in Rome, defeating former world No. 1 Karolina Pliskova 6-0 6-0 in the final. It was a statement victory, against a player in Pliskova who had made Rome her stomping ground, winning the title and reaching the final the previous two seasons. But Swiatek swept her aside in a mere 46 minutes. In Paris next, she made it to the quarter-final before falling to Maria Sakkari. All around, it was not a bad first attempt at a title defence – especially as she had only lifted the trophy seven months prior. The rest of the season went as you might expect for a player who had newly entered the world's top 10: she got to the fourth round at both Wimbledon and the US Open, and qualified for the WTA Finals for the first time. This season of hitting milestones but making gradual progress suited Swiatek. It gave her a sense of grounding that was helpful to build upon.

She wanted to make the next step up though, and that meant parting from Sierzputowski. Brown remembers her messaging him to share the decision. There were tears for Swiatek, who found it 'emotional' to make such a big change, considering how tight her team had become, but she needed someone to help her make the step up from top 10 to top five and beyond. Brown says that, upon reflection, Sierzputowski might have been putting too much emphasis on scouting Swiatek's opponents, delivering too much data to her and 'devising game plans', when she was a player who preferred figuring out her own tactics. 'You've got to be careful sometimes when implementing certain tactics, game plans, that you don't take away that natural ability that somebody has, because you kind of inhibit the way they can play,' he says.

The replacement was Tomasz Wiktorowski, previously coach to Poland's former top female player, Radwanska. He had helped guide her career when she consistently stayed at the very top of the rankings, peaking at No. 2. It appeared a savvy choice. Quite quickly he and Swiatek developed a close partnership and she trusted him enough to overhaul her tactical game. Where previously drop shots had been a feature of the way she played, he helped her simplify things. She narrowed her shot selection, became more aggressive, honed her backhand and became one of the best returners in the sport. With her trainer, Maciej Ryszczuk, she worked on her speed too. Brown says that, to him, that was by far the biggest physical improvement she made to her game after reaching the top level. 'He made a huge difference as that was the one thing that I was a little bit apprehensive of when I first met her, that she wasn't that quick. She was strong but not super quick. He did an incredible job with her, the way he's developed her to cover the court.'

This all happened just a few short months before Swiatek's world was completely shaken when Ash Barty dropped her bombshell retirement news. Swiatek told reporters the very next day that she had spent much of her pre-season practising how to compete against Barty's signature slice, such was her motivation to beat her. Now she was not going to get the chance, their record frozen 2-0 in Barty's favour. The goal of reaching world No. 1, which she had set herself only two days prior to Barty's announcement, was now within grasp in the oddest circumstances. 'When I think of the player that is really complete in terms of physicality, mentality, tennis-wise, I always thought of Ash and I always looked up to her. I mean, I still do,' Swiatek said. 'It would be really nice also to be able to compete against her for the next few years and actually try to play better and better, to be able to beat her slice.'

Without Barty standing in her way though, Swiatek went on her mind-blowing streak in 2022, which included her second Roland Garros title. Apart from a fourth round scare against China's Qinwen Zheng, where she recovered after losing the first set, she appeared to cruise through. In the final against teenage sensation Coco Gauff, it was no contest, Swiatek won 6-1 6-3. In the middle of that streak and as the newly crowned world No. 1, she also became the most outspoken anti-war player on tour, voicing her support of Ukraine during press conferences and by wearing a ribbon with the country's national colours on her cap. That July, she organised a charity fundraising exhibition in Krakow called 'Iga Swiatek and Friends for Ukraine'. She and Radwanska took to the court, with Ukraine's Elina Svitolina in the umpire's chair, in front of 12,000 people. It raised £440,000. It showed a new side to Swiatek and just how seriously she took her role as the leading figure in women's tennis. She wanted to stand for something, and – as a Polish native, the neighbouring country to Ukraine – she understood the war devastation and refugee situation better than most.

It was not the only cause Swiatek fronted from her position at the top of women's tennis, as mental health became a cause she aligned with too. It made sense, as a player who had harnessed the power of mental training and psychology in sport, but it was notable too because of where she comes from. In 2023, the World Health Organization reported that Polish children had one of the lowest rates of mental well-being, and one of the highest rates of attempted suicides in Europe. Mental health still remains a taboo in Poland, and for an athlete to talk openly about their mental health or challenges they experience is not always well received back home, says Abramowicz. 'When an athlete says something is hard, or a particular time in their life was exhausting or unbearable, in Poland they will say: "Exhausting is being a nurse, not doing sports professionally."' Ironically, she won her first major title in 2020 on World Mental Health day, which also happens to fall on Abramowicz's birthday. Coincidence or not, ever since she has used her platform to make various hefty donations of her prize money to mental health organisations around the world, and in Poland in particular. She put her money where her mouth is.

Back on the court in 2022, Swiatek's streak inevitably ended at Wimbledon in the third round. But her season kept reaching new heights as she won the US Open. This was not something she expected, as she had a subpar summer by her standards, and complained that the lighter balls and fast courts in New York did not suit her game. But those low expectations worked as she downed three top 10 opponents, including a comeback victory in her semi-final against Aryna Sabalenka. Down a break in the third set on two occasions, she somehow clawed her way back. Then, in the final against Ons Jabeur – the runner-up at Wimbledon that year – Swiatek showed the gulf between herself and the rest again, winning 6-2 7-6. It was her 10th final victory in a row but, most crucially, it was her first major title away from the clay in Paris. It also happened to be in a city which did not naturally fit with her personality. The chaotic, loud and bustling atmosphere in New York could sometimes overwhelm her, Swiatek admitted, but she found a way to make it work for her. If you can make it here, you can make it anywhere, or so they say, and after lifting the trophy Swiatek really believed that. 'I wasn't sure before the [final] if this is actually my place,' she said of the atmosphere at Flushing Meadows. 'I'm mostly proud of the fact that mentally I'm not breaking up in those important moments . . . The sky's the limit.' It capped off one of the most dominant seasons women's tennis had seen in years. She was the first woman to win two Grand Slam titles in a season since Angelique Kerber in 2016. No one had won seven titles in one season of women's tennis since Serena Williams in 2014. Backing it up was the next challenge.

*

Apart from making a public plea to her manager in 2024 to secure Taylor Swift tickets (which she got, complete with a handwritten letter from Swift herself), Swiatek remains low key about her success. There are no pictures of her on red carpets, no social media posts about swanky dinners or luxurious holidays. Fame was never a motivating factor for Swiatek, in fact it probably puts her out of her comfort zone. It wasn't until Grand Slam number five that the beauty industry came calling, with Lancôme signing her up as a global ambassador. She is actually quite private. At Wimbledon in 2024, she was staying in the village, but admitted she found it hard to walk around the area for fear of being recognised by tennis fans. 'I'm the kind of person that likes to have my peace [when I'm off court]. I'm going to parks to see some nature.' After winning the US Open, she politely declined to share which musical she was going to go see on Broadway to celebrate. She learned that giving too much of herself away had a negative effect. Even something as simple as sharing the name of the song she played in her headphones before taking to the court backfired for her. 'Everyone made such a big deal that it didn't feel like my own,' she said. For the record, she now listens to the Rolling Stones when she walks on court – but hasn't revealed which song.

Swiatek is thoughtful in her dealings with the media though, considered in her answers. She can be funny, vaguely socially awkward but also very straight-talking. As someone who is quite highly strung and a 'perfectionist', she tries to be precise in what she wants to say off the court, as much as what she says with her racket on it. In private, it can mean struggling to relax at times too. 'I used to say to Iga, it's sometimes good to be bored,' Abramowicz says. 'Don't plan, just enjoy it. But she'll have a day off, and she's asking me: "What are we doing today?" I would say: "Nothing – you can do whatever you want, but I have a day off." She would sometimes be like: "What do you mean?" So it's a constant growth process. It's not always like that, but in terms of the process, yes, she likes the routines, the structure.' So far, that approach has served her well.

Swiatek has proven throughout her career that she rises to the moment, owing to a 23-4 winning record in finals on tour. Twenty of those were straight set wins. She established herself as the ultimate front-runner. When Swiatek gets her hands on a match, and an opponent, she rarely loses. From January 2022 up to December 2024, she won a whopping 97 per cent of matches where she took the first set. It is not just the winning either, but the manner in which she does so. From January 2022 to August 2024, 6-0 and 6-1 scorelines featured in 54 per cent of her matches. If you look at her career up to August 2024, she amassed 69 6-0 sets on the WTA Tour. That equated to winning a set 6-0 in one of every five matches she plays. During her most dominant period in 2022 and 2023, it was closer to one in every three matches. Her annihilation of opponents sparked an online meme dubbed 'Iga's Bakery', referring to how she happily collected 'bagel' (6-0) and 'breadstick' (6-1) sets off her opponents. Swiatek has squirmed whenever the subject has been brought up to her though. After beating Wang Xinyu 6-0 6-0 at the 2023 French Open, Swiatek was asked about the 'double bagel'. 'Look, I don't want to really talk about that,' she said. 'I really get why people do that because it's fun and tennis is entertainment, but from the players' point of view, I want to be respectful to my opponents. You don't see the stuff that is behind the scenes. Sometimes it's not easy to play such matches . . . I don't want to talk about the bakery. Twitter can talk about it.'

Asked more widely about her ability as a front-runner though, Swiatek thinks it comes down to the mental training she has put in. 'I think all the mental stuff, I'm always kind of trying to stay present and do the same work no matter what stage of the match I'm in,' Swiatek said, speaking at the Madrid Open in April 2024. 'I think that's the main thing, because honestly, that's the only thing that comes to my mind why. Sometimes it's harder to finish [matches] or sometimes when you're leading you might lose your serve or something. It's only because you kind of lose your focus. So I just want to stay the same way.'

Throughout her success, her constant has been Abramowicz. Her mental training has been the one thing that has remained a non-negotiable aspect to the way she lives her life and career. 'She's willing to include me in her team permanently, because she felt that she can have this anchor and sense of safety and security,' Abramowicz says. She has been on-site with Swiatek at almost every single one of her victories, the person delivering pep talks 10 minutes before a match. There is the risk of over-relying on a psychologist – just in the same way as a player might be too reliant on a coach. Most sport psychologists would aim for their player to be able to cope and rise to challenges without their support eventually. So can't Swiatek figure it out for herself at this point? Abramowicz laughs, as the question and criticism has been levelled at her a lot, including on social media. 'They are saying that all the time, yeah,' Abramowicz says. 'Of course, there is the risk, when a player will become too dependent – whether it's a tennis coach, a friend, parent or psychologist or mental coach, or whoever. I think it always ends the same way: we need to teach these people, we need to empower them, we need to give them as much as possible for them to become strong and independent people. And it's absolutely necessary at some stage to let them fly in a way. Especially in tennis, when they are on their own [on court], it's a very solitary sport. But at the same time, I think they have every right to use the emotional support and support in general, especially during the matches. Sometimes a very simple clapping in the hand and saying something like a keyword can make all the difference. It's not being dependent, it's rather using the resources that are out there.'

Abramowicz believes the role of sport psychologists to be even more essential in tennis, where blurred lines in player coaching relationships remain a problem behind the scenes. She publicly voiced her support of former player Pam Shriver in 2022, when she shared her experience of an inappropriate romantic relationship she had with her long-time, much older coach when she was on tour as a 17-year-old. 'Thank you Pam for telling your story,' Abramowicz wrote on Twitter. 'I'm sure it will not only help athletes, coaches and parents, but also will contribute to raising awareness of mental health and building healthy relationships.' She believes safeguarding provisions set out by the WTA are helping to improve the situation, but as a sport psychologist she can see that things could be 'stricter'. Mandatory education for players on how to recognise abuse versus good coaching is key, she says, and 'probably more psychologists' available to players would be helpful.

Just as in the last 20 years, it has become essential for top players to travel full-time with a physiotherapist in order to help their physical longevity, Swiatek is committed to working on her mental strength full-time so that she can enjoy a long and fruitful career. In 2023, she needed that reassurance from Abramowicz more than previously as the pressure of being world No. 1 started catching up with her. That was in part because Sabalenka was chasing her like no one had before. After winning the Australian Open title at the beginning of the year, Sabalenka made the final in Indian Wells and also in Stuttgart, where Swiatek beat her in the title match. In Madrid, Sabalenka returned the favour, and was closing in on Swiatek's top ranking. It was the first time the world No. 1 and No. 2 had met in a Masters 1000 final in nine years, and it was being called the match of the season. Sabalenka's three-set win put a dent in Swiatek's confidence.

The problem with having a season as dominant as Swiatek did in 2022 was that she had so many points to defend. Every other tournament she played she had gone deep or even won the thing. There were no free hits, every match had points riding on it, and this started eating away at her. Aside from Sabalenka's charge, Swiatek also had three consecutive losses to Elena Rybakina: at the Australian Open, Indian Wells and in Rome. Like Sabalenka, 2022 Wimbledon champion Rybakina had a big baseline game, with power that outgunned Swiatek. Their height helps them neutralise the high bounce off Swiatek's topspin forehand too. The world No. 1 constantly found herself on the defensive against these two opponents, and being on the back foot was not her norm. 'It was a huge challenge,' says Abramowicz, 'to learn the thing that Serena is always describing as "having the target on your back all the time". Because Iga was not a one-year wonder any more. Girls would learn her game. She would need to adapt.'

Still, this was not exactly a crisis. She won 86 per cent of her matches that season and that included her third Roland Garros title, and fourth major overall. She did not come up against either Sabalenka or Rybakina – the latter of which withdrew from the tournament through illness – but Swiatek obliterated Coco Gauff in the quarter-final and survived the toughest final of her Grand Slam career so far, against a resurgent Karolina Muchova. As she entered the third set, Swiatek was losing her cool, hitting her hand against her head in annoyance and arguing with her box. She was a point away from going 5-2 down in the deciding set, but somehow played her way out of trouble to win the next four games. Down break point at 4-4, with the title hanging in the balance, Swiatek hit two brutal backhands to push Muchova behind the baseline and then, uncharacteristically, approached the net. The bold move paid off as Muchova's lob flew long, and then Swiatek rattled off seven of the last eight points of the match. Upon completing the 6–2 5-7 6-4 win after two hours and 47 minutes, Swiatek's emotions overflowed: she dropped to her knees and covered her face with her hands, and sobbed.

Brown sees it as a win that encapsulated what he always saw in Swiatek. 'That just characterised Iga as she found a way to win. Why was that? Because she is a great competitor. At the end of the day, she loves winning, she hates losing. It's part of the DNA of a champion; they want to win at all costs. She turned that match around. It just showed her true character. It was what I saw in her when I first saw her play: that hunger, that desire to be a great competitor.' At the end of the season, she admitted the pressure of defending all those points had been 'overwhelming', saying that she did not 'play freely' until after the US Open was done. Perhaps there was a hint of relief at relinquishing the top ranking to Sabalenka in September 2023. It ended her stunning 75-week run at the summit of women's tennis. The world did not stop turning, and she remained the player she always was, just without that number alongside her name. Perhaps that is how she managed to reclaim the world No. 1 spot so quickly (just six weeks later) by winning the China Open and securing her first WTA Finals trophy. Fittingly, the bakery reopened in the championship match as she swept past Jessica Pegula 6-1 6-0. 'I just knew I had to change this attitude and approach the next tournaments different, be a different player who didn't focus on all those things,' Swiatek said at the end of that year, reflecting on how she obsessed over the ranking points.

She spent the off-season honing new skills, revamping her service motion to try to find more of an edge. The results have not been as emphatic as she would have hoped, though. For anyone else, winning a third consecutive Roland Garros title would count as an impressive year, but Swiatek may look back on 2024 as bittersweet. It began with a third round loss in Melbourne to Czech teenager Linda Noskova. She enjoyed a lucrative February and March, winning the Doha final against Rybakina and then collecting the Indian Wells title too. Later, she avenged her loss to Sabalenka in Madrid from the previous year by beating her in a thrilling marathon final. Swiatek saved three match points in a crazily high-level competition which included 75 winners across three hours and 11 minutes. That began a clay-court streak which stretched through Rome, where she got the better of Sabalenka again, and culminated in taking the Roland Garros title for the third year on the bounce. It included a second-round epic against Naomi Osaka, where she saved match points. In that moment she saw how the anxiety she would have felt the previous season in those moments had been overcome. 'I'm really proud of myself that I didn't stop and the pressure didn't squeeze me down,' she said.

That fifth Grand Slam title meant Swiatek joined an exclusive list: she is the only player in the Open Era, other than Monica Seles and Roger Federer, to win all five of her first major final appearances. That takes some serious mental gymnastics. Somehow, though, Brown still thinks Swiatek will see the 2024 season as somewhat of a disappointment. She is yet to make her breakthrough at Wimbledon and missed out on gold at the Paris Olympics. For some tennis players, the Olympics do not feature that highly on their radar, but this was arguably Swiatek's for the taking and she had the personal connection of her father's Olympic career too. Played on Court Philippe-Chatrier, which she had not lost on in three years, there was perhaps no better time for Swiatek to have her golden moment. She was devastated to only achieve a bronze. After losing in the semi-final to Qinwen Zheng, the eventual champion, Swiatek was inconsolable. In a post-match interview with Polish media, she broke down. 'I just messed up,' she said, before turning away and facing the wall to cry. She cried for the next six hours, and described feeling like someone had 'broke her heart'. 'I actually realised yesterday that I wasn't really playing for myself, I was more playing for everybody else, for the country, for my team, for everybody that hoped that I'm going to win a medal and probably win a gold medal,' she said the following day, after winning the bronze medal – the first tennis Olympic medal in Poland's history. 'I tried to work through it but I wasn't quite aware of how deep it was in me and how much of a baggage that was.'

At the US Open, when she lost in the quarter-final to Jessica Pegula 6-2 6-4, the cameras captured her in the locker room crying too. Swiatek's tears in New York were only going to get worse. She failed a drugs test on 12 August, testing positive for trimetazidine (a medicine often used to treat heart-related conditions). She was handed a provisional suspension on 12 September, and her team were sent scrambling to find the source of the issue. Ten days later she appealed the suspension and learned that her sleep medication, which she takes for jet lag, was responsible for the contamination. After missing three tournaments and effectively relinquishing her hold on the No. 1 ranking, her provisional ban was lifted and she returned to the court for the WTA Finals and Billie Jean King Cup Finals.

Testing of her medication confirmed Swiatek's account, and the International Tennis Integrity Agency accepted her explanation, ruling that her level of fault was at the lowest end of the range for 'no significant fault or negligence'. They handed her a one-month ban, which she served in November 2024. 'The only positive doping test in my career, showing an unbelievably low level of a banned substance I've never heard about before, put everything I've worked so hard for my entire life into question,' she said in a statement at the time. It was a shocking turn of events, causing weeks of huge stress for Swiatek, who described it as the 'toughest battle of my life'.

For all her mental training, mastering her emotions is not the end game, says Abramowicz. 'We as a society think that if someone is working with psychologists or a psychologist is present, it should be healing itself – which it's not,' she says flatly. 'Why can't we think that if someone is able to recognise, accept, name and express and interpret emotions, they are mastering emotions? That's the real emotional intelligence, and that's the real and healthy emotional regulation. And some people would regulate their emotions by talking with loved ones, through meditation or sometimes with tears. Some do it through throwing their racket; we also see a lot of this behaviour on the tennis court. Iga is not ashamed to show her emotions and regulate her emotions while being able to perform on top level, to improve her tennis, to be a better athlete. I think it's all good. It's not bad.' She also adds that the focus on her tears as a negative thing remains a social construct reserved for women: 'When a man would cry after loss or after win, he would be called very sensitive. If a man breaks a racket, he will be very manly. But if a woman is doing that, she is too vulnerable, she's hysterical, she is weak and or maybe she's unstable. I'd say maybe we should treat people equally.'

*

In autumn 2024, Swiatek came full circle. Her 122 weeks at the top of the rankings (as of September 2024), put her above Ash Barty in the all-time list. Barty was the player she had hoped to form a rivalry with, a player she respected and wanted to emulate, but never got the chance to properly go toe to toe with. Swiatek has very little left to prove to anyone in terms of coping with the pressure of being world No. 1, but surpassing Barty felt significant. Her tally of weeks puts her in seventh, behind a list of tennis greats like Monica Seles, Martina Hingis, Chris Evert, Serena Williams, Martina Navratilova and Steffi Graf. With all Swiatek has already achieved, it is easy to forget that she has done it all by the age of 23.

She is not the finished product by any means. Sometimes she gets criticism for her ability to fight back from losing positions. Brown is not completely convinced by that assessment – especially after her win over Osaka at Roland Garros – but he does think those results are more likely a reflection of how she has become the one to beat. 'I think it's probably happened more in the last two years; you're going to be chased and hunted by everybody else. Everybody's after you, and that's why every player has to keep adding to their game. Once you're out on the tour for a couple of years, people know the way you play, they know your strengths, know the signature shots you like to play. Therefore you can become a little bit too predictable, unless you add a few things to the mix. In the last 18 months, the variety has disappeared from her game.'

To his mind, that may be what sparked Swiatek's surprise decision to part ways with Tomasz Wiktorowski in August 2024. It is bold to make changes when situated at the top of the rankings, and still winning major titles. She and Wiktorowski combined for 19 titles over three years. But standing still is not in Swiatek's nature, and her game – though still so effective in the majority of matches – was beginning to appear stale against some of her rising rivals. 'What happens sometimes, when she loses, she does try and hit her way out of trouble all the time, but because she doesn't have the tools, too many other options, that's her way. Working with Wim

Fissette now, hopefully he can add things to her game that will allow her to then be able to have a little bit more versatility. That's going to certainly help.'

We'll never know whether she would have won all her titles without the sport psychology methods she has ingrained into every part of her tennis life. But it remains the case that Abramowicz continues to be the most pivotal figure in her career. 'Her path, there is no line between old and new Iga,' Abramowicz says. 'I think she's a work-in-progress. I think that she sees herself that way.'

CHAPTER 16

Coco Gauff:
The prodigy

THE question was to the point: 'How far do you think you can go in this tournament?' Cori 'Coco' Gauff, 15, did not miss a beat. 'My goal is to win it.' It was met with a stunned moment's silence from the dozens of international journalists sitting in the press conference room at the All England Lawn Tennis & Croquet Club. She didn't flinch. She provided no qualifiers or additional context, nor did she think any amendments were required. That was her true assessment of the situation, so she met their stares with a quick smile and cocked her head in the direction of the next journalist with their hand up. It was a moment of self-possession from the bright-eyed teen that quite literally took your breath away.

That was not the first time Gauff had spoken aloud her goals, nor was it the first time she had said those words to a member of the press. But to do it in front of as many as that, in the vast Wimbledon media conference room took some guts. You could put it down to her being a girl swept away by the moment of winning her first ever match at a major tournament. Not only that, she had done it at Wimbledon, on No. 1 Court, against her idol Venus Williams – a woman 24 years her senior who had her name inscribed on the champions' honours board five times over. Maybe, you could think,

Gauff was getting ahead of herself. But the way in which she handled the match, the circus around it, as well as the press conference that day suggested that this was a young woman with her feet firmly on the ground – even if she was aiming high.

Every tennis fan will remember the way Gauff held her hands on her head in her moment of victory, lip quivering and looking up to her parents in the stands (who were going berserk). Some will remember the gutsy 108 mph second serve she hit when down break point to the great Williams while trying to serve out the match. But that post-match press conference is what firmly sticks in my mind. Watching it back now, it is difficult to overstate just how composed the young Gauff was. She had showered, changed and the adrenaline had worn off (slightly) as she took her seat. All eyes in the room were trained towards her. She seemed slightly nervous as the questions kept flying in her direction, but the next 14 minutes were some of the most impressive moments she showed at Wimbledon that day. 'I want to be the greatest,' Gauff said simply when asked about her hopes for the future. 'My dad told me when I was eight that I could do this. Obviously you don't believe it, and I still am not 100 per cent confident, but you have to say things and then see if it happens. I think people limit themselves too much. So I like to shoot really high and that way I'll always have many goals along the road but will have the ultimate goal.'

*

Prodigies are everywhere in sport and tennis. Most of the players in this book, at one time, would have been classed as a child star to some level or other. Gauff's introduction to the world gave her that status, but winning a US Open title aged 19 years and 180 days old four years later was not exactly a prodigious achievement. It made her the 14th youngest woman to win a major title. Hugely impressive, regardless of what age she was, but not exactly record-breaking stuff. Gauff's early years seem almost low-key when you compare her to some of the players of the 1990s. They were stacking up Grand Slam trophies on tour before they could legally drive.

Martina Hingis won the Roland Garros girls' title (for under-18s) when she was just a precocious 12-year-old. By the age of 18, she had all five of her Grand Slam singles titles. She won her first in 1997 at the Australian Open when she was just 16 years old. Monica Seles did the same in 1990 at the French Open. Tracy Austin won the 1979 US Open when she was 16 too. Unlike in the past, careers now often last well beyond the age of 30, but it doesn't mean Gauff wasn't aware of the pressure on her not to leave it too late. 'It was to the point where I remember I lost when I was 17 and there was a stat [published] that said: "She's not going to win a slam before Serena's [first slam] age,"' Gauff told reporters after her US Open win. 'I felt like I had a time limit on when I should win one, and if I won one after a certain age it wouldn't be an achievement.'

On the women's side, throughout the decades of Open Era tennis, teens have established themselves at the top of the world order with a regularity that has not been as present on the men's side. There are eight examples of men winning their first Grand Slam title as teenagers, compared to a whopping 16 women. Hingis won three at 17. Graf had eight major titles by the time she was 20. So did Monica Seles. Bjorn Borg had the highest tally in history by that age on the men's side, with three. That is in huge part down to basic biology – teenage girls are physically closer to being on par with opponents in their twenties and thirties than boys of the same age would be.

Early success has its perks, but it also invariably opened up risks for young girls on tour. Jennifer Capriati is regarded as the ultimate cautionary tale. She climbed into the top 10 at the record-breaking age of 14 years, 235 days in 1990. By the time she was 17, Capriati was taking a 14-month hiatus due to burnout and had been arrested for marijuana possession. The 'Capriati Rule', as it became known, was ushered in by the WTA as a result, limiting the number of tournaments a player could compete in each season before the age of 18, and banning under-14s from the tour entirely. The aim was to protect them from potentially pushy parents and ensure girls were not exposed to too much too soon.

It meant that for Gauff, who came of age 25 years later, the parameters were very different. Her fighting talk suggested she was hoping to establish herself at the top of the women's game as soon as possible, but that process would undoubtedly be slower while sticking to the rules around how often she could play. When she first emerged as a 15-year-old, the WTA allowed her to play 12 events. If given the option, she said she would probably choose to play more than the rules allowed, but also had a lot of development left to do on the practice court. At the time, 20-time major champion Roger Federer (who owns the management agency Team8, which Gauff was signed to) said the rule was 'counterproductive' as it just put extra pressure on young players to do well during the few tournaments they had the opportunity to play. 'I've told the WTA they should loosen up the rules,' he said. 'Maybe your best time [in a player's career] is from 14 to 20 for some reason. It's not like for everybody else from 20 to 30. So in a way you take away that opportunity, you know . . . It's up to debate. I don't have the perfect solution. I see why they did it, because we've had the history of some tough parents out there. But at the same time you're also increasing the pressure for that player each week to produce.'

Former British No. 1 Laura Robson experienced these rules as an up-and-coming player and could see the highs and lows that came with it. 'Age 14, women's side players start moving to pro tour life. It's weird to be a teenager and employ people, and fire people. It was bizarre. My first coach, when I was 18, I had to fire him. It was odd. You're living out of a suitcase most of the time because of the travel schedule; you're trying to figure out whether to play juniors still or only seniors. Scheduling is a nightmare; you want to get enough matches. In some ways I totally understand why the age eligibility rules are there, and then in others I always felt it put so much pressure on me, because you have your 10 tournaments a year and if you lose first round in one of them you're like shit, now I've only got nine – unless you're a Mirra Andreeva doing insanely well every week.'

Gauff had always existed ahead of schedule, at least in her parents' book. They had a 10-year plan for Cori Dionne Gauff, better known as Coco, from the time they decided to take the sport very seriously. She was around seven years old and had been playing for about a year. The goal was that, by the end of that decade-long plan, she would be a fully-fledged professional. But she exceeded it by two years. When Gauff was just three, her mother Candi was convinced her daughter had 'special gifts and talents' to be 'something that required a high level of discipline'. Their daughter was a naturally sporty child, owing in no small part to the fact Candi ran track at Florida State University and Gauff's father Corey played Division I college basketball at Georgia State University. When Gauff picked up a tennis racket it was clear she was mastering the strokes quicker than your average six-year-old. Not two years later, Corey and Candi made the decision to move from their Atlanta home to Florida, where they were both from and the global centre of teen tennis dreams. If their daughter wanted to make it, it was the best place for her.

The tipping point came when Sly Black, a Tampa-based development coach who had worked with Sloane Stephens (later the 2017 US Open champion), first met with Corey and Coco when she was just shy of seven years old. He went down to Boca Raton, three hours' drive across the Florida peninsula, to see this girl play. But he was not immediately impressed. 'She wasn't special then, but she had something that I liked,' Black said in a recent interview. 'She was always looking at me when I was talking to her; that's something I liked with little kids. She was very athletic. But there was nothing special then.' It was her attitude that struck Black though. Her father told Black his aim was for Gauff to win the prestigious 'Little Mo' under-eight event, but when Black asked Gauff herself, she said, 'I want to be the best in the world.' That moment stayed with him. Usually it was parents who said that to coaches, but this was a tiny six-year-old leading out from the front. A month later he told Corey he wanted to coach Gauff for three years to make her the best player in the US for her age. Within three weeks the Gauffs had packed up their home in Atlanta and moved to Florida.

Both Candi and Corey had regrets about their own athletic careers. 'Me as a child as a gymnast, I was asked to go train and live in another state, and my parents said no to that because of me living in someone else's home,' Candi said in a 2020 documentary. 'So I kind of changed my career.' Corey felt similarly about his basketball. 'I realised I could have gone further, but I didn't have a father like me,' he said, laughing softly. On the outside, it may have seemed rash and a huge punt to take on a seven-year-old. In reality, it was. It meant leaving their comfortable home and stable life to move into Candi's parents' home in Delray Beach with their daughter and two younger sons. Candi would also have to leave her teaching job to homeschool Gauff. Her mother, Yvonne Odom, initially questioned the move. 'I was not totally in favour of her quitting school. Candi had been working 19 years and, as a mum, I'm concerned about my kid,' Odom said in the documentary. But Candi and Corey were adamant about their plans, and their family supported them.

If their story – child excels at tennis, top coach believes in child, family moves across the country to pursue long-shot career – sounds familiar, it's because it is. The Gauffs built their master plan around countless other examples of aspiring tennis players who went professional. 'This is what had been done by other parents,' Corey said. 'I think you see that with the Williamses. Nadal, his uncle [Toni] was highly involved in his career. So it was no different with Coco's. We kind of looked retrospectively back at many of the women that were successful on tour, some of the more famous ones, trying to look at how they trained, what their parents did, what decisions they made, what kind of formula, and what would be our plan to getting her there based on her interest, athletic abilities and our finances.'

The Williams sisters are the prime example, and the Gauffs literally moved to Delray Beach, where Richard and Oracene had set up with their daughters way back in the early 1990s. The courts at Pompey Park where Corey coached Gauff were the exact ones that he and Candi had played sport as children, and where the Williams sisters often frequented themselves. The symmetry was undeniable, as was these parents' certainty in their daughter's potential. 'What I have is an undeniable belief in my daughter that she can achieve great things,' Corey said in 2020. 'Not only do I believe that she can do it, I raise my hand as willing to participate to help her get there. I don't question one thing. I think she has everything she needs to get to the lofty goals she set for herself. I'm not going to allow her to not focus, not give it her all, to set targets that are too low. If you want to call it pushy, I guess it's pushy.'

Black remembers Corey was pivotal in her development. When he said Gauff needed a new racket, Corey had one by the following day. When he said he needed a hitting partner for Gauff, Corey had found someone suitable within days. 'He was all-in, the mum was all-in, even the grandma was. The whole family is in,' Black said. 'It was just me and her [out on the court], in the sun and she would just go all day long if I allowed her to go all day.' One year in, Gauff played the 'Little Mo' Nationals. 'I looked at the dad and said I don't think we need to go to this tournament; in one year she's already way ahead of where we were predicting, and of all the girls,' Black said. 'She went, and I think she lost one game in the final. She beat everyone else 6-0 6-0 in the tournament.'

Gerard Loglo first met the Gauffs when she was just about to turn eight. Togo-born Loglo was a former player who had worked as a hitting partner with the Williams sisters in the early noughties. He headed to Rainberry Bay Tennis Club to watch Gauff as his coaching friend Black had implored him to take a look at her. Within a couple of hours of hitting with her, he was brought into the inner circle. Like Black, he saw her athletic ability as paramount to her talent at that point, but was more taken by her mentality. 'You see a champ and you might know right away, depending on their attitude, the way they carry themselves,' Loglo says. 'I see a lot of girls and they want to be champions. Yeah, they have potential, but they don't have that mentality like they want to push themselves beyond what they have. So that's the difference. Coco had that already. You can't teach that too much with a kid. We'd just do the hour session, and she'd want more. She was there 100 per cent and that's amazing for a girl of seven years. You have to push it; you have to give them more if you see a girl like that.'

Gauff has said since that her self-discipline came from her competitive nature. 'I love winning, I love being at the top,' she said in an interview with *Forbes*. 'One of my pride and joys when I was younger is I loved being the first to go into school. I realised very quickly at a young age that, if you want to do all these things, it takes work. Things don't come easily but things can seem easy if you put the work in. My parents just put in the structure, because you can work hard but work stupid.' Loglo's favourite memories of working with Gauff were when she would shock older players: 'One time we had a practice match with a girl who was 18 when Coco was nine. The girl sees Coco, who was tiny, and told her coach, "I'm not going to play a junior; it's not fair for her." The coach and I were laughing. Eventually we convince her to get to the court. Coco beat her 6-1 6-1. Because she was so tiny, young, everyone thinks they'll beat her, but when they start hitting the ball, they always got surprised. Everyone we played, it was the same thing. Sure, she was younger, but they're forgetting she was training with me. She was sparring with a guy. She's that strong.'

Between the age of eight and 10 years old, Gauff won in every year group she played in: under-8s, under-10s, under-12s, under-14s, under-16s and under-18s. 'This was one of the most unbelievable things I've seen as a tennis coach,' Black said. Then, aged 10, she became the youngest ever USTA Clay Court national under-12 champion too. After she reached the Orange Bowl final, which pitted her against international players for the very first time, Black turned to her father. 'I think there's a possibility that Cori [Coco] is the best 10-year-old tennis player in the history of tennis,' he said. He estimated that she was beyond her age by maybe four or five years.

She was invited to train at Serena Williams's coach Patrick Mouratoglou's training facility in Nice, France, in April 2014 when she had just turned 10. 'The fitness test was incredible for her age,' Mouratoglou told CNN in 2023. 'Her competitiveness when it came to playing matches against other players was impressive. She was able to beat players that were technically better than her because of her competitiveness.' But it was how believable she was when they sat her down in the office to ask about her hopes, dreams and goals that sold it for him. Loglo remembers Mouratoglou being taken aback by how bold Gauff was. When she left the office, Mouratoglou turned to his colleagues and said: 'This one, we take her with us and she can be great.'

Her performance in Nice meant she received funding from the Champ'seed Foundation (which Mouratoglou served as president for) thereafter, to help put towards her travel and training costs. The USTA started supporting her development too, with the resources they could provide at their Florida base. But still her father Corey was leading Project Coco. Her first big moment came at the US Open in 2017 when she played in the girls' junior event. She was still only 13, playing in a draw that included 64 of the world's best under-18s, but she breezed through to the final without dropping a set. She was the youngest ever finalist in the tournament's history. Martina Navratilova called her a 'phenom'. In the final against 16-year-old top American Amanda Anisimova, Gauff was finally brought back down to earth, losing 6-0 6-2. But she caught attention for saving a phenomenal nine championship points before finally folding. Loglo had seen her perform like that from match point down before, at the Orange Bowl, and go on to win. 'Me as a coach, I'd think we were done, but she could turn it around from nowhere. If she's under pressure, that's how she puts her best tennis together. That's weird, right? It was in life too. In school or in tennis, if she's under pressure or thinks she's gonna fail, that's when she's gonna ace it. She can be nervous, but when she gets up on the court, she's not gonna be nervous any more.'

That fight is something Gauff continued to show upon turning professional. It has been the central part of her game, and something her parents refer to as innate in her personality. Loglo says Gauff could often cry during practice sessions if she did not pick things up immediately, but he said it was just because she wanted it so badly. Alongside her fight, her physical prowess has made her one of the best movers on tour too, defending against more powerful opponents and shrinking the court with her agility and long wingspan. Her topspin forehand proved temperamental at times (which we will get to), but her strong serve was powerful beyond her years. Her most reliable shot, her two-handed backhand, was a weapon. It all put her on course to level up to the professional circuit quicker than most. That trip to Flushing Meadows in 2017 was the last tournament Loglo worked with Gauff in an official capacity, but he continued to track her progress from afar and is in contact with the family still. Gauff takes her roots seriously, he says. Even while working on becoming the child prodigy she was, her values always came first and continue to do so: training always had to fit around church Sundays, her brothers and cousins remain very close to her and, even now, she still visits Loglo's academy to have a hit with the children there.

Everything started to click into gear for Gauff in late 2017. She signed with Team8, Roger Federer's management agency headed up by Tony Godsick (his business partner and superagent, who had worked with the likes of Monica Seles and Anna Kournikova). The power of the Gauff brand was clear to see on the outside, and her family had some of the most experienced people in the business to help them navigate all the offers already coming her way. She had a setback at the Australian Open in early 2018 when she lost in the first round of junior singles and doubles, a moment her mother Candi has recalled as the only time she ever saw doubt creep into her husband's mind, ever so briefly. Federer personally called Gauff to give her 'a pep talk'. By the French Open juniors that year, she had picked herself up and more, becoming the youngest person to lift the trophy in 25 years. She did so by launching a 1-6 6-3 7-6 comeback, despite trailing 0-3 in the final set against fellow American Caty McNally, who was two and a half years older than her. Gauff was making a habit of breaking records. Early in 2019, she played some of her first ITF professional events (a level down from the WTA Tour), where most players spend their teenage years, testing themselves while they continue to develop. But by May 2019 she had played her seventh and final lower-level event. She may not have fully known it yet, but she was about to graduate to the big leagues at 15 years old.

*

At the French Open she lost in the second round of qualifying before heading to Roehampton to play in her first Wimbledon qualifying event via an unexpected wildcard. She was only ranked 313th, but made light work of her opponents, taking out world No. 128 Greet Minnen 6-1 6-1 to qualify for her first Wimbledon main draw. She was the youngest person in the Open Era to do so. That would have made headlines in itself, but when the draw was done at the All England Club, the stars aligned to give Gauff an opening round date with her idol: Venus Williams. Not only was Williams the oldest player in the draw (39), she was also a five-time champion at Wimbledon. She won four of her seven major titles before Gauff was even born in 2004. Williams and sister Serena were the players Gauff's family had tried to emulate in making her a tennis prodigy. Gauff, Serena said, reminded her of Venus. The long limbs, the court coverage and the way she aggressively went for her shots were all Venus-esque. Her self-assuredness in front of a microphone too. Except, against Williams that day, she was just better.

Loglo spoke with Gauff before the match. 'I used to work with Venus in the past, so we spoke and I told her what she needed to do. Venus was not moving well, so I said you've got to keep moving the ball. In that match I'd seen the champion coming out of her.' She admitted later that a small part of her wondered just what she could achieve against this giant of the game. She was thinking 'let's see how many games I can win'. Before the match, though, Mary Joe Fernandez – former top American player and Gauff's agent Tony Godsick's wife – pulled her aside. 'No, you have to go into that match and think you can win,' she told her firmly. 'That mindset changed my life,' Gauff said in a 2024 interview with *Forbes*. 'I thought, I'm going to beat her. I believed it before I walked on court.'

Gauff looked and played like she was relaxed. The only sign of tension was how, after each changeover, she ran around the umpire's chair on her way back to the court, seemingly in an effort to avoid crossing paths with the statuesque figure of Williams. Serving out the first set, she won a 15-shot rally with a smash at the net and hit an ace. In 33 minutes, she had hit two unforced errors and 10 winners and made nearly 80 per cent of her first serves. Gesturing to her parents in the stands, she shouted, 'C'mon!' when Williams's backhand hit the net. She didn't face a break point until 63 minutes into the match, but then had to fight to close it out, doing so on her fourth opportunity. She was overwhelmed by emotions at the moment of victory, but had the grounded sense to hold on to Williams with a prolonged handshake at the net. She had previously been too shy to speak to Williams when she had met her briefly, and she knew it was 'now or never' to approach the elder stateswoman of Wimbledon. 'Thank you for everything you've done,' she told Williams, who smiled graciously. 'I wouldn't be here without you.' Then, while the crowd continued to applaud her on their feet, she sank to one knee in front of her chair, leaning on her racket for support, and prayed.

CHAPTER 17

Coco Gauff:
Practising patience

AHEAD of her momentous match against Venus Williams at Wimbledon in 2019, Gauff finished her final practice session at Aorangi Park and headed back to the player area. This short walk is where fans gather behind some fences, waiting to catch a glimpse of their favourite athletes. Sometimes they're lucky enough to get them to stop and chat. Gauff was stopped that day by one young boy, who probably had no idea who she was, but asked her for a picture. By the following day, the throngs of people behind the barriers were shouting: 'I love you, Coco.' It's funny how quickly things change. On No. 1 Court the previous day, the crowd had willed her on with 'Let's go Cori!' No one yet knew she preferred to go by Coco. Between games, she stared at the ground in what looked like complete focus, but revealed afterwards that she had a silly thought about whether her father, also called Corey, thought they were cheering for him. Within 24 hours, Gauff had stamped such an impression on the Wimbledon fans that they quickly adapted and she was now known solely by her nickname.

On Instagram, her follower count was ticking up in the thousands and her 12-year-old brother sent her a message to congratulate her. Coco-mania took over Wimbledon that fortnight in a big way.

Walking around the grounds, all eyes were on Gauff. As a top jun-ior talent, she had been meeting professional tennis players for years, but now the news television cameras at Aorangi Park were trained on her court rather than the more experienced stars. When she walked, her competitors' heads turned. She was polite and said hello to those she knew. A quick 'Hi' to Serena Williams and a hug from her coach Mouratoglou. She said 'good luck' to her compa-triot Taylor Townsend. And Roger Federer told her to 'play well' as he stopped for a quick catch-up. She was still being her 'goofy' self, despite the attention, playfully trying to juggle tennis balls court-side, her mother teaching her as they waited for their practice slot to start. When she reached the third round later that week, her star power was such that the club committee decided to schedule her on Centre Court to face Slovenia's Polona Hercog, the world No. 60. Waiting in the grand, traditional entrance to the most hallowed court in tennis, she had her headphones firmly on, to blast hype songs by rappers Jaden Smith and J. Cole in her ears. It was jarring but somehow Gauff also felt like she belonged.

The Tennis Podcast was recording their episode that evening on the picnic benches above Court 18 as usual as it helped them soak up the last of the atmosphere on-site. The spot is adjacent to Henman Hill, where punters without tickets for Centre Court sit each day to watch the action on a big screen. That evening, it was packed and rocking as if home favourite Andy Murray was playing. The num-ber of fans trying to catch a glimpse of Gauff's third round match meant they were overspilling beyond the Hill itself. 'There was no bench available that evening because they were all being stood on by people who had been moved to the back of the Hill,' Catherine Whitaker says. 'They were standing on the benches to get a glimpse of the screen to watch Coco Gauff against Polona Hercog. Polona Hercog nobody had heard of and Coco nobody had heard of three rounds before. It was so intoxicating that David [Law, her co-host] and I ended up standing on the benches and just looking around going, wow, this is absolutely wild. It was a total moment in time.'

The fans were rewarded with a near-three-hour complete fight-back from Gauff. This was not the flawless and nerveless performance of the previous two rounds, but rather a more raw and defiant effort from Gauff. She was 5-2 and match point down in the second set, but willed herself back into contention to win in three. In the UK, 5.2 million watched BBC coverage – more than any other match in the first week of the championships, including Rafael Nadal's win over the mercurial Australian Nick Kyrgios. Gauff was only the fifth player to ever reach the fourth round of a major before turning 16. In the commentary booth, nine-time Wimbledon champion Navratilova marvelled at this teenage superstar: 'I have a feeling Coco Gauff will transcend the game.'

In the fourth round, Gauff finally showed she was human. Eventual champion that year Simona Halep beat her 6-3 6-3. Gauff said she had struggled with a stomach bug during the match and she fought back the tears during her press conference. 'I'm going to continue to watch the tournament and try to learn some more,' she said. When asked what she hoped to do next, she showed the same laser focus she had earlier in the week: 'My next goal would be to win the next tournament I play.'

Whitaker recalls that week as the making of a star. 'The general feeling was, if this is what she's doing at 15, imagine what she'll do next year.' Gauff jumped from 313th in the world to 139th. Before Wimbledon, her sponsors included New Balance, Barilla (pasta brand) and Head which, according to *Forbes*, was worth $1 million combined. That was about to seem quaint. Her audience shot up too, with her Twitter following rising from 17,000 to 119,000 by the end of her run. Life had completely changed for Gauff in the way she and her family had hoped it would. It was a wonderful and wild run for everyone watching, and the kind of introduction to the world most players can only dream of. How she coped with it going forward was the question on everyone's lips.

She answered it almost immediately by reaching the US Open third round on her main draw debut that September, beating two opponents ranked above her. That summer she had been busy with her tennis and also became the cover star for *Teen Vogue's* glossy September issue. Somehow she was taking it all in her stride and still delivering results beyond her years, and set up a tantalising encounter with world No. 1 Naomi Osaka. At that point, Japan's Osaka had won two majors in the calendar year and was reigning champion in New York. It was an enormous test, and Osaka duly defeated Gauff 6-3 6-0, quashing all the pre-match hype. She was, quite frankly, in a different league. The tennis match was unremarkable, but the memorable moment came after the final point was played. Osaka gave a tearful Gauff a warm hug and asked her to stay on court for the post-match interview, to address her thousands of new fans on Arthur Ashe Stadium. 'I'm literally going to cry,' Gauff said, shaking her head, but Osaka reassured her. 'No, I think it's better than going into the shower and crying,' the 21-year-old said. 'You have to let these people know how you feel.' Gauff complied. 'She did amazing, I'm going to learn a lot from this match,' she said, fighting back her emotions. 'Thank you, Naomi. I don't want people to think I'm taking this moment away from her because she really deserves it.' 'You guys raised an amazing player,' Osaka added, addressing Gauff's parents. 'I remember I used to see you guys – I don't want to cry – training in the same place as us and for me the fact that both of us made it is incredible.'

Gauff was humbled that night by Osaka when it came to the tennis, and she has admitted since that her confidence took a bit of a hit. Interviewing her in 2022, she laughed at the audacity she had at 15. 'It wasn't that I believed I could win the US Open, it's that I expected to,' she told me. 'She was crazy,' she added, referring to her younger self. And yet, in her very next event, Gauff came through qualifying as a lucky loser at the Linz Open and won her first title. She did it by securing her first top 10 victory over Kiki Bertens and slugging her way past 2017 French Open champion Jelena Ostapenko. It was only her fourth time competing in the main draw at a tour event, but Gauff was not exactly taking things slowly.

At the Australian Open in the new year, she astounded again. First, by beating Venus Williams again in the opening round, before taking defending champion Osaka out in the third round in straight sets, 6-3 6-4, on Rod Laver Arena. 'Honestly, what is my life? Oh my gosh. Two years ago I lost first round in juniors and now I'm here; this is crazy.' She added a reminder that she was still continuing her schooling: 'My teachers are letting me submit some assignments late.' She was defeated in three sets by eventual champion and compatriot Sofia Kenin, but this run was another signifier of just how quickly Gauff was climbing up into the top. She finished the Australian Open ranked 51, jumping up 262 places in the space of her first seven months playing WTA events. It was mind-boggling, especially considering there were restrictions on how many tournaments she could play. But the pandemic saw the tour come screeching to a halt and Gauff was forced to slow down.

Though tennis was on hold, Gauff continued to show the world what she was made of. When Black Lives Matter protests sprung up across the United States and beyond, after the brutal police killing of an unarmed Black man George Floyd, Gauff put herself front and centre. She gave an off-the-cuff speech at a protest in her Delray Beach home town, saying she was sad to be speaking out about the same things her grandmother had to '50-plus years ago'. 'If you are being silent,' she said, standing at a lectern with a microphone in hand, 'you are choosing the side of the oppressor.' She was only 16, but she was proving herself a leader in a sport where very few players beyond Osaka were standing for something beyond tennis.

Loglo was not surprised by what he saw. This was a feature of the Gauff he knew. 'That's her character. She's a young lady now, and she stands for her values. If you're wrong, she's going to tell you you're wrong, and if you're right she'll say you're right. It comes from her background, the Black American story. You have to stand up for yourself. She's standing and speaking the truth. On the tennis court she does it too; she'll talk to the umpire because she wants to speak her truth. She's only one way, and people can hear her voice. It's not like she's making it up; that's just her.'

When the tour started up again, her next big result at a major came at Roland Garros 2021, where she made it to her first quarter-final. It was perhaps helped by her winning her first clay-court title in Parma earlier in the month and reaching the Rome semi-final before that, which featured a win over world No. 1 Ash Barty. In Paris she was beaten by eventual champion Barbora Krejcikova, but it served as a precursor to the following season, where she would finally make it to a major final. It feels perverse to write 'finally', as Gauff was still only 18 when that happened. But she felt like a feature of the tour at that point, someone who was aiming so high and being so vocal about those aims that anything but the big-time was a disappointment – to her and to those watching. After the heavy heights of 2019 and early 2020, she had steadily built her way into the top ranks over 18 months, but the expectations only mounted. There were some setbacks as her loopy forehand faltered occasionally, and she had some serve malfunctions too, but this Paris run was the step up she and her team – which still included her father as her head coach – had been working towards. It was also her very first major tournament in which she had no homework looming over her head as she had celebrated her high school graduation the week before, even gaining a congratulatory message from former First Lady Michelle Obama.

Her wins in Paris included a quarter-final defeat of Sloane Stephens, one of the players she most admired growing up. After her semi-final, she wrote 'end gun violence' on the camera lens, following news of a deadly school shooting in Texas. There was no fairy-tale ending though as Gauff came up against former French Open champion and newly crowned world No. 1 Iga Swiatek, who was on a winning streak for the ages. She lost 6-1 6-3 in a soberingly one-sided final, her third straight loss to Swiatek, in what would turn into a dismal head-to-head for Gauff (which stood at 2-11 as of December 2024). Wiping away the tears, she referred to Obama's message for her. 'I think it reminded me that people are proud of me outside of tennis,' she said. 'That moment really changed my perspective going into the tournament.'

For all the growth she gained, she was still mad about losing. Speaking on reflection two years later, Gauff described how she used the loss to fuel her. 'Honestly, I don't know if they caught it on camera but I watched Iga lift up that trophy and I watched her the whole time. I said, I'm not going to take my eyes off her, because I want to feel what that felt like for her.'

*

In June 2022, I met Gauff a couple of weeks after her run in Paris, at the Berlin Open. I was writing a feature for the *Telegraph*. She is one of those athletes who has an aura about her. It doesn't stem from entourages (there were no agents or even parents around when we sat down – a rarity) or how she presented herself (in her workout gear). Rather, it was her ability to be warm while also having this extremely strong sense of self, despite only being 18.

'Hi, I'm Coco,' she said by way of introduction, extending her hand. I'd watched her walk into the player lounge moments earlier, signing autographs with fans and even patiently taking selfies with security staff who should probably know better. She had addressed a press conference room earlier that day and moved fluidly between talking about her forehand issues to how ironic it was that, as an

18-year-old in America, she could legally buy an assault rifle at the supermarket but not a bottle of champagne to toast her French Open final. When she sat down for the one-to-one interview, she was just as comfortable talking about bingeing *RuPaul's Drag Race* on Netflix, how she finds nail salons around the world to keep her set 'fresh', and prioritising speaking out about issues like race, violence and equality.

'I think that really came from my grandmother,' she said of the latter, referring to her maternal grandmother Yvonne Odom. 'When she was younger, she was actually the first to integrate her high school [after segregation ended]. She – actually my whole family – always encouraged me about speaking on whatever issues you believe in. Not just speaking off of emotion, but taking time to reason and look at both sides. You realise there are issues going on that are much bigger than just you. For me I'm thankful that I have a platform people can kind of listen to. I think I like to speak on issues that I believe have nothing to do with politics, more so just being humans in general. My grandmother especially has pretty much [always] been an activist, so I'd feel like I'm doing a disservice to her and to the people that came before me, my ancestors.'

Unlike many big-name athletes, Gauff had a refreshing amount of perspective. She also had an ability to laugh at herself – especially 15-year-old her, whom everyone so admired for her maturity, but whom she looked back on as grossly unrealistic. 'I almost had main character syndrome,' she said. 'I think I got too caught up in tennis, tennis, tennis. Now people come up to me and say they support me regardless, and it almost brings me to tears. When I was 15 or 16, I would think people would only like me if I won.' She added that her parents were the key to reeling her back in too: 'We've heard some horror stories in tennis regarding tennis dads. I'm so thankful my dad – while he is a tennis dad – never has been in that aspect.'

While she said there was relief in making a Grand Slam final, the

pressure to actually win one still loomed large in the background. It
was not instant and change came first. About a year later, she added
Pere Riba to her coaching staff. She suffered her first ever first-round
exit at Wimbledon a couple of weeks later, in a particularly low
moment, and then helicoptered in Brad Gilbert – who famously
coached American great Andre Agassi. Commentators continued to
urge Gauff to make technical changes to her extreme forehand grip
and her volatile serve, which was prone to collapsing under pressure in recent months. It was why she was coming undone against
the top players like Aryna Sabalenka and Iga Swiatek. But getting
Gilbert involved was a sign she was doubling down as his ethos was
not based on technical tweaks but rather on 'winning ugly'. It is a
term he coined and honed in Agassi and Andy Roddick. It refers
to winning tennis matches not by being the perfect player, but by
playing percentage tennis, winning by being smart and in spite of
your flaws, not by eradicating them entirely. He literally wrote a
book on this philosophy, self-describing it as 'an invaluable combat
manual for the court'. '*Winning Ugly,*' so reads the blurb, 'will help
you beat players who have been beating you.' That was exactly what
Gauff was looking for.

In the reshuffle, her father took somewhat of a back seat. He
was still ever-present, but Gauff admitted he was sometimes not her
favourite person to hear from during matches. He duly noted the
feedback and watched from more covert areas in the stands. This
was a significant shift, but within weeks of linking up with Riba and
Gilbert, Gauff went on a remarkable run during the 2023 American
hard court swing. First she won the Citi Open in DC, then reached
the Montreal quarter-final, before taking the title in Cincinnati too.
It felt particularly significant as she beat world No. 1 Iga Swiatek in
a match that spanned three brutal hours. She had lost all seven of
their previous meetings, never winning even a set against her. This
was a confidence-inducing victory, and one which put her on the

path to her first ever WTA 1000 title, the biggest of her career. It was the perfect preparation as she headed to the US Open.

There, more pressure rested on her shoulders than ever. With Serena Williams's retirement the previous year in New York, this time the tournament made Gauff the face of the event, gracing billboards all over the city. She was a big enough name to attract celebrities in the way the Williams sisters had during their careers too and even former US President Barack Obama and First Lady Michelle attended her first round match. There were instances in New York where Gauff pushed the limits of winning ugly, like her three-set slug-fest with former Australian Open champion Caroline Wozniacki in the fourth round. It may not have been pretty, but it made her the first American teenager to reach back-to-back quarter-finals in New York since Serena Williams in 2001. She was indomitable at other times, including over fellow teen sensation Mirra Andreeva in the second round and against Jelena Ostapenko in a 6-0 6-2 quarter-final drubbing.

Her fight was never clearer than in the final though, against the favourite Aryna Sabalenka, a fearsome opponent who could be unplayable on her day. Gauff owned a 3-2 record against her, but lost their last meeting earlier in the year 6-4 6-0 at Indian Wells. Down a set, and with the match running away from her, Gauff dug in and defended like her life depended on it, scrambling around the court with awe-inspiring tenacity. It turned into a dogfight, but that suited Gauff just fine. While Sabalenka faltered, Gauff reeled in her unforced error count to just two in the final set to Sabalenka's 16, and she let the Belarusian hit her way out of contention. Some credited Gilbert's winning ugly method as she clawed back the match 2-6 6-3 6-2, but Loglo saw that fight as pure, vintage Coco Gauff. 'You know, everyone can talk, but I know Coco very well, how she developed, how she needed to play,' he says. 'The whole tournament, she was not playing the way she knew how. When she won, in the final, that's the way I taught her how to play tennis. The consistency, the heavy ball and using her backhand as a weapon.'

As Sabalenka's final shot sailed over the baseline, Gauff fell on her back in the middle of the court. The home supporters were on their feet, her mother jumped up and down, delirious and overcome with the moment. When Gauff ran up to celebrate with her father, who had been watching out of camera shot from a corporate box, he cried into her embrace – a fact she teased him for during the trophy ceremony. As stunning as the victory was, the winning speech was eye-popping, as Gauff took a swipe at her haters. 'I want to say thank you to the people who didn't believe in me,' she said. 'A month ago, I won a [WTA] 500 title and people said I would stop at that. Two weeks ago I won a 1000 title and people were saying that was the biggest title I would get. Three weeks later, I'm here with this trophy right now. I tried my best to carry this with grace, but honestly to those who thought you were putting water on my fire, you were really adding gas to it and now I'm burning so bright.' In fitting Gen Z fashion, she revealed afterwards that she was reading people's negative comments online up until 10 minutes before the match.

Her win made her the third American teenager to win the title, following in Serena Williams's footsteps in 1999. It marked her 18th win in her last 19 matches too. When she came home to Delray Beach, as is her way, she invited Loglo to grab some food with the family. 'I said, "Girl, why you want to give me a heart attack?"' he laughs, but then adds: 'I'm so proud of her.' Away from the court, more than 100 sponsors contacted her agent. She now counts New Balance, UPS, Bose, Head, Barilla, Baker Tilly, Rolex, L'Oréal, Naked Smoothies and Carol's Daughter (a beauty brand) as sponsors.

In 2024, there were no Grand Slam titles, but there were semifinal runs in Melbourne and Paris, plus four titles, including the WTA Tour-end Finals. It capped off an up-and-down year where her forehand played up and she had an early exit at the Paris Olympics.

She broke ties with Gilbert after the US Open, and her new coach, Matt Daly, is advising her alongside Jean-Christophe Faurel, whom she has known and worked with throughout her young career. Daly's impact, as someone known for tweaking technique issues, has already seen marked improvements in her wayward forehand. The WTA Finals win in Riyadh, Gauff's biggest title since New York and where she beat Swiatek, Sabalenka and in-form Qinwen Zheng in a classic final, provided a positive reward. The Saudi deal to host the Finals through to 2026 has proved controversial, due to concerns over human rights in the region. Navratilova and Chris Evert have opposed the move. Billie Jean King is more supportive. Gauff said she would only play there as long as she 'felt comfortable'. This time she did, and she pocketed $4.8 million in prize money for her efforts. According to Sportico, it contributed to making her the highest paid female athlete in 2024, with $9.4 million in on-court earnings, and $21 million in endorsements. She is just the third woman in sport to earn more than $30 million in a year, following – you guessed it – Serena Williams and Naomi Osaka's lead.

As prodigy stories go, Gauff's has turned out sublimely so far. But she wants more, and has previously said she wants her trophy cabinet to house 'double figures' worth of majors. Asked recently what she wants her empire to look like at the end of her career, Gauff said 'timeless'. 'I feel like a lot of my career is associated with my youth,' she said, in a revealing moment. 'I'm not going to be young forever. A lot of the stat lines are "the youngest to do this" or "that". The older I get the less of that will happen. Not only on court, but off court, I want to appear timeless.' Loglo has no doubt that she will come good on that. He may be biased, but he believes her potential is 'unlimited'. 'She's not playing at least 60 per cent of her game yet. So imagine, soon she's gonna cross that bar to 60 or 70 per cent, she's going to dominate a lot of girls on tour. People need to watch out now.'

CHAPTER 18

Aryna Sabalenka:
The serve bot

ARYNA Sabalenka always aims for the top. Top of the rankings. Top seed at Grand Slams. Top prizes at all tournaments. Top winner count. Top speed on her serve. Top spin on her groundstrokes. If she is not in first place, she is not satisfied. For a while though, that overflowing ambition was scuppered by claiming the top of a less desirable list: the double fault rankings. One of her team members, Shane Liyanage, is her numbers man. His job is analysing the data to help make improvements to her game and suggest effective tactical approaches. In January 2022, though, a year into forming part of Team Sabalenka, you did not need to be an expert to know that her numbers were atrocious. 'At that point, the serve was not reliable,' Liyanage says, in somewhat of an understatement.

In her first two matches of the season, she leaked 39 double faults on her serve. One of those was a 21-double fault loss to qualifier Rebecca Peterson, where she smashed her racket to the ground in despair and was sobbing between games and even between points. As she desperately resorted to underhand serving, the umpire intervened to ask if she was injured. 'Nothing is wrong,' Sabalenka said flatly. 'It's a technical problem. I cannot serve better.' A couple of weeks later at the Australian Open, she hit six double faults in the very first game of her second round match. Somehow she still won and, when she reached the fourth round later that week, her first reaction was that she was 'mostly happy that I made only 10 double faults'. This was one of the best players in the world, ranked inside the top five, but she was operating at such a dire level that 10 double faults were considered a good day at the office. 'Even though, for her, it felt like a horrible time, she still made the fourth round at the Australian Open averaging 20 double faults – a lot of people would trade their season for that result,' Liyanage says. 'It meant she did other things quite well and that was the messaging we tried, and we saw that in the data.'

Getting that message across to Sabalenka was difficult. She was a player who possessed one of the most fearsome serves on the whole tour and she liked relying on it. When she was hot, few could match her in those stakes. Her average serve speed regularly outperformed her rivals, her placement could be stellar and she should have been racking up free points by simply bringing down the hammer. Instead, she was literally giving away dozens of points. In a sport like tennis, where matches are often won and lost on the swing of two or three, this was a huge issue. Sadly, that Australian summer marked only the beginning of one of the infamously bad serving seasons in recent memory. Throughout 2022, Sabalenka racked up 428 double faults across 55 matches – 139 more than any other player on the women's tour. One in every 10 points on her serve resulted in a double fault.

There was precedent for such shaky serving form for Sabalenka. For three consecutive years, she had the dishonour of being the WTA player with the most double faults per season. In 2021 she hit 338 in 61 matches. In the shorter Covid season of 2020 it was 166 in just 37 matches. The year before that she ranked second with 350 in 57 – only surpassed by Jelena Ostapenko's abysmal tally of 436. Away from the raw numbers, the impact this was having on her self-esteem was disastrous. Sabalenka is six foot tall, has broad, strong shoulders and is a real presence on the court. She competes fiercely, and she is one of the loudest players too. On the outside, she was the picture of confidence. Commentators, including former champions Kim Clijsters and John McEnroe, have compared her big-hitting abilities and imposing style to Serena Williams, who was perhaps the greatest server the game has ever seen. But Sabalenka was starting to be known by opponents as the kind of player who beat herself. All they had to do was hang in during matches against her, and she would almost inevitably get tight and completely lose control of her biggest weapon, the serve, as well as her groundstrokes.

Sadly for her, 2022 topped all of her previous woes. It was the year from serving hell. She had reached rock bottom and could only try to make light of the situation by nicknaming herself 'the queen of double faults'. By some miracle though, just a month into 2023, she found herself at the Australian Open lifting the first of her three Grand Slam trophies. She did so by only hitting 29 double faults across the entire tournament in Melbourne (an average of four per match). To Liyanage's mind, that torturous previous season turned out to be the absolute making of her. 'It was a blessing in disguise,' he says. 'That year is critical. What she went through and the help she got is the reason she's a three-time Grand Slam winner. I feel like she wouldn't have got there without going through that year.' It was a swift turnaround that perhaps she does not receive enough credit for, but just how did Sabalenka vanquish the serving yips?

The yips are a common occurrence across world sport. Defined as 'a psycho-neuromuscular impediment interfering with the execution of fine motor skills during sport', the term originated in golf to refer to players suddenly being unable to make easy putts. Sport psychologist Dr Misia Gervis has worked with athletes across football, golf, gymnastics and tennis, and has seen it all: from young gymnasts afraid of performing a simple backflip on the beam to a top division footballer unable to shoot a penalty after the yips take over. 'Generally by the time I get to work with an athlete, they've had hundreds of unsuccessful attempts at doing it,' Gervis says. 'It's often a case of too much explicit monitoring of what you're doing, in other words overthinking. When movements are automated, we just press go and our brain talks to our body, which carries out the instruction. That mind-body connection is a thing of loveliness. But when the yips happen it's like the wiring gets rerouted so everything becomes stuck.'

Take an automated movement like walking, for example. 'There's very little conscious thought to doing it, you just do it,' Gervis says. 'But imagine if you were thinking, "Oh my goodness me, I can't walk, I have to think about what I need. I need to put the right foot in front of the left foot," then it impedes the movement. It makes it sticky. Most of the movements that we're talking about with the yips are actually happening at speed, and if you're explicitly monitoring the movement, then it gets in the way of the flow.' In a sport as isolating and high pressure as golf, there are many excruciating examples of talented athletes being overcome by the yips. Former world No. 1 golfer David Duval won his first major title at the British Open in 2001, but his game completely fell apart the following year as seemingly simple shots became impossible for him. His career never really recovered. Ernie Els also had a brief and brutally timed case of the yips when he had six failed putts on one hole at the 2016 Masters. Away from golf, darts player Eric Bristow coined the yips as 'dartitis' in his own sport, while snooker world champion Stephen Hendry had a similar problem which stopped him from performing at the top level. In individual games of precision like these, it is a nightmare scenario to completely lose your touch.

Perhaps the most famous recent case of the sporting yips was at the Tokyo Olympics in 2021. All-time great gymnast Simone Biles suffered from her sport's version: the twisties. She described it as a 'mental block' and loss of spatial awareness while somersaulting through the air, leaving her unable to complete her usual high-level skill set. It can also be extremely dangerous because gymnasts perform such complex and risky routines. Imagine losing track of your spatial awareness while airborne and upside down? This was not a case of jitters and worrying about poor scoring, Biles literally could have broken her neck if things went badly wrong. She likened it to forgetting how to drive a car while going at breakneck speed on a highway, except without the relative safety of a seat belt or airbag to soften your crash. Her case of the twisties was so severe that she abruptly pulled out of the team event while representing the United States in Tokyo, after struggling during what should have been her strongest rotation, the vault. Though she was tipped to win multiple gold medals she withdrew from a number of events at those games.

In tennis, the physical danger is not nearly as high; that goes without saying. But the mental anguish experienced by a player with the yips cannot be underestimated. Seventeen-year-old Anna Kournikova famously suffered from them between October 1998 and January 1999, recording a whopping 182 double faults across just 10 matches. Sabalenka's own start to 2022 was a continuation of a long period in which her serve had been running hot and cold, with no real way to know when it would suddenly fail her. 'A serve for Sabalenka is simple, automated, because she's done it a gazillion times before,' Gervis says. 'When it went well, she probably wasn't thinking. Bounce, bounce, throw, boom. The thing that stops her is the threat and the fear, the anxiety response, the possibility it will go wrong. When the body is under scrutiny or potential failure, it gets cautious and, in being careful, we change our motor movements slightly.'

The serve is the staple of any tennis player's toolbox. It is literally the only shot in the whole sport that they can be fully in control of, with no outside influence from their opponent. Choosing exactly where they stand on the baseline, the height of their ball toss, the arch of their back, their tracking of the ball, the point of contact and the power, speed, spin and placement of the ball, there is no other moment in a tennis match where the player has as much agency as when they are serving. A strong serve can prop up other weaknesses, guide the flow of a rally and help a player get into their opponent's head too. An unruly serve though can cause all sorts of problems, as Sabalenka was finding. She was getting broken by opponents more often than usual, lost her nerve while serving in the tough moments and was dragged from winning positions into lengthy deciding sets as a result. Instead of the serve helping her out of troublesome moments, it was getting her into trouble in the first place.

Interestingly, Sabalenka's panic response is not to shy away. Instead of holding back or reeling in the power, she tries to hit through the issue. Her response to danger is to hit harder – whether that is in groundstrokes or in her serve. Call it brave or foolish, what is for certain is it can make her erratic at times. In 2022, it was altogether catastrophic. As well as hitting through the issue, she did try to find solutions. At the beginning of that year, when Sabalenka's serve first started blowing up, she very briefly worked with Australian Mark Philippoussis. He was famously one of the best servers in the game during his ATP career in the late 1990s and early 2000s and he had previously weighed in on her serve at Wimbledon when she was similarly affected by the yips. Immediately after she played that horrendous 21-double fault match in Adelaide, Philippoussis was at the tournament and felt compelled to drop her a note. 'Girl, you've got to stop thinking so much on your serve,' Sabalenka later recalled him saying. 'If you have some time today before you leave to Melbourne, I can help you.'

At 9 p.m., after Philippoussis finished his commentary duties on-site, Sabalenka joined him on the practice courts. He gave her some much-needed tips and the following week she credited the time spent with him in helping her 'survive' her first round match against Storm Sanders at the Australian Open. She even admitted to being surprised when her serve landed within the lines that day. 'You see how bad it was, so it surprised me and I wasn't ready for the next shot,' she said bemusedly. The frustrating part of it all was how much she had worked on the serve during the off-season, she added: 'We worked a lot on serve. But it's not about my serve. If you see me serving on the practice court, it's perfect. It's an amazing serve. I think it's all about in here,' she said, pointing to her head. 'I was thinking a lot on my serve. I tried to control everything and this is not how it works. I have muscle memory and I just have to trust myself.' She ended up staggering through to the fourth round at that Australian Open, but this bumper set of results were merely a Band-Aid for a problem that cut much deeper.

There is something perversely fascinating about watching an elite athlete suddenly find themselves unable to perform an action that should be simple. At her worst, Sabalenka was serving without even rising to the ball, her feet planted to the ground, her left hand tossing up the ball and her right arm merely going through the motions. Even hitting at 50 per cent power, with an aim to simply get the ball over the net, she still often failed. The ball would either hit the middle cushioning of the net or it would sail over and far beyond the service line. She groaned and grunted with every miss, rolling her eyes in that animated way of hers, gesturing exasperatedly up at her team in the stands or chastising herself in Russian. Sabalenka went from being one of the fiercest competitors in the sport, prone to wild shouting and big, bold celebrations, to being a shadow of herself at times. It was hard to watch, but you almost couldn't look away either, so unfathomable was it to see this firecracker server reduced to such lows.

'That failure is being reinforced, and the fear factor of "I can't do it" starts to take over,' Gervis says of the toll taken by athletes experiencing the yips on the global stage. 'Tension appears in places that it shouldn't; maybe our gut starts working, because our body responds to the threat of "I can't do this". The risk in golf or tennis is different to gymnastics; it's about other people's perception of you, that feeling of failure, inadequacy and humiliation. These are big feelings that start to show up. Your body responds to the feelings, and not in a helpful way. Your mind is saying "alert", and your body is trying to protect you from it so it puts the brakes on things. Which is really the opposite of what you want.'

Putting herself through that every couple of days, in front of thousands of spectators and more watching on television, only exacerbated the issue for Sabalenka. With every match she won or lost, she was asked about her serve by the media. Unlike in some other sports, tennis players face questions post-match more than athletes in team environments, for example, when the task is shared among members of the squad or coaches. If Sabalenka was requested by a journalist, win or lose she was required to speak, and the questions inevitably had one main arc: what on earth is going on with your serve? How did you keep it in check today? What felt different? What kind of solutions are you finding? How are you coping mentally with the issue? Do you ever feel like giving up? Win or lose, even if she wanted to try to put her serving issues to the back of her mind, it became increasingly difficult.

An unusual bonus factor that season was that the Netflix cameras were following her around as she had agreed to be one of the focal figures in *Break Point*, a fly-on-the-wall documentary series about tennis. The external scrutiny was higher than ever for Sabalenka, and the yips became the driving focus of her story – at least from the outside. The episodes were not released until early 2023, but watching them back provides great insight into the turmoil in the Sabalenka camp. 'I couldn't see the ball,' she said of those dire matches in Adelaide. 'I was panicking. It's like you don't feel your body, you don't control your arms, your legs, nothing. After that I couldn't play. This is the worst feeling I'd ever had on a tennis court. For me it's really emotional, because I want to do really well.'

She kept powering through and looking for solutions, mostly via direction from her team, which included head coach of two years Anton Dubrov and her trainer Jason Stacy. They convinced her to work with a sport psychologist eventually, but by the end of 2022 she concluded that it was only making things worse. 'I realised that nobody than me will help, you know?' Sabalenka said a couple of months later. 'I spoke to my psychologist saying: "Listen, I feel like I have to deal with that by myself, because every time hoping that someone will fix my problem, it's not fixing my problem." I just have to take this responsibility and I just have to deal with that – I'm my psychologist.'

Sabalenka's mindset was always about pushing through; taking a break never really came into the equation. At that stage in her career, she had never retired from a single match through injury or otherwise. Even when her serve was at its worst, she still found ways to win. In fact, for all of the bad moments she had on court that year, she still won 33 of 55 matches that season. She relied on her brutal groundstrokes and leant into her first-strike, big bash tennis trademark – just without the booming serve to match. It was a measure of her stubborn refusal to succumb to an obstacle. Giving up was not in her DNA.

*

Sabalenka grew up in Minsk, Belarus, where her father, Sergey, began her love of tennis. She has referred to him as one of the great influences in her career, saying she is '100 per cent' the person she is today because of him. He was a former ice hockey player but introduced Sabalenka to tennis by chance. 'One day my dad was just driving me somewhere in the car, and on the way he saw tennis courts,' she has previously said. 'He took me to the courts, I really liked it and that's how it started.' Her junior career was unremarkable, never playing any Grand Slam events and only reaching a 225 career-high ranking, as she competed sparingly. She started playing on the ITF women's circuit in 2012, when she was just 14, but failed to win a single match in every one of her first five tournaments, all played in Belarus. She trained at the Belarus National Tennis Academy in Minsk from the time it opened in 2014 and recorded her first ever professional win that year.

Sabalenka made a big leap from outside the top 550 to just shy of 150 over a 12-month period from 2015 to 2016. It mostly went under the radar though as it happened at low-level ITF circuit events, but she was methodically making her way as a young professional. In 2017, when she was 18, she made her first main draw appearance at a WTA tournament in Dubai and also won her first Grand Slam match after coming through qualifying at Wimbledon. But her real breakthrough moment on the world stage came at the Fed Cup that year. Along with compatriot Aliaksandra Sasnovich, she helped her country reach the final of the team competition for the very first time. They were both ranked outside of the top 75, but Sabalenka managed to get wins over players well above her in the pecking order – including reigning US Open champion Sloane Stephens, her first top 20 win. She won her first WTA title later that month, at the Mumbai Open, to cap off the season. It meant that by 2018 she was inside the top 75 and able to enter WTA events on a consistent basis. She had qualified to the big leagues.

A run to the final at Eastbourne that summer, where she beat three top 20 players plus former world No. 2 Agnieszka Radwanska, caught people's attention. Then three top-five wins in the US hard court swing helped her make her top 20 debut and put her on course to reach the fourth round at the US Open, where she lost a three-set thriller to her contemporary and the eventual champion

Naomi Osaka. In a foreshadowing of things to come, Sabalenka double-faulted on match point in that encounter. Overall though, the picture was rosy and Sabalenka was firmly in the conversation as a rising star, named the WTA Newcomer of the Year for her efforts. Dmitry Tursunov was the coach working with her in the summer of 2018, and he saw how Sabalenka responded to her progress. Her hunger and drive were insatiable, and she was impatient. 'Even in 2018, she was freaking out, saying: "I'm so behind; I'm late; I need to win a slam,"' he says. 'She was so anxious about winning a slam, she always was.'

That desperate longing saw her succumb to pressure at times, even as her game became more aggressive and solid. Tursunov saw it play out during that Osaka match in New York. 'She could have won a slam, but her game was raw at that time. You can have all the individual strokes, but learning how to use them, when to use them, and trusting in your own ability, it happens as you get older. The freshman becomes sophomore and then senior at high school; she knows where the bathrooms are, she can hustle a freshman for lunch money, so to speak. Now she's a more mature, more confident player. Then, she might have felt like: "I'm good, but I'm not as good as these girls,"' he says. 'Everyone has imposter syndrome, you know? It's how many times you are going to be proved wrong before you start believing in yourself.' That underlying crisis of confidence crept on to the court at key moments, despite her charismatic, brash on-court persona.

There was another layer of pressure clawing at her. She and her father Sergey had plotted a secret goal: win two Grand Slams by the time she was 25. That goal only became more important to her in 2019, when Sergey died suddenly at the age of 43 of meningitis. She wanted to win for him, and it weighed heavily. 'I lost my father. We had one dream. When he passed away, I started thinking too much about it,' Sabalenka said, in one of the most revealing moments on

Break Point. 'Now I'm 24 and there's zero in my pocket. I feel like I just put so much pressure on myself. I was overthinking about everything. I was feeling like I just have to fight through it.'

It explained some of the reason why Sabalenka is not easily satisfied, but Tursunov said it was as much instilled within her personality, as she possessed that mindset even before she suffered such great personal loss. 'Everyone sets a standard for themselves; she felt like she was unaccomplished when she wasn't winning slams,' Tursunov says. 'She was top 10, and she felt like a failure – I know girls who are 60 in the world and feel like a success. So that to me is an indicator of internal motivation. If a person is unhappy where they are, they're going to move their ass. They're going to do something to change their environment. She expects to win many slams. If she doesn't win them she would consider herself a player who didn't achieve what she was meant to. If Aryna would win a 250 or 500 she would not feel complete. Something was missing. For her winning a slam is what's going to fill that hunger. I think she's just hungry for more than most other players.'

Even as she got closer to those goals, her serve troubles were already creeping into her peripheral vision in 2018 and 2019. Tursunov says 'she's definitely not an overthinker', but even back then had 'good days and bad days' on her serve. 'I don't think she was ever getting to these stages of 20 double faults, but a lot of it is just psychological,' he says. 'You can tweak things technically, but it's the understanding that things can go wrong. When you're aware of your shot that potentially is a liability; of course you're going to be worried that at the important moments it's going to fall apart. It's almost a self-manifested thing. It can fall apart, but when she starts freaking out about it then it falls apart even more. The fact that she was relying on it as her main weapon had more to do with it than anything else.'

At the time, Sabalenka barely worked on her serve at all in practice. It was not something she was willing to let Tursunov tweak or tinker with. 'The serve was not something to be touched,' he says. 'As a coach you let some things slide; you don't want to work on the serve then fuck it, we're not going to. There's plenty of other ground to cover and improve. In reality, her serve is just one part of her game; everything else was also a weapon. When she starts figuring out how to put these things together, how to win without a serve being online, how to win only playing second serves, that's all part of maturing and actually a big part of being a slam champion. Not because you possess certain shots that no one else knows how to make, it's just being able to survive two weeks while some things are not working. Something's going to fall apart, you're going to have a bad day and as a slam contender, you have to know how to win matches when things are not working well for you.'

That shift started to happen for Sabalenka as far back as those years with Tursunov. 'I think it was kind of an important period for her because she was actually one of the better returners on tour at the time in terms of statistics. My guess is she slowly started realising that she can win without her serve being on. Also moving away from the belief that if my serve goes wrong, I'm going to lose.' The reality is, Sabalenka was winning far more than most players, but she was falling short at the majors. Despite being ranked around the top 10 mark, she failed to make it past the first week at the Grand Slams for all of 2019 and 2020. Every one of those early-round losses were to lower-ranked opponents who, on paper, she should have been beating.

After parting ways with Tursunov and promoting her young hitting partner, Dubrov, to the head coach role, she finally reached her first Grand Slam semi-final in 2021 at Wimbledon. Though it was a breakthrough, it only brought with it another mental hurdle: losing semi-finals. She lost that semi-final as well as the next two from winning positions. The worst was against Leylah Fernandez at the US Open in 2021, a surprise package semi-finalist whom Sabalenka was the outright favourite to beat. But Sabalenka was anxious to finish points, going for too much, and made 52 unforced errors as a result. She lost a match that was firmly on her racket. In the final game of the match, in what had been a tight third set, she hit back-to-back double faults and then blasted an error on the final rally. 'I would say that I destroy myself,' she aptly summarised afterwards.

Perhaps, considering a loss like that – in what was arguably her best chance to win a slam, as qualifier Emma Raducanu ended up taking the title – it is not surprising that Sabalenka returned at the start of 2022 with the serving yips. The psychological toll of coming up short in the big moments was likely wearing her down. One person was about to give her the solution she so needed.

CHAPTER 19

Aryna Sabalenka:
A new queen

DURING 2022, much was written about Aryna Sabalenka's chronic case of the yips and plenty of theories abounded about what could be done about the problem. Gavin MacMillan was watching from afar, and he was unconvinced: 'You had everybody in the world telling her it's a mental thing, she's got the yips. That is such an extraordinary disservice to her and to what's going on. It's not the yips. It's not mental. She's flat out doing it wrong. And the fact that she was having any success at all is shocking.' MacMillan is a biomechanics specialist, and founder of the Sports Science Lab. His previous client list includes all-time great boxer Manny Pacquiao, Super Bowl champion Will Blackmon and nine-time major champion Monica Seles. He is also as straight-talking as they come. Before his career as a trainer, he was a keen athlete, playing baseball, ice hockey, basketball and tennis as a teenager. There was always one frustration that plagued him in tennis: by his own admission, he could never hold serve. Years later, and once he was studying biomechanics, he watched videos of Pete Sampras – widely considered one of the most technically sound servers of all time – and it hit him that he had simply been doing it wrong. The irony is not lost on him that it was partly his own abysmal serving record that motivated his career in biomechanics, and had now led him to be the go-to man to fix the world No. 2's serve.

He was first introduced to Sabalenka's coach, Anton Dubrov, in Indian Wells, March 2022. A few weeks earlier, Dubrov had literally told Sabalenka: 'I don't know what to do. I think you need to find someone else who's going to help you.' She immediately rejected his resignation. He couldn't quit on her, she argued; they would work through things. That solid, reliable team in her corner has been the only stable aspect to her life. When her serve failed her and her game struggled, at least she had a team she trusted alongside her. 'She genuinely values having Anton around,' team data analyst Shane Liyanage says. 'I think he's almost a big brother to her. He tells it to her pretty straight, but he delivers it in a constructive way. So I think she was mature enough to recognise at that age that you could have had any other coach in there, and it would probably be the same. She stuck with him at that point. I know it would have been stressful for Anton as well. He would have felt like "what can I do to improve this?" And it wasn't that we weren't doing anything. We looked at things like ball toss contact, for example. It wasn't that we were thinking it'll fix itself. We were digging. I think Aryna valued that, and ultimately she made the right decision to go with stability.'

But she was reluctant when Dubrov brought up the idea of getting MacMillan involved. It took five months for her to come around. MacMillan got a second call from Dubrov after Sabalenka suffered a three-hour-11-minute loss to Coco Gauff at the Canadian Open in Toronto that August. Sabalenka had been losing in the early rounds of most tournaments that summer. She hit 18 double faults in that epic against Gauff, after notching up a grand total of 59 in the previous three matches. She had reached breaking point. After that match she sat on the floor in tears, rueing how she had tried just about everything to fix her serve and nothing had worked.

Her trainer Jason Stacy gave her some tough love, calling her out. 'There is still one thing left to try,' he told her, 'a complete rebuild of the serve.'

To Sabalenka, it had always been a terrifying prospect. Tinkering and changing technique can come with risks and complications. For one, tennis players have very little downtime in the schedule to learn, practise or implement changes. The 2025 tennis calendar literally started in December 2024, and runs through to November, leaving barely one month of off-season. It has been a point of complaint for players for decades. If you're experiencing serving trouble in the middle of the season, like Sabalenka was throughout 2022, taking yourself off the hamster wheel has to be a conscious choice. It can be hard to do, with mandatory tournaments dotted across the calendar for top players and skipping events can mean losing ground if you give up ranking points you earned in the previous season. The tour is built around the premise that consistency pays off.

Then the actual relearning of an automated skill is not easy. You have to reroute the neural pathways that you have been accessing for years. It can feel clunky and unnatural to make even the most subtle of alterations. Then, at the end of it all, it might not actually work out much better. You may never be able to regain your swing. But Sabalenka was desperate at this point. She gave Dubrov the nod and he made the call to MacMillan. MacMillan was at his friend's ranch in Fresno, California, when he picked up the phone. He told Dubrov he needed to speak with Sabalenka herself to make sure she was on board and after asking her if she was okay ('No,' was the reply), he laid out his pitch. 'The fact that you still compete so hard tells me everything I need to know,' he told Sabalenka. 'And I can 100 per cent promise you this isn't mental.' Sabalenka, confused, asked: 'How can you promise that?' 'Because you're doing it so wrong,' MacMillan said of her technique. 'How would anyone say it's mental if they look at your film properly and look at what your left arm's doing – it's dropping so far down, pulling your right shoulder down. And your right arm's wrong too, you're not doing either one of them right – and I can prove it. I can fix this.'

The next day, he was on a plane to Toronto. By Saturday, 36 hours after their initial call, he was on the court with Sabalenka. He started by getting her to make some simple physical adjustments and gave her a task to hit 10 serves in a row at a specific target, using his new tip. She was not allowed to stop until she hit his mark without fail. 'She did it the second time she tried,' MacMillan says. 'I told her: "Well, it's not mental or you wouldn't be able to do this."' That was the first time Sabalenka had even practised serving during a training session in weeks. 'She stopped doing it in training,' MacMillan says. 'She was like, it's pointless; it's not going to change.' Psychologists might raise an eyebrow at this assessment, as a training environment does not have the psychological pressures associated with competing, which is where Sabalenka was consistently being failed by her serve. The truth is, Sabalenka's issues were neither totally technical nor totally psychological: the two were coexisting together. It became clear to MacMillan just how deep this serving issue ran for Sabalenka who, he claims, had experienced some particularly harsh coaching from a young age. 'I couldn't have predicted what I was dealing with. You're dealing with such a huge amount of fear of her not being able to do it, of previous coaching that had been done with her – which was nothing short of what I'd call abusive, I guess. The information she was given was dead wrong, but childhood coaches would yell at her. What happens is when a coach doesn't know what they're doing, then you blame the player. She had that experience.'

From Dr Gervis's viewpoint, in the majority of cases of the yips, they are rooted in some kind of trauma or negative experience – either on or off the court. 'In the instances where I've worked with people, there's something that sits beneath it. It doesn't just come in a vacuum of everything's fine and lovely. Once you dig a little deeper, and deal with the underlying trauma, often then that resolves the issues.' Off the court, Sabalenka had been experiencing a lot of turbulence. As well as still grieving her father's untimely death three years prior, in 2022 she was subject to a whole new unexpected challenge when Vladimir Putin launched Russia's invasion of Ukraine in February of that year. As news bulletins were dominated by bomb attacks and stories of heartbreak and casualties in Ukraine, Belarus remained a major ally and supporter of Putin and Russia. Sporting bodies were urgently told to make geopolitical decisions about who could and should be competing on the international stage, as Russia and Belarus both had long-standing reputations for using sporting success as propaganda. Where other sports delivered bans which blocked those national teams from taking part in major events, tennis took the decision to allow players from both Belarus and Russia (a significant portion of the top 100) to continue to play, as long as they agreed to do so under a neutral flag.

Ukrainian players complained about being forced to compete against their country's enemy on the court. Sabalenka and fellow Belarusian and Russian players were asked about the war at great length during press conferences at events. It was obviously a difficult topic to navigate. The Belarusian government had a history of cracking down on athletes who chose to speak out against President Aleksandr Lukashenko's increasingly autocratic leadership. The war had only heightened those fears. Two Russian players, Andrey Rublev and Daria Kasatkina, stood out for boldly denouncing the war. But Sabalenka came under scrutiny as she had attended Lukashenko's New Year address in 2021, even after the authorities violently repressed mass protests in Belarus and imprisoned multiple top athletes who participated in them.

When Wimbledon went against the grain and issued a blanket ban of Russian and Belarusian players for the 2022 tournament, in an act of solidarity with Ukraine, Sabalenka was one of the athletes directly affected. Speaking on *Break Point* that year, she gave some insight into how the war had been playing on her mind throughout 2022. 'I'm from Belarus so I felt really bad,' she said. 'It's really tough what they're [those affected by war] dealing with. If I could have any control then of course I would do everything I can to stop everything. Everyone started talking about "you have to ban all the players from Russia and Belarus". I thought everyone is looking weird to me, you know? I felt like everyone hates me because of my country.'

These feelings were bubbling beneath the surface when MacMillan joined her camp that summer. He could see the mental toll that year had taken on Sabalenka, but remains adamant that this was a physical issue that was the result of poor coaching advice she had received during her developmental years. Beyond Sabalenka's specific case, MacMillan does not mince his words when it comes to describing the level of coaching he thinks exists in tennis. As he works in other sports, he says he is immune to the tennis bubble, and says the standards vary massively. 'You get these people who are beyond incompetent – they are making it up as they go along,' he says. 'If you are witness to this, you can't believe how unprofessional most of it is, and the fact that these girls still find a way to succeed is shocking. What they do on the women's side – and it happens more on the women's side – is they establish emotional relationships with them, and they develop a connection that way. When you don't have knowledge but you get lucky enough to stumble upon somebody that's good, well, then you cling to them, because you know that's your only way of surviving. It's like a lifeboat. But if you know what you're doing, the last thing you're worried about is getting fired.'

He says Sabalenka was lucky to have a stable coaching team in Dubrov and Stacy, but had specific expertise to add to the mix and help overhaul her serve. His view is that there's a dearth of coaches in tennis who actually understand the biomechanics involved, and it causes technical issues across the sport. 'You see it in baseball too; you'll see it with the pitching coaches, who mostly have been hired because they know the manager, not because they know what they're doing. In tennis, they're this messed up because so few people are out there actually teaching the mechanics right. Here's why: they teach what they think they see. They don't learn how a human throws something. They don't learn how a human runs. They don't look at the actual physiology of what someone's doing and then match it to that event.' He adds: 'I'm not saying that to brag, because there's other people that are doing this for sure. Roger Federer did not get to the way he hits a tennis ball without somebody teaching that to him. No one figures all this out. It's impossible. [Carlos] Alcaraz, if you looked at his serve three years ago, it's night and day better [now]. Somebody fixed it. There are guys out there, but they're not running around on Instagram telling everybody how great they are, or the minute somebody famous walks into their gym, they've got 50 Instagram posts about it. The people that are doing the change in development aren't the ones out there bragging about it. I think in tennis, at that level it's pretty bad.'

When it came to working with Sabalenka, MacMillan saw immediate improvements. Her four matches prior to working with him, she averaged 19 double faults per match, the next four she averaged seven. But not every element of the service motion was a quick fix. Showing her how to lift her left arm further in the toss and get her to twist her right arm to get the racket facing the correct way was his main aim. To the average person, these changes may be more subtle, easy to miss. For MacMillan, the mistakes were glaringly obvious. 'The right arm has been a really long process to try to fix because she's always opened it and pointed her racket to the back fence. Like, you're screwed the minute you do that. And getting her brain around trying to change that, that has not been simple.' Getting her to do that consistently right was a challenge. As well as the technical adjustments, there is also the mental impact of years spent lacking trust in a shot that should be your strongest. With MacMillan's help, she turned a corner in the latter stages of that season. She reached the semi-finals of her first two events with him in her team, at Cincinnati and the US Open, to help her qualify for the WTA Finals, where she finished runner-up. 'This year I was fighting with myself, which is a completely different fight,' she said. 'I learned a lot about myself. I think this season started as the worst season, but at the end I think it was the best season for me because I learned a lot, and I became even stronger, and like mentally stronger.' But behind the scenes, her perception was still negative. 'She had such a warped look at what she was doing. I said to her after: "Do you realise what you just did?" And you know what she says to me? "Well, it doesn't matter, I lost."' There was plenty of work left to do.

*

As much as technique came into play in helping Sabalenka fix her serve, so did tactics. And the numbers were telling Liyanage that Sabalenka's problem was overhitting. She is a full-throttle, 100 per cent on every point tennis player. Her decision-making let her down in key moments and she had a stubborn tendency to try to blast her opponents off the court. Sometimes, it worked, and winner after winner, as well as aces rained down. Other times, like in that US Open semi-final loss to Fernandez, it went catastrophically wrong – with a big chunk of her 52 unforced errors coming during very short, one to three shot rallies. Most people watching Sabalenka or having a quick look at the post-match statistics could have told you all of that. But identifying the problem was not the difficult part. Helping Sabalenka understand the value of reining in her power was. That was partly Liyanage's job.

Tennis has not opened itself up to data as quickly as other sports. In baseball, their 'moneyball' moment changed the way players were scouted and valued way back in 2002. It also influenced the rest of sport. Formula One has embraced data as a fundamental way to make marginal gains, in a sport where every second counts. Football has adopted data over the last 15 years, to help with analysis, improve injury rates and it plays a huge part in the transfer market. Unlike team sports, tennis players have relatively small entourages and almost all costs come out of their own pockets (unless you're receiving funding from your national federation too). The amount of data you have access to directly depends on the resources you can afford. In tennis, it was only in 2023 that the ATP began setting out plans to open up ball-tracking data to all of their players and coaches – a practice that until then had only been available to top players with bigger budgets. The WTA does not provide the same data to its players, so they either only access that information at joint-1000 events, via the ATP, or by purchasing the data directly from the electronic line calling provider. The other option is employing a full-time data analytics firm, as Sabalenka chose to do in early 2021 with Liyanage.

He started his business in 2017, and had previous experience working for Cricket Australia and Tennis Australia, but Sabalenka was one of his first big-name individual clients. He said tennis was 'slow in uptake', compared to other sports he has seen. 'The first couple of years, it was trying to just sell the idea that data is useful,' he says. 'I think tennis has a very traditional history, so it's very slow at changing. The catalyst I think that's helped is the on-court coaching, or the softening of the rules around communication. Now you're getting live data into the player box. And I think some high-profile examples of players using it, like Roger Federer – I know he wasn't a big fan, but his team used it – Novak, Nadal didn't use it, but his coach Carlos Moya was using it with him, leaves a footprint, to get other players thinking we need to adopt something similar.'

Whereas before Liyanage says coaches were using data to upskill, now there are more and more players using a data analytics expert alongside their coaching team to help inform and find things that are actually actionable on the court. Liyanage does not travel full-time with Sabalenka, but he is present at the slams, sitting in the player box alongside Dubrov and the rest of the staff. His role ranges from clipping together 20-minute video packages of Sabalenka's matches, removing the dead time between points, plus similar scouting videos of her next opponents. These reports highlight patterns of play, how the opponents respond to pressure on certain wings, what tactics they deploy against heavy-hitting opponents like Sabalenka, or where they serve in the big moments.

Dubrov wanted this to be a long-term project. The focus, Liyanage says, was mostly on what the data told them about Aryna's Grand Slam performances, compared to other events. One of the first things he pointed out was that her record could be improved if she stopped playing doubles. It was a bold suggestion to make, especially immediately after she won the Australian Open with her partner Elise Mertens and subsequently rose to world No. 1 in doubles. But her team trusted Liyanage's message, and that was the last Grand Slam doubles tournament she competed at. 'I think it helped her stability, managing the weeks at the slams,' Liyanage says. 'It was a big decision, because I'm sure that the prize money was good and she was world No. 1, but to give her singles the best opportunity, that was a good decision.'

Later that year, as if by clockwork, she made her first two semi-finals at major tournaments at Wimbledon and the US Open. That might have helped give her the breakthrough to make a real run at a slam, but her decision-making in tough moments remained questionable, and her serving form was continuing to nosedive.

When things came to a head in 2022, Liyanage says delivering the data reports was not always easy. He always communicated through Dubrov, and Dubrov decided what information to relay to Sabalenka, both during matches as well as pre- and post-match. 'He would have to be very mindful of the situation with the serve,' Liyanage says of Dubrov. 'There's an art to it in coaching, to pick your moments on when to get that information to the player. We wouldn't have tried to overcomplicate what was required on the serve at the time. I do remember actually making a video for them in the middle of the year, and it was more a positive reinforcement video where I just selected clips of her serving amazingly, on both first and second serves. When it was played back to her she was able to see, okay, actually, my service is still pretty good.'

That was only a short-term solution, though. To Liyanage's mind, MacMillan was the missing piece for Sabalenka. 'Of course, getting Gavin involved was critical. What he rightly identified was there were issues with the technique and, while she got away with it and served amazingly some days, I think the flaws in the technique were really showing under pressure. I really credit the work he's done improving the serve, but also the other strokes. He doesn't get the recognition for the work he did on her forehand, even the backhand, just resetting under pressure. Anton as well, the work he did throughout the year to reinforce that. We all played a little bit of a role to get that information to her, and she had to mature as a person to accept that help as well.' The biggest piece of information they all delivered was that she was not at her most effective when she played at 100 per cent. Her sweet spot, where she won the most points and caused her opponents the most issues, was actually 85. The data was showing Liyanage that if she hits her forehands with the shape her new technique was giving her, at 85 per cent power and with a 2,400 revolutions per minute (nearly 300 above the rest of the tour), she is only losing 30 per cent of points. 'She's dominating,' Liyanage told MacMillan. 'That makes the ball a lot more challenging, jumping out of her opponents' strike zone and still faster than most other girls on tour can hit,' Liyanage says. 'I had talked to Gavin at the 2022 US Open about the data showing us the optimal spin rate and ball speed for her. It's a really nice sweet spot where opponents actually win a lot fewer than if she hit really flat, hard and took that high risk – or she played really heavy, but not with a fastball. That was the message that had clearly been given to her by Anton and Gavin.'

MacMillan describes it as increased heaviness on her forehand shot in particular. 'The change in her forehand has been more dramatic than her serve,' he says. After those initial few months with MacMillan at the end of 2022, Liyanage's job turned to more positive reinforcement, like 'you made the changes, and look at your numbers now, you're on the right track'. Sabalenka put it into practice in a big way during the Australian swing in 2023. Liyanage firmly remembers her playing against Liudmila Samsonova at the Adelaide International, the first match of her season, where it all clicked. 'Samsonova gives her trouble. I think it's an awkward match-up. She was down 5-1 but she was really calm. I remember sitting next to Andrei Vasilevski (her hitting partner) and saying: "Right there, this is different, she's different." She just trusted her game in that moment and she turned it around.' She fended off seven set points to take the match 7-6 7-6. 'She trusted her game and her patterns. I could see there's a confidence in her game, to be able to come back from wherever. I trust my game. I trust my technique. I maybe haven't played my best, but I know I've got what it takes to turn this around.'

Next, at the Australian Open, things continued smoothly. One big difference in the numbers was that her first-serve speed dropped by 10kmh on average from the previous year. It meant she was following Liyanage and MacMillan's 85 per cent rule, and the results were more consistent. On her way to the final, she did not drop a set. With the trophy on the line, she was up against one of the supreme servers in the game: Wimbledon champion Elena Rybakina. Going into their final, 51 per cent of Rybakina's serves had gone unreturned that tournament, envy-inducing form for someone with Sabalenka's history. Sabalenka won the toss and elected to serve first. It was her first Grand Slam final, and she wanted to take it by the scruff of the neck, as is always her way. She immediately double-faulted on the very first point. Raising her eyebrows, and looking to the sky with a wry smile on her face, she shook her head and let herself laugh. It was a palpable moment of irony, but she was not about to crumble. The next point was an ace down the T, to help shake off the nerves. Another ace in that game settled things. But she was quickly down a break in that opening set. Rybakina attacked her second serves and Sabalenka went for too much, hitting another double fault to gift her opponent the break opportunity. She lost the first set.

It could have been the moment where she spiralled out of control. But Sabalenka emitted a sense of steadiness throughout that match that few had seen from her previously under such pressure. 'We were trying to get some information to her from the box, but she went back to what they had been working on,' Liyanage says, 'that 85 per cent of power, spin. Just find that ball and make it uncomfortable for Rybakina, but not taking crazy risks trying to hit them necessarily. She went back to that in set three. I don't know if my contribution was 1 per cent or 5 per cent of what happened, but it gave me some satisfaction that the work we had done over a number of years, it felt like the penny had dropped, and she was applying it in the big moments intuitively.'

After clawing her way back into a match many regard as one of the best women's finals in recent memory, Sabalenka showed some of the traits of old while serving for the title. On her first championship point, she hit a double fault. She screamed at herself. On the second match point, when she missed her first serve, the crowd groaned. She didn't double fault, but she hit a wild error. The nerves were jangling, and she sent another backhand long on her third match point. When she eventually clinched it by finally making a first serve and drawing the error from Rybakina, she lay on her back and cried with relief.

MacMillan watched from home in South Africa. He can rattle off her stats from that match from memory: 17 aces, seven double faults, won 72 per cent of points on her first serve and hit nearly double the amount of winners to unforced errors (51-28). But the main thing that stood out was how Sabalenka problem-solved her way out of that opening set deficit and committed to that new shape she had switched to on her forehand side. 'I think it's one of the best women's tennis matches I've seen – I told that to Elena because I really respect that kid,' he says. 'After the first set, Aryna was so all over the place mentally; obviously the stress of the moment was getting to her. Once her brain switched over to I can do this, and was not terrified of I can't, she turned it around. What we'd been working on so much was the shape of her forehand to keep pushing people back. Hit semi-open, as hard as you want, but you have to accelerate this way so there's spin. In those really big points she really trusted it and got an error from Elena out of it. If you looked at where she was four months before, and said: "We're going to win the Australian Open." Like, no, that's not an option. And you're going to be in the finals and semi-finals of all the others for the rest of the season? Again, no way. But it happened.'

*

In 2023, Sabalenka won the Australian Open, reached two semi-finals at Roland Garros and Wimbledon and then reached the US Open final. They were impressive results by any standards, but winning a Grand Slam title was not the magic pill to solve all her problems of course. Tennis does not work like that. She had dips in 2023 amid those runs, and off-court controversy played a part. At the French Open, the Ukraine war became a big talking point, especially as Sabalenka faced two Ukrainian opponents. When Marta Kostyuk refused to shake her hand after their first-round encounter, and was booed by the Paris crowd, Sabalenka became the story of the day. As a newly crowned Grand Slam champion, and not far off becoming world No. 1, Sabalenka now faced new scrutiny. After fractious exchanges with the media that week, including with a Ukrainian journalist in which her previous support of President Lukashenko was questioned, Sabalenka then opted out of traditional open press conferences for the rest of the tournament, as she 'did not feel safe'. She still reached the semi-final in Paris, but it was a low point of the season. She had two match points to reach the final and squandered a 5-2 lead in the deciding set against savvy Czech player Karolina Muchova. Most disappointingly, when serving at 5-5 40-15 in the final set, she produced back-to-back double faults to eventually be broken.

In the US Open final later that year, she got similarly tight and let Coco Gauff back into the match. It stung, but 2023 remained a year of significant progress. She was rewarded with reaching the world No. 1 ranking at the end of the tournament. It was a huge milestone, if only lasting for a few weeks. MacMillan was brought in and out of her camp sporadically during that season to provide guidance when her technique started slipping up at certain points. It lacked consistency on the one hand, but Sabalenka was also problem-solving on court on her own. The following year she defended her title in Melbourne without dropping a single set, including in her semi-final revenge over Gauff. Throughout the entire tournament, she hit just 10 double faults. For a player who two years ago was celebrating keeping her tally per match to 10, that was a show of solidity she could only have dreamed of before.

Off the court, she suffered more heartbreak. In 2024, ahead of the Miami Open, news broke of her ex-boyfriend Konstantin Koltsov's sudden death. He fell from the balcony of his hotel room in Miami in a suspected suicide. Sabalenka tried to power through her shock, taking to the court the day after she heard the news. Eventually her body stopped her from continuing on tour as a shoulder injury hindered most of her grass court season, including Wimbledon. Later that summer, in an interview with the *Guardian*, she admitted she probably should have taken some time off after Koltsov's death.

MacMillan was with her and her team for the American summer though, where Sabalenka had her mind set on revenge in New York. Things started coming together for her in Cincinnati, and MacMillan points to another Liudmila Samsonova win. 'She's a player she struggles with, and she absolutely kicked her ass,' he says of the 6-3 6-2 victory. Then she beat Iga Swiatek in straight sets, ending a three-match losing streak against the world No. 1. She lifted the title after beating Jessica Pegula, and had been mostly unplayable for the duration of that week. That form continued through to New York. Apart from dropping one set to 29th seed Ekaterina Alexandrova in the second round, Sabalenka was hardly troubled during her run to the final. There were only brief wobbles, moments where she was ahead and started trying to speed to the finish line, rather than sticking to the percentage tennis her team had tried to instil in her. 'She tries to do more,' MacMillan says, 'she doesn't grasp how much pressure she's putting these people under. She doesn't need more – they have to do more.'

Instincts are hard to temper, but Sabalenka had proved yet again that she was capable of doing so over a two-week period. In the final against a home favourite Jessica Pegula, she kept her cool. There was symmetry there with the previous year's loss, where the crowd got behind Coco Gauff and seemed to send Sabalenka into overdrive.

But this time, Sabalenka held fast. The title felt different to her Australian Open wins as it proved she could do this at other tournaments. She was now the undisputed queen of hard court tennis, with 27 match wins from her previous 28 matches at the slams on that surface. Notably, she hit only 20 double faults across the entire tournament at Flushing Meadows in 2024. It was not even a talking point any more. She has shaken off that reputation she had, of the erratic player who blasted her way out of fulfilling her true potential. MacMillan believes she can dominate the sport over the next few years, especially if she continues to 'get over the mental hurdle of letting somebody help her through it, and getting past that fear of it not working'. He adds: 'Hopefully this last little run she's had changes this permanently.'

Liyanage says her 2022 experience was integral to this success, and her former coach Dmitry Tursunov agrees. 'One of the things about Aryna which makes her the whole package is that she bounces back fairly quickly. In this sport, it's super important, as you're going to take some losses. Obviously she would get upset when she lost. But she would be ready to work pretty quickly. She wouldn't let it get her off track. She was like a Goliath who felt like David during a certain period. To become like David for a little bit can show you a different perspective and where to improve. In retrospect, it helped her.'

Three slams is already a haul most would be delighted with. Sabalenka's high standards suggest she is aiming for much more though, and it is hard to see her stalling. From when she first started dismantling her serve in August 2022 up to the end of 2024, she won three major titles, and reached at least the semi-finals of seven out of eight Grand Slams played. In the one she didn't, she still made the quarter-final. No player in the sport can boast such an emphatic record in recent years. For someone who had previously only been beyond the fourth round at a major twice in her career, it is all the more impressive. She has gone from flaky to the most consistent player in women's tennis. 'If there's a better turnaround in sports in the last 25 years,' MacMillan says, 'I want to know what it is.'

Postscript

WHISPER it, but women's tennis feels on the cusp of something novel: a bit more stability. The era of messy, unruly draws may not have ended completely, but it's definitely showing signs of waning, especially at the majors. A small group of players you can bank on are beginning to reign. From 2022 to 2024, four women won at least one major title and made at least three major semi-finals in that time too: Iga Swiatek, Aryna Sabalenka, Coco Gauff and Elena Rybakina. This consistency started talk of a 'Big Four' in women's tennis. That's perhaps a slightly premature statement, but it is fair to say that the pool of players reaching the latter stages of Grand Slams has become somewhat easier to predict than before.

In these three seasons, Sabalenka led the charge with seven last-four appearances (and three titles), while Swiatek had five (four), Gauff had four (one) and Rybakina had three (one). Other notable mentions were Karolina Muchova and Ons Jabeur, both three-time semi-finalists in that period, but failing to make the final step to clinch a trophy. Add four-time major champion Naomi Osaka to that mix, as she continues her return from maternity leave, and there's potential for a solid group of five or six players to consistently challenge each other in the second week of Grand Slam tournaments for the foreseeable future.

There are still sudden spurts of magic from unexpected rackets. Jasmine Paolini surprised the tennis world in 2024 with runs to two major finals despite never previously going beyond the second round. Or take Barbora Krejcikova's unlikely Wimbledon title in 2024, and her compatriot Marketa Vondrousova's the year before that. Then there's Madison Keys and her maiden slam victory in Australia in 2025, at the age of 29. These curveballs remain possible because of the depth in the sport, but the balance finally seems to be evening out, as regular contenders are proving more reliable than in previous years.

Swiatek and Sabalenka are the obvious top two. At least one of them featured in six of the last eight major finals and they have shared ownership of the No. 1 ranking since April 2022. Their consistency is impressive, but crucially their matches almost always produce fireworks. Rivalries need enthralling contests, not just players going toe to toe in a stats race or for ranking points. As the top two players in the world, all but one of their 11 matches since 2022 have come in the semi-final or final of an event. That sense of jeopardy has cultivated a healthy rivalry, making their matches essential viewing. Swiatek and Sabalenka's most notable battle in the Madrid Open final in 2024 delivered in every sense, lasting more than three hours before it was clinched by Swiatek 7-5 4-6 7-6(7) – but not before she saved three match points. Sabalenka's overwhelming power is slightly less effective on the slower clay, Swiatek's most-favoured surface, and the combination created a high-intensity duel as both players tried to outmanoeuvre each other.

A similar burgeoning rivalry between Sabalenka and Rybakina has emerged in the past two seasons, with three of their seven encounters in that period coming at the championship match of a tournament – including their sublime Australian Open final in 2023. There is something mesmerising about watching the fiery Sabalenka contend with a much more measured opponent in

Rybakina. They have polar opposite on-court demeanours but their baseline exchanges are a match made in tennis heaven as they each possess the most ferocious groundstrokes on the tour. As for how Gauff fits into this quartet, she holds winning head-to-head records against Sabalenka (5-4) and Rybakina (1-0), while the tide seems to be turning on her previously dire results against Swiatek. Their two meetings at the 2024 WTA Finals and the United Cup to kick off the 2025 season were won by Gauff, lessening Swiatek's favourable record to 11-3. If Gauff can keep her shaky forehand and serve in check, her superior movement will cause problems for the rest of this group.

Women's tennis has had a few false starts in trying to fill the shoes of an irreplaceable champion like Serena Williams – from Angelique Kerber and Simona Halep briefly taking their opportunities for a season or two, to Ash Barty and Osaka making a play for the top, only to both take permanent and temporary hiatuses. This current crop may just be the generation to maintain that quality for years to come. No one can say for sure how long their careers will run. Motivations could change or momentum could swing away, but this time feels different. If it does all go awry, the sport will move on as it always has done. More academy hopefuls will pummel forehands in the Florida sun, or parents will drag their children to dilapidated public courts in the cold, or tiny girls will hit tennis balls against their garage doors, dreaming of match points, crowd roars and trophy lifts. The only guarantee in this game is that there will be a steady stream of talent chasing that same goal, and continuing to find new ways to get there.

Acknowledgements

BUILDING Champions would not have been possible without the help of every single person who spoke with me in person, on FaceTime or over the phone. Thank you to the tennis players, coaches, pundits, agents, journalists, data analysts and psychologists who took the time to share their versions of events, opinions or simply pointed me in the right direction. You significantly enhanced this book and helped me to paint a fuller picture of the crazy world and vivid characters that make this sport so interesting to cover.

Thank you to the great Billie Jean King, for the lifelong inspiration and for doing me the honour of writing the foreword to this book. It's a complete dream come true. Tip and Josh, my thanks go to you too. This book came to life with significant help from my literary agent Melanie Michael-Greer – thank you for working on this idea with me, answering my many questions and for having faith in my writing. Another huge thank you to everyone at Birlinn for believing in this book and making a commitment to elevating the stories of women in sport. In particular Paul Smith, Andrew Simmons and Ian Greensill for the meticulous edits, welcome advice and tons of patience.

Thanks also to my colleagues over the years who have pushed and supported my writing about women's sport and tennis. Special mention to Simon Briggs for always lending an ear over the phone (whatever the time zone!) and Anna Kessel for your continued guidance. Last but not least, thank you to my friends and family for encouraging me to pursue this project: everyone on the 'Family' WhatsApp group (you're the real MVPs), Aida and Bobo (who asked me if I'd finished writing my book almost every single day), and Mum and Dad (I would never have loved sport if it wasn't for you both, thank you). And Ollie, thanks for always reminding me that I can do hard things and dragging me on long beach walks on the days I'm not so sure.